The Absolute Shado

This book explores Jung's central concept of shadow from a particular configuration that the author calls "Absolute Shadow," placing it in relation to the idea of destiny as catastrophic.

Clinically based and supported by a vast number of therapy cases, the book exemplifies how the Absolute Shadow is a result of the projection of the most fragile and destructive parts of ones psyche. In some cases, it may cause loss of identity and, through the mechanisms of false/double personality, is bound to result in psychosis. Other aspects of the Shadow, like the intergenerational shadow, are also examined in depth.

The Absolute Shadow is the well-informed result of Caramazza's fifty years of study and clinical experience. It is important reading for Jungian and depth psychologists, as well as for psychoanalytic students, trainees, and clinicians of all schools of thought.

Elena Caramazza, MD and Pediatrician, is an IAAP member, AIPA preceptor and Jungian analyst. She has published several papers and reviews concerning Jungian thought and analytical psychology and practices privately as an analyst in Rome. She is the author, with Murray Stein, of *Temporality, Shame, and the Problem of Evil in Jungian Psychology: An Exchange of Ideas,* (Routledge). She is the author of the book *Silenzio a Praga* (Moretti e Vitali) and also wrote a chapter "L'Ombra" in *Trattato di Psicologia Analitica,* UTET, 1992.

The Absolute Shadow

Destiny, Fate, and Intergenerational Processes in Analytical Psychology

Elena Caramazza
Translated by Susan Ann White

Routledge
Taylor & Francis Group

LONDON AND NEW YORK

Cover image: The cover image portrays the Cumaean Sibyl, a plaster sculpture by Elena Caramazza

First published 2023
by Routledge
4 Park Square, Milton Park, Abingdon, Oxon OX14 4RN

and by Routledge
605 Third Avenue, New York, NY 10158

Routledge is an imprint of the Taylor & Francis Group, an informa business

© 2023 Elena Caramazza,

British Library Cataloguing-in-Publication Data
A catalogue record for this book is available from the British Library

Library of Congress Cataloging-in-Publication Data
Names: Caramazza, Elena, author.
Title: The absolute shadow: destiny, fate, and intergenerational processes in analytical psychology / Elena Caramazza; translated by Susan Ann White.
Description: Abingdon, Oxon; New York, NY: Routledge, 2023.
| Identifiers: LCCN 2022025560 (print) | LCCN 2022025561 (ebook) | ISBN 9781032200118 (hardback)
| ISBN 9781032200095 (paperback) | ISBN 9781003261872 (ebook)
Subjects: LCSH: Shadow (Psychoanalysis) | Jungian psychology.
Classification: LCC BF175.5.S55 C37 2023 (print)
| LCC BF175.5.S55 (ebook) | DDC 150.19/54--dc23/eng/20220715
LC record available at https://lccn.loc.gov/2022025560
LC ebook record available at https://lccn.loc.gov/2022025561

ISBN: 978-1-032-20011-8 (hbk)
ISBN: 978-1-032-20009-5 (pbk)
ISBN: 978-1-003-26187-2 (ebk)

DOI: 10.4324/9781003261872

Typeset in Times New Roman
by SPi Technologies India Pvt Ltd (Straive)

To Mino Vianello
my life companion
who encouraged me to write this book

"Men at some time are
Masters of their fates:
The fault, dear Brutus is not in
Our stars,
But in ourselves."
W. Shakespeare
Julius Caesar Act I, Scene III.

Contents

Foreword

Elena Caramazza's *The Absolute Shadow*

If in the future the human race becomes extinct, it will not be the first species to fall to such a fate, but it will be the first to do so with foreknowledge of its doom, the means to prevent it, and the lack of sufficient will to act accordingly. A million years from now, a boy will ask his father: "Papa, why didn't humans save themselves?" And his father will reply: "They were helplessly overshadowed by a power greater than themselves. Thank goodness we are not in that position anymore. Their candles were too dim to bring enough light to the darkness of their nature." In short, the shadow determined the destiny of the species.

Jung chose the term "shadow" as a metaphor to refer to several aspects of the unconscious, which are more or less equivalent to what Freud meant by the Id, as he writes. In some ways, it is a useful term and quite easy to communicate to students and patients. But it also has a serious drawback because, unfortunately, it implies something dependent and insubstantial. Naturalistically speaking, shadows are not autonomous; they are nothing more than passive appendages to the objects between themselves and the light. They do nothing but follow; they do not lead or block or instigate the behavior of the object they are shadowing. Jungian psychology is somewhat handicapped by this metaphor for the awesomely powerful unconscious force that so frequently controls our lives, whether by preventing us from doing that which we know to be "the good," or by enticing us to do that which we know to be evil. Traditionally, this would be called the Devil or Satan. In the cold eye of Justice, there is no excuse for failure to act on behalf of the good or to do evil. In the deeper psychological account of Jung, however, there is a reason for this human failure. It is the dark side of the self. The problem of evil is more than a problem of ignorance, or the absence of good (*privatio boni*). Evil is an archetypal Will that has the capacity to determine an individual's destiny. It is the god referred to in the adage fixed above the doorway of Jung's house in Kusnacht, Switzerland: *Vocatus atque non vocatus, deus aderit* ("Called or not called the god is present"). That is what is meant by the rather tame word "shadow."

Elena Caramazza has written a book that pays careful and scrupulous attention to this powerful feature of the self. She calls it appropriately, "the Absolute Shadow," in direct reference to a similar term used by Jung in his account of the shadow in his late work, *Aion*. What makes this present work so important is that humanity today is facing an unprecedented crisis, and the question is: are we up to the task of meeting the crisis with any measure of success? Without much greater attention to the shadow, the answer is: absolutely not!

Stories of how this force for evil works in human life are to be found everywhere in the literatures of the world – in myths, Scriptures, fairytales, and all kinds of other works of imagination. I will cite only two examples. The first is from the Hebrew Bible. In the Book of Genesis, there is a tragic story of two brothers, Cain and Abel, the children of Adam and Eve, who were destroyed by the shadow. When Abel's offering of meat is accepted by the Lord with satisfaction, and his brother Cain's sacrifice of vegetables is not accepted, Cain becomes enraged and violently envious of his preferred brother. At this moment, the Lord comes to Cain and speaks with him:

"Why are you incensed,
and why is your face fallen?
For whether you offer well,
or whether you do not,
at the tent flap sin crouches
and for you is its longing
but you will rule over it."[1]

The image of sin crouching at the tent's door is arresting. It's like a wild beast, perhaps a wolf or lion, waiting for its prey. And Cain succumbs despite having been made conscious by the Lord of the dangerous being waiting for him at the flap of his tent. Even with the benefit of consciousness and the assurance that he has the freedom to gain mastery over the shadow, Cain succumbs to it and lets it possess him: he invites his brother into the field and murders him. In modern times, this story was replayed by the Nazis in the Holocaust. The Jews were the "chosen people," and the envious Germans were taken over and possessed by the sin that was waiting for them at the flap of their tent. As Cain was forever branded with a mark on his forehead, so have those who participated in the evil of murdering six million Jews in the twentieth century.

This biblical story gives us a sobering realization that parental advice and education are not sufficient, the voice of conscience is not sufficient, in fact nothing short of physical intervention would be sufficient to forestall such strong shadow enactments. The message is that the shadow can override consciousness and good council. It is embedded in and empowered by a more potent motivational charge of psychic energy than is the ego. Freud called this force Thanatos; Jung called it Absolute Evil. Both are a reference to the shadow aspect of the Self. Nevertheless, there is punishment, so it is also the case that the shadow is not the ultimate power in the psyche, personal or collective. That more pessimistic view would be left to Schopenhauer to develop in his philosophy of the World as Will. Jung, who studied Schopenhauer's works carefully, was not quite so pessimistic. There is another side to the Self, and it may outweigh the effects of the shadow aspect.

Another literary example offers further and more detailed information about how the shadow operates in human life. It is Goethe's great work, *Faust*. The protagonist is a brilliant scholar and physician, Faust, a character modeled somewhat, according to Jung, on the Swiss alchemist and healer, Paracelsus. Early in the play, Faust acknowledges that he is divided between two personalities:

> Two souls, alas, are dwelling in my breast,
> And one is striving to forsake its brother.[2]

The one soul is sensual, the other spiritual; the one tends to seek pleasure, the other seeks after meaning and transcendence. It is agony for Faust to contain the tension between the two, as he confesses to his student, Wagner:

> You are aware of only one unrest;
> Oh, never learn to know the other![3]

Wagner remains a dedicated scholar; Faust leaves his study to experience other pleasures than the intellect has on offer.

Meanwhile, the Lord in heaven has given permission to Mephisto (the Devil, i.e., the Lord's shadow) to approach Faust and test him. The story echoes the Book of Job. The Lord places his wager on the conviction that Faust will not lose his way and fall totally under the spell of Mephisto:

> A good man in his darkling aspiration
> Remembers the right road throughout his quest.[4]

To which Mephisto replies with characteristic cynicism:

> Enough – he will soon reach his station;
> About my bet I have no hesitation...
> ......
> Dust he shall ear, and that with zest,
> As my relation does, the famous snake.[5]

Mephisto approaches Faust in disguise, as a black poodle, a friendly and harmless-looking dog, which Faust naively befriends and allows to fol-low him home. The relationship between Faust and Mephisto begins in all innocence but quickly evolves into a conversation that appeals to Faust's repressed sensual worldly desires and latent ambition for power. Mephisto promises Faust magical fulfilment of all his wishes if, in exchange, he agrees to forfeit his soul to Mephisto upon his death. Faust does not hesitate to sign the contract in blood because as a modern intellectual he has no belief in the afterlife, and so his adventures in the world outside of his stuffy study commence. He has made a contract with the Absolute Shadow, to use Elena's terminology, and Mephisto keeps his side of the bargain, supplying Faust with every wish-fulfillment he asks for.

By the conclusion of Faust's life at the age of 100, he has committed murder, acted out sexually to an astonishing degree, been responsible for infanticide and suicide, participated in a war among emperors, committed fraud on a massive scale, and, as a grand finale, has overseen the death-by-fire of the innocent aged couple, Philemon and Baucis, in order to eliminate the aesthetic eyesore of their humble cottage from his visual horizon. One could say that the Absolute Shadow had directed his life completely from the moment of his contracting for the assistance of Mephisto. It was a cooperative effort, however: on the one hand played out by one of Faust's two souls and on the other by the archetypal shadow figure, the Devil. One does hear Faust speak from time to time about guilt feelings and remorse, but such moments of reflection in no way deter him from satisfying his further ambitions and desires. His life is characterized by a kind of narcissistic triumphalism at the expense of everyone around him.

What about the other soul inhabiting his breast? The one that aspired to higher things, to the spiritual, to the ideal? Did the Lord lose his wager with Mephisto? Apparently not, because in the end Mephisto is left without possession of Faust's soul, which is transported by angelic figures into the Empyrean and thus slips out of Mephisto's grasp. Mephisto meanwhile is distracted by pretty angelic boys with naked bottoms and loses track of his prey, Faust's immortal soul. It's a strange and surprising ending to the story. Goethe could not explain its meaning when asked and could only say that he was not capable of writing a tragedy. One is left wondering what guided his imagination to this result. It was something irrational and inexplicable. Goethe was not Christian in any usual sense of the word, but rather prided himself on his often flamboyant and outrageous paganism. Yet something whispered to him that the Lord is more powerful than the Devil, that in the end goodness and mercy overcome evil and punishment. The last verses of *Faust* are a hymn sung by the Chorus Mysticus about transcendence and Divine Love, who is figured as the Eternal Feminine.

> What cannot be attained
> Here it takes place;
> What cannot be described
> Here it is done;
> The Eternal Feminine
> Draws us up on and on.[6]

Faust's soul is thus redeemed in the end, thanks to the gracious Eternal Feminine, who is equivalent to the Sophia aspect of the biblical Lord, a strong counterforce to the nihilism and malevolence of the Devilish aspect, Mephisto. It is a close escape.

Elena Caramazza's work is a deeply considered and extremely timely book on the archetypal shadow, the most dangerous factor at play in the world today. It answers to a challenge Jung laid down in 1959, some two years before his death, when he was interviewed for the BBC by John Freeman. In response to Freeman's question about the possibility of nuclear war at the time, Jung answered:

Jung: I have no definite indications… One thing is sure. A great change of our psychological attitude is imminent. That is certain.

Freeman: And why?

Jung: Because we need more psychology. We need more understanding of human nature, because the only real danger that exists is man himself. He is the great danger, and we are pitifully unaware of it. We know nothing of man, far too little. His psyche should be studied, because we are the origin of all coming evil.[7]

Elena's work is a significant contribution to the type of understanding Jung was calling for. Without more awareness of the shadow, personal and collective, our species will probably become extinct within a few generations. Perhaps our souls will escape to heaven à la Faust, and planet Earth will be free of its most violent, destructive species ever. Plants and other creatures will gratefully be left in peace to grow back to their full potential and perhaps find their way to a better evolution of consciousness.

Richard Leakey, the renowned paleoanthropologist, when considering humanity's future, once wrote: "As we peer back through the fossil record, through layer upon layer of long extinct species, many of which thrived far longer than the human species is ever likely to do, we are reminded of our mortality as a species."[8] Can this mortality be extended given humanity's failure to take responsibility for itself as a species burdened with the affliction of unconscious shadow enactments such as have brought about global warming and devastation of nature due to blind arrogance and greed?

Our hope for further survival as a species now hangs by a thin thread, as Jung warned, and that thread is the marvellous resource we have for developing consciousness. I salute Elena's passionate attempt to bring the bright light of her analytic mind into the darkest corners of human nature and thus assist not only with human survival but with an enhanced capacity to thrive as individuals and as a global community.

Murray Stein

General concept of the shadow in Jung's thought

It is not my intention in this book to exhaustively explain the theme of the Shadow and its multiple aspects in Jung's work, but rather to focus on a particular configuration that I call the "Absolute Shadow," placing it in relation to the idea of destiny as catastrophic. Since this theme is central to Jung's thought and pervades his whole concept of the psyche, but has never been systematically treated, I shall begin with a brief overview.

The Shadow: Defining the problem[9]

The first difficulty we encounter in approaching the concept of Shadow in Jung's work stems from the fact that it embraces two dimensions. On the one hand, the Shadow is part of the psychic reality – and hence a circumscribable phenomenon; on the other, it is also the expression of a relationship between the different parts of that reality. This is, however, a crucial relationship, because without Shadow the psyche would not only be incomplete, but could not even exist. Indeed, it is the reciprocal relation between light and shadow, or rather the dimensions represented by these images, that both makes them real and constitutes the totality of the soul.

In the first place, with the birth of consciousness, i.e., the capacity to psychically represent the reality of the outer and the content of the inner world, the Shadow expresses all that is unknown, thus becoming a pole of the antithesis between known and unknown, representable and irrepresentable. Once these antitheses have been established, the human being immediately experiences attraction and repulsion. The exercise of consciousness enables intellectual judgment, which permits us to distinguish and conceptualize things, but also value judgment. Thus the Shadow becomes a condensation of everything unknown, and also everything unacceptable. This is also the time of ethical activity to which a contrast between value and disvalue is indispensable: "There is no good that is not opposed by evil" (Jung 1927, 1970, p. 131). At this level, recognizing the Shadow does not simply mean becoming conscious of it, but also placing it in the sphere of practice, i.e. combining reflection with action. In effect, this means choosing to act according to what we judge to be good and to refrain from doing things we consider bad, though it may often signify committing a lesser evil to avoid a greater one; for example, it would surely be more ethical to lie in order to save a life, than to abide by the absolute rule of telling the truth.

Ultimately, the Shadow is a provocation for man in that it forces him to question not only the images he has of himself and the world, but also the ideas he has formed about the motivations for his actions. When the Shadow manifests, "bringing into consciousness" also means "bringing into existence." In this sense, the theme of the Shadow is the great challenge issued by Jung to contemporary culture, at least to the extent that it has been assimilated to the legacy of Enlightenment (Horkheimer and Adorno, 1947). By its very nature, in fact, the Shadow cannot be grasped or totally "illuminated" solely through a concept, since our subjectivity is rooted in its unfathomable aspect. The Shadow is also the principle of individuality that makes us unique, which cannot be shaped by any abstract plan, let alone by laws dictated by absolute power, whether political or deriving from a religious faith, and can only be embodied through freedom and taking the risk of experiencing of life.

However, it seems to me that in Jungian thought there is in the Shadow another, more subtle ambivalence. As we have seen, it is both part of a whole and relation between its parts, but I would also add that it is relation itself, and hence exchange between two opposite poles that leads to their gradual transformation, as well as the expression of the undifferentiated remainder from which those poles have not yet emerged. The task of the Ego, therefore, is to distinguish, to position and, where possible, to develop the various unconscious contents; but above all to make the Shadow of "before" all differentiation (which, as I shall explain later, can be considered a kind of "Absolute Shadow" if one remains imprisoned by it) evolve into a Shadow of "after" all differentiation. Here we find ourselves in a more mature phase of the evolution of consciousness: a phase that should see the human being working to reconcile the opposites, and which Jung saw as occupying the second half of our life. It is a question of finding a product of synthesis that expresses and goes beyond the antitheses –without, of course, annulling them – after the discriminating activity of judgment has irreversibly identified them. This new product, for Jung, is the symbol, wherein the opposite poles of light and shadow (representing knowledge and ignorance, for the intellect; good and evil, for the moral sense) once again become harmonious interpenetration, obtained, however, through the participation of consciousness. Now, in fact, we are dealing with a shadow that generates light and light that does not forget shadow. The union does not take place in an indeterminate primordial place, but in a continuous and dynamic transition between origin and present, between known and unknown, between destructiveness and renewal. It results from an ethical commitment by the Ego, which agrees to fully develop the most evolved faculties of consciousness. Not by making it the sole protagonist of psychic life, but by engaging with the Self and the Unconscious, both personal and collective, and courageously taking the constant risk of losing itself, and by nurturing the hope of attaining redemption through gradual growth.

Places and moments of the Shadow in the topography and dynamism of the psyche

More than a notion, the Shadow is an image charged with affectivity. If considered as an existential entity, it is difficult to assign to it an exact place in the structure of the psyche. The Shadow is extremely mobile. We could see it as a shifting surface or volume, located on increasingly deep levels in the inner world. In the upper psychic layers, i.e., those closest to the Ego, and when it is unconscious, the Shadow coincides with the personal unconscious. Although some of the Shadow can enter the field of consciousness and thus become known to the Ego, for example when a removal is suspended or when, in the flow of life, we suddenly discover a characteristic of our personality of which we were not completely aware, we are usually dealing with its outer layer, while its body and roots are immersed in the depths of the soul. This is why I believe that the Shadow should essentially be considered as an unconscious phenomenon.

By contrast, in the psychic layers furthest from the Ego, in the heart of our interiority, the Shadow's activity merges with that of the collective unconscious. Hence we can speak of the Shadow both as part of the restricted personality, which develops on the basis of individual experience of life, and as part of the extended personality, where the Ego engages with the millenary experience of the species and of life in general, including the pre-human, by interacting with the archetypal world. In this case, however, rather than identifying the Shadow with a series of contents potentially accessible to consciousness, the accent should be placed on the symbolic charge it brings to the structuring of images.

Personal aspect of the Shadow

If we consider the Ego as the center of the field of consciousness and as the body of contents and functions that give us the sense of our unique and unrepeatable identity, then for Jung the entire unconscious layer constructed during an individual life. i.e., the personal unconscious, is Shadow, although not all of the Shadow is personal unconscious: "The personal unconscious contains lost memories, painful ideas that are removed (i.e., deliberately forgotten), subliminal perceptions, by which are meant sense-perceptions that were not strong enough to reach consciousness, and finally, contents that are not yet ripe for consciousness. It corresponds to the figure of the shadow so frequently met with in dreams" (1917/1943, 1966, p. 66).

In *Psychological Types* Jung explains that the psychic function, or functions (thought, feeling, sensation, intuition) insufficiently exercised at a conscious level, are part of the Shadow, as is the less developed type of attitude assumed by the Ego in adapting to reality (introversion or extroversion). Positive or negative events can make the inferior function emerge, causing susceptibility, "the sure sign of the presence of inferiority," to manifest (1917/1943, 1966, p. 58). The more the inferior function is removed by a unilateral attitude assumed by the Ego that identifies with the most developed or socially accepted function or functions, the more it is deprived of conscious energy and finds itself undergoing a shadow experience, activating the unconscious in an unnatural way. In the first place, this means that the inferior function, which is always associated with an archaic side of the personality, becomes autonomous, exerting a possessive action on the Ego. Consequently, the purpose of consciousness and the exercise of free will are disturbed. "In our inferior functions we are all primitive; in our differentiated function we are civilized, convinced that we possess free will, whereas in our inferior function we are completely without it. Our inferior function is a weak point, an open wound through which anything can enter" (Jung 1943/1987, 2015, p. 73). In the second place, the inferior function is unsuitable for orienting oneself in the inner and outer world because it expresses itself univocally, without nuance. A truly differentiated function, as Jung states, is always marked by a shadow of contradictions. An evolved thought is able to proceed by paradox, just as a refined feeling contains an element of doubt (ivi, p. 71). It can therefore be said that a superior function has integrated the Shadow principle, while the inferior function embodies a type of Shadow which, having no contact with light, is split from the rest of the personality, and thus condemned to stasis. For example, an intellectual type, who uses thought as a dominant function to adapt to reality and who may, therefore, fall victim to archaic feelings, has a tremendous fear of falling in love. And quite rightly, as he could set his sights on a woman who is unsuitable for him, "since his feelings are only aroused by a femme fatale, that is a primitive female (ivi, p. 73).

In *The Psychology of the Unconscious*, Jung explains his concept of Shadow, considering it from another angle: "By shadow I mean the 'negative' side of the personality, the sum of all those unpleasant qualities we like to hide, together with the insufficiently developed functions and the contents of the personal unconscious" (1917/1943, 1966, p. 66, note 5). Here, the affective movement of the Ego is the principal lens through which the Shadow can be observed. The Shadow is not dark solely because it is unconscious and unknown, but also because it has been valued negatively. As Trevi writes, the Shadow can be understood as "the unaccepted part of the personality (commonly defined as the 'dark side' of an individual): the sum of the tendencies, characteristics, attitudes, and desires that are unacceptable to the Ego" (1975, p. 13). In this case, however, the Ego does not only reject the truly inferior or bad aspects of one's nature, but may also spurn an inability to be corrected or a limit to be overcome. Then, the meaning of the Shadow is strictly linked to the Ego's need to construct a false image of itself. Rather than being what the Ego does not know or what it holds in contempt, the Shadow becomes what the Ego does not want to know, and the immorality of the Ego, which thus configured is the real Shadow, lies in its having ceased to genuinely seek its own truth, insofar as it is painful and difficult. Everything we do not like, rightly or wrongly, is refused and goes to constitute the secondary personality, which thus seems unpleasant and extraneous, even though intrinsically bound up with us. In fact, the Shadow represents not only specific unconscious contents, but also a particular relation that the Ego establishes with them. In other words, if the Ego uses the defense of removal and does not enter into contact with its inner sphere and the archetypal world, the personal unconscious and the collective unconscious become Shadow, i.e., a negative part of the personality and of the psyche in general (Carotenuto 1977, p. 110). In this event, we may also speak of a "white Shadow" (Gallard-Drahon, 1987), since we are dealing with a void, an absence of images, which is the opposite of the "black Shadow," a principle charged with corporeality, and therefore very real. Thus, the negativity of the Shadow would be a consequence of the refusal of consciousness to contemplate it. The Ego's failing to pay attention to its Shadow deprives it of various opportunities to discover the potentialities hidden beneath its surface. From this standpoint, the Shadow would behave rather like our inner child. The more the Ego inhibits the Shadow through its criticisms, the more the Shadow is forced to react, charging itself with apparently negative and hostile elements: "The educated man tries to repress the inferior man in himself, not realizing that by so doing he forces the latter into revolt" (Jung 1938/1940, 2014, p. 79).

Another positive aspect of the Shadow is linked not so much to its contents as to its function of correcting the orientation of consciousness: "In analytical psychology, the *Shadow* is the sum-total of all the personal and collective psychic dispositions which, due to their incompatibility with the consciously chosen way of life, are not experienced and merge in a relatively autonomous partial personality with opposed unconscious tendencies. With regard to consciousness, the Shadow has a compensatory function and its action can, therefore, be positive" (Jung 1927, 1963, p. 93 n.). This particular beneficial function of the Shadow in promoting the maturation of the personality emerges clearly in the following observation by Jung: "This 'sliding' consciousness is thoroughly characteristic of modern man. But the one-sidedness it causes can be removed by what I have called the 'realization of the shadow' [,...] the growing awareness of the inferior part of the personality, which should not be twisted into an intellectual activity, for it has far more the meaning of a suffering and a passion that implicate the whole man" (1947/1954, 2014, p. 208).

This does not, however, prevent inferior aspects of our nature, which can be very painful to accept and position in our conscious personality, from emerging during the exploration of the Shadow. Jung's term for them was the "statistical delinquent," that is, the general predisposition toward evildoing inevitably present in human nature (a knowledge of which makes us more human, enabling us to better comprehend the blame and errors of others).

Hence the Shadow, with its multiple meanings, gives our life both depth and authenticity. From "negative part of the personality" it becomes the pole of an energetic relationship, a term of the eternal dialectic between value and disvalue (Trevi and Romano 1975, pp. 17–19).

The collective aspect of the Shadow

Coming into contact with the collective aspect of the Shadow means subjectively retracing the experience of human and pre-human history that took place during phylogenesis, as well as penetrating the primitive modes of psychic functioning that express the events and aims of our biological substrate formed during ontogenesis. In order to accomplish this, the Ego must reconnect to the Self, i.e., to that psychic greatness which comprises the single individuality but goes beyond it to embrace the human collectivity of every age, and the whole world. As Jung maintains, in fact, the Self is both the center of the field that comprises the Ego, consciousness, the personal unconscious and collective unconscious, and the totality of that field. The Jungian concept of "Ego" and of "Self" is well defined in the following passage: "By ego I understand a complex of ideas which constitutes the center of my field of consciousness and appears to possess a high degree of continuity and identity. Hence I also speak of an *ego-complex* The ego-complex is as much a content as a condition of *consciousness*, for a psychic element is conscious to me only in so far as it is related to my ego-complex. But inasmuch as the ego is only the center of my field of consciousness, it is not identical with the totality of my psyche, being merely one complex among other complexes. I therefore distinguish between the *Ego* and the *Self*, since the Ego is only the subject of my consciousness, while the self is the subject of my total psyche, which also includes the unconscious. In this sense the self would be an ideal entity which embraces the Ego" (Jung 1921, 2014, p. 425). Since the first approach to the Shadow is always an approach to unconsciousness, there is an analogy between collective Shadow and collective unconscious. Just as the Shadow is superimposed on the personal unconscious at an individual level, it is superimposed on the collective unconscious at a trans-individual level. For Jung, the collective unconscious is not a product of individual experiences: "… it is innate in us, just like the differentiated brain with which we are born. This is simply the same as saying that our psychic structure, like our cerebral anatomy, bears the phylogenetic traces of its slow and constant edification that has taken place over millions of years. We are born, in a certain sense, in an edifice that has been constructed since time immemorial, which rests on millenary foundations, and which we resurrect. We have climbed all the rungs of the animal ladder and our body bears countless traces of this; for instance, the human embryo still has gills. We have a whole series of organs that are none other than ancestral throwbacks. In the organizational plan of our body we are still segmented like worms, whose sympathetic nervous system we also possess. Hence we carry our complete genealogical history within us, in the structure of our body and of our nervous system. This is also true of our soul, since it too reveals traces of its past and of its ancestral evolution.

Theoretically speaking, we could reconstruct the story of humanity starting from a psychic structure, since everything that once existed is still present and alive in us. [...] In the psychic sphere, the collective unconscious is constituted by a series of past existences" (Jung 1943/1987, 2015, pp. 159–160).

Here, I shall refer to three different moments in the process of approaching the collective unconscious, and hence the archetypal world. These, of course, are not moments that are over and done with, since they can be experienced more than once; thus, it would be more correct to consider them not as chronological stages, but as positions assumed by the Ego during its relationship with the great originary images.

In the first phase, given the enormous distance that separates us from the collective unconscious, the images will appear unusual, and even monstrous at times; in the second, they will embody the opposite poles of the archetype, which may even split, exercising a possessive action on the Ego; and in the third, the opposites will be reunited in a single image.

First moment

The first moment consists primarily in the encounter with our body, when our evolved consciousness engages with the most archaic psychic structures, i.e., the sensitive motor spinal cord and sympathetic nervous system that regulates visceral sensibility and the metabolism of the internal organs (Jung, ivi, p. 161). This is a difficult encounter, since it seeks to reestablish the harmony interrupted by the one-sided orientation of consciousness. If, as Jung states, a philosophical system or religious doctrine cause physical illnesses in us, such as a gastric disorder, this is the clearest evidence of their falseness: "When I wish to know if a truth is bona fide and beneficial, if it is an authentic truth, I incorporate it, I assimilate it, so to speak... if it collaborates harmoniously... with the other elements of my psychism... if I continue to function properly, to behave well and nothing in me rebels against the foreign body, I tell myself that it is a bona fide truth ... the things truly worthy of man are so complete to him that his whole being is perfectly expressed in them" (ivi, p. 163). This stance is clearly indebted to American pragmatism.

The archetypal images that correspond to this level of psychic functioning are generally represented by archaic animals with fantastical and mythological characteristics, like the snake or dragon. In fact, such animals share our spinal and sympathetic nervous system, and condense everything that seems extraordinary, unpredictable and, in a certain sense, incommensurable, to a puerile logic holding that reality can be eliminated simply by considering it insignificant. Modern man should contemplate behaving in a way that would earn the approval of the saurian, the cold-blooded animal dormant in him; otherwise, this creature, which represents the biological process, the instinct that has not been called upon, will rise up in a hostile manner against a consciousness that has become too rigid and ill-equipped for life. In this case, there would be a deep Shadow in our very body and in the archetypal images that represent it, which would threaten us.

For Jung, bringing our body into experience also means stimulating instinct: "Our rational philosophy does not bother itself with whether the other person in us, pejoratively described as the 'shadow,' is in sympathy with our conscious plans and intentions. Evidently it does not know that we carry in ourselves a real shadow whose existence is grounded in our instinctual nature" (Jung 1957, 2014, p. 290). The instinct can be likened to a band of energy which, rooted in *bios*, moves the organism toward the outer world in relation to the vital process.

As an innate behavior model, instinct definitely has an element of the obligatory and of automatism, at least in what Jung refers to as the physiological aspect of instinct, which corresponds to the "partie inférieure des fonctions" (inferior part of functions) described by Pierre Janet (Jung 1919, 2014, p. 180). This is composed of impulses that proceed, without any conscious motivation, from an inner constraint. Since instinct is not subject to will and drives us to perform actions that are not premeditated, which may be judged primitive or violent by ethically-oriented reason, it can also represent a Shadow. We should bear in mind, however, that for Jung bringing instinct into experience also means bringing it close to its opposite archetypal pole, where blind movement can be psychicized and thus more aligned with the intention of the soul. The archetypal image is, in fact, a mental representation of instinct: "The primordial image might suitably be described as the *instinct's perception of itself*, or as the self-portrait of the instinct" (ivi, p. 136). But since the archetypes are part of the spiritual sphere and the spirit is the archetype of meaning, retrieving the Shadow potentially contained in the instinctual impulse enables us to reconnect the image of the action to the sense of its purpose. While, for Jung, the instinct is a model of behavior, the archetype is a model of representation. "In spite or perhaps because of its affinity with instinct, the archetype represents the authentic element of spirit, but a spirit which is not to be identified with the human intellect, since it is the latter's *spiritus rector*" (Jung 1947/1954, 2014, p. 206). This would enable man to rid most of his behavior of blind determinism and to shape a capacity to act with purpose.

Can it be said, therefore, that spirit and instinct, sense and force are linked by the Shadow, or must necessarily pass through it to evolve? Jung seems to think so when he speaks of the need to reconcile intellectual and moral judgment with the demands of life. In *Psychological Types*, he holds that instinctive forces are of an "impure" nature:

> Seen from the heights of a differentiated point of view, whether rational or ethical, these instinctive forces are "impure." But life itself flows from springs both clear and muddy. Hence all excessive "purity lacks vitality. […] Every renewal of life needs the muddy as well as the clear.
>
> (Jung 1921, 2014, pp. 244–245)

The moment of the integration of instinct could be represented by the mythologem of the "trickster," an expression of the collective Shadow. In an early phase of the mythological cycle, in fact, this figure's behavior is characterized by coarseness, vulgarity, foolishness and, at times, maliciousness, all deriving from a lack of consciousness. However, in later more developed stages the figure becomes increasingly dense with meaning, and even the bearer of salvific functions. Possessing ambivalent traits that are both animal and divine, the trickster in his clearest manifestations "is a faithful reflection of an absolutely undifferentiated human consciousness, corresponding to a psyche that has hardly left the animal level" (Jung 1954, 2014, p. 260). Also in this case the transformation is made through contact with archaic aspects of the soul, especially with regard to praxis.

A dream referred to by Jung clearly illustrates how the Shadow can be encountered at the level of both the personal unconscious and the collective unconscious. This dream, which I shall describe briefly, was had by a young man a few months before succumbing to a manic-depressive psychosis: Beneath Toledo Cathedral there is a cistern full of water, with a subterranean connection to the River Tagus. In the cistern, which is like a small dark crypt, there is a huge snake with eyes glittering like precious stones. The reptile is guarding a golden bowl containing a key-dagger, a precious object because it will give its possessor sovereignty over the whole city. Instead of going down himself into the snake's lair to take the talisman, the dreamer sends a male friend, a Moor, who fails to carry out his mission and, consequently, is left there as if he were a decorative object (summary based on the text in 1943/1987, 2015, pp. 176–177).

According to Jung, the Moor represents the dreamer's personal Shadow, which embodies the pagan culture that was judged inferior and later supplanted by the Christian vision of the world. At a symbolic level, this signifies that after a whole body of values had been disavowed they were separated from consciousness and constituted a Shadow from that moment on, since the Ego was unable to recover their sense and function. The fact that the Moor was abandoned as something useless and devoid of life evidently means that the Shadow, with its hidden reserves of energy and wisdom, was lost. Thus, the first task in the individuation process failed, namely the recognition of the personal Shadow, a threshold we must cross to make contact with the most hidden contents of the psyche. The young man entrusted to the unconscious part of the soul a task of vital importance, which he should have carried out himself, using all the available resources of his personality.

The snake, on the other hand, represents a much more archaic part of the psyche, and therefore a collective image of Shadow. Recognizing the snake as a part of oneself is much more difficult than recognizing the Moor as one's alter ego, because the latter, though judged inferior and thus rejected, at least has a human face. "The snake [...] is a cold-blooded vertebrate that embodies the inferior psyche, dark psychism, and the unconscious. But also what is rare, incomprehensible and monstrous, and can rise up in us, as our enemy, capable, for example, of making us mortally ill" (ivi, pp. 179–180). However, it guards a secret that the elders still knew, but to which the Christian Church has remained impervious: "It is the earthly secret of the *inferior soul*, of the *natural man* who does not live in a purely cerebral way, and in whom the spinal cord and sympathetic system still have something to say" (ivi, p. 194). The dream represents an attempt to remedy but, at the same time, prefigures failure. Jung also sees it as a message for contemporary Western culture: an invitation to reflect on our diseases and our failings, in order to emerge from the sterility and violence to which a certain way of thinking has led us. It may be said, in fact, that since Parmenides postulated the equivalence between being and thinking, the knowledge of reality, acquired mainly through reason, has been progressively utilized to possess and exploit that reality. Thus, a more profound vision of the world, which cannot be perceived through the senses alone, nor explained solely by the intellect, has been lost. In fact, the whole of reality has a subjective dimension that, in a certain sense, demands and invokes empathic interaction with every human being, in order to pursue its creative process.

In the world of literature and theatre we also find the drama of a splitting between knowledge and life. In the play *The Rules of the Game*, Luigi Pirandello demonstrates that the defensive use of reason, which seeks to avoid the suffering that comes with accepting knowing along with living, warps human relationships to the point of activating irrepressible murderous instincts. Leone Gala sets his emotions aside and becomes a "spectator" of life. For him, the intellectual game is a tremendous thrill "that clears away all the sentimental sediment from your mind, and fixes in calm, precise orbits all that moves tumultuously within you." Leone likens the "concept" to which things and people can be reduced if one refuses to invest feelings in them, to an empty egg shell that can be turned around at will. His wife, Silia, succumbs to the toxic effect of her husband's gaze, as he anticipates every step of any initiative she might take, to the extent of paralyzing her spontaneity. Silia's emotional and instinctual world, which erupts through her vengeful act, is no less destructive than Leone's lucid observation, devoid of emotion, which scatters a lethal poison over life. The symmetry between the break in interpersonal relationship and that in intrapsychic relations could not be more evident and dramatic. Indeed, an irreducible enmity is created between Self and other than self, and likewise between reason and passion.[10]

Lastly, for Jung, passing through the Shadow that envelops the collective unconscious also means breaking through its exterior and making contact with those "hidden values" which consist of "increasingly numinous figures" (Jung 1954, 2014, p. 270). If this is the case we must expect that after making this descent into the depths of the Shadow, the Ego will have to confront the images and forces that inhabit the primordial Self. As Jung states, the risks involved in such an undertaking are that the Ego will be assimilated to the Self, which would imply a loss of personal differentiation, or the Self will be assimilated to the Ego, through the accentuation of the world of consciousness and

the reduction of the figures of the unconscious to mere psychological existence, i.e., to a subjective invention (while, far from being a product of the
imagination, they would possess a relative autonomy and reality deriving from
the "objective" psyche). Either way, the result would be "inflation," that is, a
loss of ego boundaries (Jung 1951, 2014, pp. 24–25). This danger could be
symbolized by the Shadow of the collective unconscious in the mythical
themes of being swallowed by a dragon or poisoned by a snake. Which is perhaps why, in Jung's clinical example, the snake asks the dreamer to send him a
child. Of course, this does not mean that one should "remain a child," "but
that the adult should summon up enough honest self-criticism admixed with
humility to see where, and in relation to what, he must behave as a child – irra-
tionally, and with unreflecting receptivity" (Jung 1942/1948, 2014, p. 183).

With regard to the Self, the Ego has not only to sacrifice its puerile dependence, but also to forego exclusive independence, and to learn, as a child does,
to allow a whole world to live within without paralyzing it with judgment and
censure. As Jung writes: "as he grows, the individual forgets the secret of
infantile totality [...] of the child who lives in a kind of Garden of Eden
where all beings grow peaceably alongside each other" (Jung 1943/1987,
2015, p. 183).

Second moment

During the second moment of contact with the collective portrayals of the
Shadow, the archetypal images split violently into antagonistic representations. Where religion is concerned, there appears a good God, the expression
of supreme good, and a devil, bringer of all evil. In fairytales and myths,
we see the good and bad magician, the fairy and the witch, the figure of the
savior and that of the antagonist. I think there is a similarity between this
second moment and the stage of psychic development in infancy that Klein
associates with the "schizoparanoid position" (1946).

We may suppose that the splitting of the archetypal image into apparently
irreconcilable poles, in order to reinforce one of them, results from an attempt
by the unconscious to compensate a one-sided attitude of Ego consciousness.
But it can also be the response to a person's renunciation of individual differentiation, due to his feeling overburdened by acute misery, i.e., by a psychological situation characterized by the dominance of emotions such as despair,
doubt, anxiety, and fear. According to Jung, these emotional reactions always
imply regression and lead "... to group formation, or rather to clustering
together in masses for the sake of gregarious security" (1957, 1970, p. 594). In
the group common human traits, and especially instinctual qualities of a
primitive nature, are agglomerated, while the more evolved and differentiated
individual capabilities elide each other. Hence, as Jung states, the psychology
of the masses is always inferior to that of the individual, and the whole of a
nation never reacts like a modern individual, but always like primitive group
being (ibid., p. 595): "Man in the group is always unreasonable, irresponsible,

emotional, erratic and unreliable. Crimes the individual alone could never stand, are freely committed by the group being" (ibid., p. 595). Moreover, the masses need to identify with a "charismatic leader" (Weber), who both represents them and embodies the "state," thus easily exercising the "absolute power" required by the collectivity. It follows, therefore, that individuals who identify with the nation are dominated precisely by the "absolute power complex," and that this complex attracts the negative pole of one or more archetypes, exerting a possessive effect on the individual Ego. This would benefit the individual in the sense that it would shatter the illusion of his having rid himself of all feelings of inferiority, weakness and anxiety, and of his having acquired a position of superiority and unassailable strength. However, the archetype's negative pole would become the energetic support of an omnipotence complex with which a formerly fragile Ego would identify. I think that this mechanism may also be likened to a form of Shadow that we may call "absolute," as I shall explain below.

The concatenation of such psychic events is tellingly conveyed by Jung's reflections on the behavior of the German people during the period between the two world wars.

At the end of World War I, the Paris Peace Conference saw the stipulation of the Treaty of Versailles and the founding of the League of Nations, whose purpose was to protect weak countries from attack by aggressors, and to guarantee their right to self-determination. The Peace Conference was presided over by French Prime Minister Georges Clemenceau, whose radical implementation of his plans earned him the nickname "Le Tigre." The treaty adopted strict measures against Germany, requiring the country to make large reparation payments to the nations it had attacked and to restore to France the territory of Alsace and Lorraine, annexed during the Franco-Prussian War in 1871. Other measures adopted against Germany included: the reduction of its army by limiting the number of soldiers; the release of prisoners of war; control of German factories and goods produced for import and export; the demilitarization of the Rhineland; the setting up of a naval blockade around the country; and the renouncement of sovereignty of former colonies. In addition, the former German emperor Wilhelm II ran the risk of being tried by an international court for supreme offence against international morality and the sanctity of treaties, and Germany had to acknowledge sole responsibility for the outbreak of the world war.

Understandably, these events caused the German people to feel severely impoverished, humiliated and oppressed, to the extent they became extremely resentful and angry, and thirsted for revenge against the victorious nations. This may well have led individuals to abandon their autonomy and independence of thought to merge with the masses, and thus to identify with the power of the many of which they had become part, which could explain the birth of National Socialism and the acclamation of Hitler, i.e. of a supreme leader, endowed with totalitarian powers to redeem his people from the misery and inferiority to which they had been reduced.

According to Jung, the sociopolitical configuration and the historic events in Germany during the years that followed World War I, which we now know led to another more devastating war, cannot be understood simply through a rational explanation based on economic and political factors, or even on the laws governing the psychology of the Ego complex. Far deeper, and in a certain sense unfathomable, psychic factors linked to the collective unconscious would have had to have been activated to reawaken a great archetypal image belonging to the German people: the god Wotan. In 1936 Jung wrote: "... laying aside our well-meaning, all-too-human reasonableness, [and if we may] burden God or the gods with the responsibility for contemporary events instead of man, we would find Wotan quite suitable as a causal hypothesis. In fact, I venture the heretical suggestion that the unfathomable depths of Wotan's character explain more of National Socialism than all three reasonable factors put together" (1936, 2014, p. 184). Jung sees Wotan as an irrational psychic "factor" and a fundamental attribute of the German psyche, which acts on "the high pressure of civilization like a cyclone and blows it away" (ivi, p. 186). As an archetypal image, Wotan is an *Ergreifer*, "one who seizes," and thus would have possessed the psyche of each and every German. "All human control comes to an end when the individual is caught in a mass movement. Then the archetypes begin to function..." (ivi p. 189). Jung accurately describes, drawing inspiration from Ninck, the characteristics of the god Wotan (1935):

> ... the berserker, the god of storm, the wanderer, the warrior, the *Wunsch-* and *Minne*-god, the lord of the dead and of the *Einherjer* (fallen heroes who dwell in Valhalla), the master of secret knowledge, the magician, and the god of the poets. Neither the Valkyries nor the *Fylgjur* (companion spirits that often assume the form of animals) are forgotten, for they form part of the mythological background and fateful significance of Wotan).
>
> (ivi, p. 287)

This portrait ... "shows that Wotan is not only a god of rage and frenzy who embodies the instinctual and emotional aspect of the unconscious. Its intuitive and inspiring side also manifests itself in him, for he understands the runes and can interpret fate" (ivi, p. 188).

This portrait ... shows that Wotan is not only a god of rage and frenzy who embodies the instinctual and emotional aspect of the unconscious. Its intuitive and inspiring side also manifests itself in him, for he understands the runes and can interpret fate".The god Wotan is clearly an archetypal image with two different sides: on the one hand he is "restless, violent, stormy"; on the other, "ecstatic and mantic" (ivi, p. 192).

We may therefore conclude that the poles of the archetypal image embodying the god Wotan were violently split in the psyche of the German people and that the unconscious of single individuals was possessed by the god's negative aspect, namely the furious warrior who implacably storms the enemy to annihilate him; whereas his divinatory powers, which see beyond appearances and can set in motion and produce the endless becoming of beings and the world, was completely scotomized. The identification of single individuals and of an entire people with the negative pole of the god served to repress an inferiority complex, but led to the assertion of an absolute power and a domination complex whose terrible Shadow fell across the entire collectivity.

Third moment

The third and last moment is characterized by the reconciliation of the opposites inherent in the archetypal world. The primitive unconscious ambivalence becomes conflict that is consciously experienced and overcome. For Jung, this stage is symbolized by Job, the man who reveals the contradictory nature of God.[11] A divinity capable of inflicting the cruelest and undeserved calamities on man, in order to test his faith, his constant worship and his persistence in considering him a just god, clearly still possesses an element of unconsciousness and amorality on which he has not reflected. From the two, the one. In Job's case, God either foresaw the consequences of his acts, and thus had to come to terms with his injustice, or he used his faculty of omnipotence, forgetting that of omniscience, and had to come to terms with his blindness: "For Job, the God-image split and he became conscious of the divine ambivalence" (Jung 1948/1975, p. 118).[12] Job discovers God's Shadow without succumbing to the hubris of consciousness, because he intuits that the Shadow, with its multiple aspects of ignorance, primitiveness and evil, occupies an important place, albeit obscure to reason, in the cosmos. When faced with the temptation to abandon a god who is incomprehensible and amoral, or unaware of himself, and to set himself up as the sole judge on Earth, Job's deeply religious spirit recognizes its limits, and chooses to prostrate itself and worship the Mystery:

> Therefore have I uttered that I understood not;
> things too wonderful for me, which I knew not.
> Hear, I beseech thee, and I will speak:
> I will demand of thee, and declare thou unto me.
> I have heard of thee by the hearing of the ear:
> but now mine eye seeth thee.
> Wherefore I abhor myself,
> and repent in dust and ashes.
> (Job 42, 3–6 KJV).

In acting thus, Job avoids the two grave dangers which threaten him from above and below: the refusal to use the tool of judgment, and identification with ethical reason. In the first case, he would have doubted his innocence and betrayed his human truth, his guilt feelings would have destroyed him physically and psychically, and nothing new would have happened in the world because the dialogue between God and man would have been permanently interrupted (in fact, the collective voice insinuated that as God was unquestionably good, the tragedies that had befallen Job could only have been brought about by his having sinned). In the second case, he would have found himself in a sterile, rarefied limbo, and deprived of all vital contact with the emotional and the irrational sphere.

If life provokes consciousness through its chaotic madness, consciousness provokes life by demanding consistency and sense: "God is obliged to have recourse to human sin to know what is good and what is evil, for his purpose of salvation" (Jung 1948/1975, p. 165).

The *Deus absconditus* of nature gives a terrible lesson to Job but, in his turn, he teaches God justice and compassion.

We may conclude, therefore, that Job's reflections and actions cause the divine and human dimensions of reality to interpenetrate and, in a certain, sense complete each other; thus, as Jung states, God's answer to Job can only be the former's future incarnation. This means that, rather than splitting and excluding each other, the great archetypal poles of "knowledge and ignorance" and "good and evil" merge and are both transformed by the incommensurable reality of the "Self." In fact, when the Ego is at its level of greatness, we cannot be simultaneously conscious and unconscious of a given psychic content; while at the level of the Self, consciousness no longer identifies solely with reason or with sensory perceptions, but comprises the profound intuition of realities that embrace the Mystery, going beyond the visible and describable concrete datum. Similarly, with regard to the good/evil dichotomy, at the level of the Ego we are required to choose, because we cannot simultaneously perform an act that we consider good and one that we consider evil, while at the level of the Self the principles of evil and our "so-called good" are assimilated and transformed. Thus, evil relinquishes its sting and becomes the force, determination and truth of good, and good, in its turn, drops its mask of conformism, acquiescence and unconditional obedience, providing the impetus to becoming that leads to a feeling of completeness, of joy, and freedom.

Obviously, the synthesis and transformation of the poles of the antitheses can only be effected at highly advanced stages in the individuation process, which not all human beings are able to reach. Consequently, knowledge and ignorance, good and evil, remain realities to be faced when antithetically configured.

Shadow and evil

Evil is certainly part of the Shadow and, as well as being perhaps the most brutal provocation in life, is also the enigma that sparked most of Jung's speculations on the relationships between psychology and religion. It is an inexhaustible theme that can be addressed from many different perspectives: metaphysical, ontological, ethical, psychological and historical, to name a few.

First of all, Jung dissents from the conception, characteristic of some Christian thinkers, which considers evil from an apotropaic standpoint to avoid dealing with an issue that is both inconvenient and disturbing. Evil is not simply the "absence of good," but something real and substantial. Just like the Shadow, in fact, which exists in itself and is not merely an effect created by projected light.

Indeed, if there were no evil, good would not exist: "as psychological experience shows, 'good' and 'evil' are opposite poles of a moral judgment which, as such, originates in man. A judgment can be made about a thing only if its opposite is equally real and possible. ... How can one speak of 'good' at all if there is no 'evil'? Or of 'light' if there is no 'darkness,' or of 'above' if there is no "below?" (Jung 1942/1948, 2014, p. 168).

Hence, an apparent evil can only be opposed by an apparent good, and an evil without substance by a good without substance.

However, Jung also distances himself from the Manichean stance, being of the opinion that evil is not an absolute principle that can be hypostatized and placed in opposition to the principle of good, but an aspect of the originary entity itself. The devil, identified with evil by another school of Christian thought, can also be seen as the antagonist within the dialectical process of God: "In every monotheistic religion everything that goes against God can only be traced to God himself" (ivi, p. 167). For Jung, this metaphysical aspect of evil is inseparable from the psychological aspect, because God and archetype of the Self are indistinguishable and, since all reality is experienced through images, the representation of God corresponds to that of the Self: the soul is to God what the eye is to light. The following passage is significant in this regard: "Consequently, man's achievement of consciousness appears as the result of prefigurative archetypal processes or – to put it metaphysically – as part of the divine life-process. In other words, God becomes manifest in the human act of reflection" (ibid., p. 161). All this would lead us to think that good and evil are actually intertwined and that one pole of the antithesis they constitute cannot eliminate the other; however, if we cannot eliminate the predisposition to evil from the individual soul and from the human collectivity, neither can we eliminate the principle of good which, paradoxically, flourishes in the most unjust and evil situations. Recently, I was struck by an episode recounted by Edith Bruck, a Hungarian Jewess, writer and poet, in her book *Il pane perduto* (The Lost Bread). From the age of thirteen, Edith was interned in various concentration camps, where she lost her entire family: parents, grandparents and a brother. Then she had an experience in Dachau that eased her desperation. "And there, one day, a miracle happened! After he had finished eating, a soldier threw his mess tin at me, ordering me to wash it, like every other day. And inside, on the bottom, he had left me some jam, which for me meant hope, the goodness of heaven and earth, the strength to keep going, the will to survive and to believe that in the depths of darkness there is light. And as evil begets evil, good begets good" (*Il pane perduto*, La nave di Teseo, 2021 Milan, p. 46). At the heart of one of the most atrocious manifestations of collective cruelty that history has ever known, a human being participating in the extermination of an entire people was miraculously moved to tenderness and compassion, seeking in some small way to make amends to a defenseless young girl who was suffering and confused.

In the context of the Creation, evil manifests as the transgression of God's will, first by Lucifer and then by man. But if evil also exists in God, if evil is the Shadow of God, then we may suppose that this transgression is in keeping with a more deeply hidden divine will. The manifest will would resemble the commands a father gives to his children, also in the hope that in time they will disregard them, in order to become adult and self-responsible. Hence, disobedience was the initial act that established an autonomous reality. Without it, the unity of the absolute would never have been divided, and the multiplicity of beings, the flow of energy projected toward the future, and freedom, would not have originated. The Creation would have remained a mere emanation of God, a kind of machine in the hands of its builder, and God himself, confined to a boundless uniformity devoid of space and time, would not have been able to reveal himself through his work. "Lucifer was perhaps the one who best understood the divine will struggling to create a world and who carried out that will most faithfully. For, by rebelling against God, he became the active principle of a creation which opposed to God a counter-will of its own" (Jung 1942/1948, 2014, p. 196). Ontological evil also fosters the coming into being of reality because, in a certain sense, it constitutes the limit, the space-time boundary within which phenomena can unfold. We could also say that a world without evil, and hence without suffering and death, would be perfect, but we would be forgetting that it could never exist. As Trevi observes, the fundamental philosophical question, "*Si Deus est, unde malum?*," can be reversed: "*Si malum non est, unde Deus?*" (1975, p. 32). Illuminating in this regard is a Sufi legend recounted by Panikkar: "... Allah once addressed himself to a Sufi who was spending his life in a hermitage in the desert, heaped with honors and veneration by the local populace, who would supply him with food in return for his counsel. 'Were I to tell the people what a great sinner thou art, no one would wish to have anything to do with thee any longer.' 'Yea, Lord," replied the Sufi, and added, 'But were I to tell them how merciful thou art, neither would anyone wish to have anything more to do with thee.' And so it was agreed that neither would betray their common secret" (1985, p. 199, note 182). This legend clearly demonstrates that the antinomy of good and evil can be eliminated from neither the human nor the divine dimension, which is also the foundation of our being, because it performs an essential and transformative role in the becoming of the world. In other words, one can pardon, indeed forgiveness is a fundamental act in exercising goodness, but this does not mean that one should forget the wrong or forego judgment and the application of justice. The Italian root of pardon, *per dono*, means to give back to someone, "as a gift," on a symbolic level, all the missed opportunities and the paths not taken, which help to rebuild the sense of one's own being and trust in one's own creative abilities.

At the end of analysis, a female patient had a dream in which she was present, with her analyst nearby, at surgery performed on a man's brain: the centers of evil had to be reconnected to the peripheral nerve pathways. At a certain point the surgeon broke out in a cold sweat and, seized by profound anxiety, said to his assistant, who had the analyst's face: "If the operation is unsuccessful, the man could become a delinquent, a murderer when he regains consciousness. Perhaps it would be better to give up and let him die." The assistant protested, exclaiming in a loud voice, "We have to risk it, let's keep going!" In relation to this dream, we might imagine divine wisdom as a female spiritual figure who assisted God when he doubted the goodness of his creation. Out of a love for life, she would have borne the wounds inflicted by all future violence, by all sin and by all the suffering that would have been experienced, to prevent the world from being plunged into gloom without time and without hope.[13] We may suppose that when there is no conscious awareness of evil, together with the possibility and, eventually, the desire to perpetrate it; that is, without those functions represented and rendered efficient by the connection of the nerve pathways to the cerebral cortex, nothing can be held responsible for that evil, as in the case of natural disasters. But in this event its transformation, which always implies the exercise of consciousness and the attribution, to oneself or others, of the acts carried out, would not be possible.

Moreover, if evil did not exist atonement for sin, and consequently redemption, would never be possible. At a psychological level, this perhaps means reconnecting evil to the opposite root of good, and suffering their contradiction within the soul. Instead of being expelled or resolved by excluding one of the poles, the conflict would thus be completely assimilated to the inner self which, like an alchemical still, would trigger a reaction between different elements and the birth of a new substance. Hence, the redemption of evil does not mean ignoring, defeating or destroying it, or even projecting it onto a scapegoat who will be obliged to pay for our sin; but assimilating it and willingly and consciously accepting the fact that we will be transformed by the clash between opposing factors. The god Shiva is depicted in blue or violet in various representations because he has swallowed all the poison in the world, in order to metabolize it and to neutralize its destructive power. According to myth, when the world had just begun, demons and gods together extracted the elixir of immortality, or life, from the ocean's churning depths. But once the elixir arrived on Earth, it turned into a potent poison that would have destroyed the entire universe if Shiva had not offered to swallow it and render it harmless through the suffering of his body, which reacted to the effects of the poison by setting in motion a biological process to degrade it. We may suppose that the elixir of immortality represents the aspiration to omnipotence, to immunity to the limits of life that necessarily ends, and to exemption from the possibility of committing error and sin, and that this impulse itself is the poison of an evil that tends to spread rapidly, becoming a kind of "Absolute Shadow." As a god, Shiva can obviously host boundless evil within, whereas man, a limited creature, can only accommodate the amount of evil he is able to metabolize without perishing from it.

However, if we consider that the psyche consists not only of the Ego but also the Self, that it contains "collective man" who participates in the destiny of the whole of humanity, we can also see ourselves as the link in the chain of the global redemption of evil. In *Aion* Jung states: "It is quite within the bounds of possibility for a man to recognize the relative evil of his nature, but it is a rare and shattering possibility for him to gaze into the face of absolute evil," where "absolute evil" should be understood as all of existing evil (1951, 1982, p. 10). In *Answer to Job* Satan embodies the threats to human beings issued by God himself, as if he were "a destructive demonic principle firmly anchored in the plan of redemption" (Jung 1948/1975). Through the actuation of his Shadow and through sin, God sought to set in motion a process aimed to transform the world. The Original Sin is nothing but the human continuation of that first divine sin, through which evil ceases to be absolute and is relativized, becoming the pole of an antinomy. "We know of course that without sin there is no repentance and without repentance no redeeming grace, also that without original sin the redemption of the world could never have come about; but we assiduously avoid investigating whether in this very power of evil God might not have placed some special purpose which it is most important for us to know" (Jung 1944, 1968, p. 61).

But why was sin so important in triggering the story of salvation? Could there have been a world that did not need saving? Firstly, it should be said that, in some cases, a negative act performed and recognized as such (which obviously can also occur at the inner level, in the form of fantasy or intention) circumscribes evil, while a state of continuous temptation, rejected in the belief that one is superior to others, acts like a poison that contaminates the whole of life. Jung cites in this regard the Neoplatonic philosopher Carpocrates: "No man can be redeemed from a sin he has not committed" (1927, 'Woman in Europe' 2014, p. 131). This means that in order to be forgiven one must have experienced falling into sin, a conscious and complete understanding of the act committed, a sense of one's own frailty, and regret for the evil caused. This process will likely lead us to develop a more mature humanity than we would have had by preserving our innocence. Secondly, reality, offended by sin, demands that the debt be made good, and the price paid (which obviously involves shouldering a moral burden, as well as making amends) can restore an inner balance and check the destructive forces; in fact, as Jung states: "one can miss not only one's happiness but also one's final guilt, without which a man will never reach his wholeness" (1944, 1968, p. 61).

Clearly, it is most important to avoid an opportunistic misunderstanding of the problem, such as the belief that sin is desirable in itself, or that one can remain indifferent to a moral dilemma because it is inevitable. Jung shows no indulgence whatsoever toward those who wish to remain "beyond good and evil," and to cut, rather than untie, the Gordian knot (1934/1954, 2014, p. 21). Evil is always evil and man must make a superhuman effort to seek to avoid it. In practice, however, it can be extremely difficult to evaluate what is good and what is evil, since the codified norms of behavior are not always appropriate to the circumstances. "On paper the moral code looks clear and neat enough;

but the same document written 'on the tables of the heart,' is often a sorry
tatter, particularly in the mouths of those who talk the loudest" (1944, 1968,
p. 63). According to Trevi and Romano, it is important to avoid adopting two
extreme positions: the identification with evil and the moralistic rejection of
sin (1975, p. 33). In both cases, the Ego would attribute to itself a form of
absolute power: all-out destructiveness or unadulterated pureness. Apropos
of the latter option, Jung observes that there are actual cases in which a sin,
which has been unavoidable, has marked a positive turning point in a man's
destiny: "Yet if you had not taken this step, if you had not trodden this path,
perhaps it would have been a psychic regression, a retrograde step in your
inner development, a piece of infantile cowardice" (1959, 1970, p. 460).

Now, I shall deal briefly with the problem of unconscious sin.

In Jung's view, unconsciousness is a sin in itself when it covers contents
that require only a little effort to be known. In fact, man has a moral commitment to develop consciousness, and so removal as "a sort of half-conscious
and half-hearted letting go of things ... or a looking the other way in order
not to become conscious of one's desires" (Jung 1938/1940, 2014, p. 75).
Moreover, the consequences of unconscious sin are no less serious than those
of its conscious equivalent. As Jung states, human beings are usually rather
indulgent toward sinners who are unaware of their sins, whereas nature is
not: "She punishes them just as severely as if they had committed a conscious
offence" (ivi, p. 73). People who are unconscious of their Shadow have an
ominous aura, engendering inferiority complexes in more fragile individuals
and encouraging immoral behavior in those less morally equipped. These are
situations in which we are contaminated by a projection of Shadow that possesses us, probably by blending with characteristic traits of our own unconscious Shadow, which makes us unable to recognize and to distance it.
According to Jung, many children are compelled to commit the sins from
which their parents have refrained to maintain their respectability (*Le
Conferenze di Basilea*, 1934).

Concerning the question of collective sin, history presents an endless series
of horrors, such as devastating conflicts between states and religions, the bar-
barity of dictatorships, man's exploitation of man, and the destruction of
countless peoples and cultures. There emerges an overall picture of the
human Shadow that, according to Jung, could not be painted in blacker
colors. The evil that comes to light in man is of such gigantic proportions that
speaking of it in terms of the original sin is almost euphemistic (1957, 2014,
p. 296). Even though the individual cannot hold himself personally responsible for all crimes, he shares to some extent the common guilt; for example,
when he adopts a passive attitude and is not capable of protesting against the
directives of leaders. But in every case, it is because human nature itself is
predisposed to evil: "None of us stands outside humanity's black collective
shadow" (ivi, p. 297). On the other hand,

> The evil, the guilt, the profound unease of conscience, the dark foreboding, are there before our eyes, if only we would see. Man has done these

things; I am a man, who has his share of human nature; therefore, I am guilty with the rest and bear unaltered and indelibly within me the capacity and the inclination to do them again at any time.

(ivi, p. 296)

If we do not recognize all this, if we do not personally experience affliction every time the sin is renewed, we cannot develop an image of evil or learn how to deal with it, which could also help us to prevent it: man "regards himself as harmless and so adds stupidity to iniquity" (ivi, p. 296). Shared unconscious responsibility constitutes a serious risk for the collective Shadow, especially today when minds are manipulated by mass propaganda. If man, as an individual, feels he is the victim of uncontrollable forces, he does not realize that his Shadow is a dangerous inner adversary, "involved as an invisible helper in the dark machinations of the political monster" (ivi, p. 299).

Notes

1 Genesis 4: 6–7. Translation by Robert Alter, *The Hebrew Bible*, Volume 1. New York: W.W. Norton, 2019.
2 Goethe, *Faust*, Part I, 1112–1113. Translation by Walter Kaufman.
3 Ibid., 1110–111.
4 Ibid., 323–324.
5 Ibid., 330–34.
6 Ibid., 12105–11. Translation by Paul Bishop at author's request.
7 W. McGuire (ed.). (1977). *C.G. Jung Speaking*, Princeton, NJ: Princeton University Press, p. 436.
8 R. Leakey (with R.A. Lewin). (1977). *Origins: What New Discoveries Reveal about the Emergence of our Species and its Possible Future*, p. 256.
9 I am including various extracts from my chapter 'L'Ombra' in *Trattato di Psicologia Analitica* (UTET, Turin 1992, (ed.) Aldo Carotenuto.
10 This comment on Pirandello sheds light on a type of thought which, as I shall explain later, can be described as "male chauvinist," and is also dealt with in my Preface, p. 29, in the book, edited by myself, entitled *Introduzione alla Psicologia Analitica. Le Conferenze di Basilea (1934) di C.G. Jung, trascritte da Roland Cahen*. Bergamo, Moretti e Vitali 2015, private edition.
11 This passage concerning Job appeared, along with extracts from the following paragraph, in the treatise on analytical psychology (1992, pp. 170–119) in my book *Silenzio a Praga*, Moretti e Vitali, Bergamo 2017, and my correspondence with Murray Stein, *Temporalità, vergogna e il problema del male*, Moretti e Vitali, Bergamo 2019, translated into English under the title *Temporality, Shame and the Problem of Evil in Jungian Psychology. An Exchange of Ideas*, Routledge, London and New York 2021.
12 The citations from Symbolik des Geistes. Studien Über psychische Phänomenologie (Jung 1948), on pp. xxx, xxxi, and xxxv have been translated into English from the Italian version titled La simbolica dello Spirito. Studi sulla Fenomenologia dello Spirito, published by Einaudi, Turin, in 1975.
13 I described this dream in the volume *Temporalità, vergogna e il problema del male, carteggio con Murray Stein*. Moretti e Vitali, Bergamo 1919, translated into English under the title *Temporality, Shame and the problem of Evil. An Exchange of Ideas*, Murray Stein and Elena Caramazza, Routledge, London and New York 2021.

Introduction

The ideas that have inspired this book derive from two sources: on the one hand, my research on the Shadow in Jung's work, which is summed up above, and on the other, my clinical activity in which I have long been concerned with situations where apparently unsolvable problems emerge and all the defenses of the psyche seem to conspire to deny the possibility of arriving at a new and free approach to existence. Hence I have chosen to draw a parallel between a particular way in which the Shadow may be structured, giving rise to the configuration that I have called the "Absolute Shadow," and its phenomenological manifestation that, I believe, is expressed through a negative idea and sense of destiny; indeed, it is as if destiny were a pre-established design that permits no choice, and hence neither the development of a creative dimension nor the exercise of freedom. We may call this a *negative destiny complex* that blocks the possibility of hope and often leads life toward paralysis or catastrophic developments. I am referring to situations in which a person feels oppressed by an inscrutable design, devised in realms outside the Ego's competence and decided by suprapersonal, and sometimes superhuman, powers, which deprives the individual of his sense of freedom and brooks no exception, mediation or negotiation in the implementation of the plan imposed on his existence.

Part 1

Chapter 1

Destiny as a sense of the inevitable

The clinical situations in which the dominant feeling is that of a negative existential path, as if a shadow had fallen across it, seem to be characterized by the emergence of powerful emotions. At the beginning, at least, these require of the analyst more sympathetic listening and greater empathic involvement than is usually necessary, since the patient's need to relive the experience prevails over that of working through the memory of it. The person in question has probably been impacted by traumatic experiences that, while weighing on the corporeal memory, have also barred the possibility of mentally representing the events and of describing them in words. It is as if the patient wished to reproduce in the analytic setting the vicissitudes and difficulties of his primary relationships by entrusting them to a mind (understood as "psychic wholeness") that can understand and contain them, but without thought intruding at this stage. The possibility of making analysis a process of knowing, interpreting and revisiting one's own story will only develop later, when the time is ripe. Thus, the analyst often finds himself thrust into a contradiction that he is required to manage, because the patient asks him, on the one hand, to descend with him into the deepest layers of the psyche in a kind of joint active regression, which means virtually abandoning his consciousness and personal differentiation; and, on the other, to remember every single thing that has happened and to continue to think. These two demands of analytic work may be said to correspond to what C. Bollas calls: "The need to know and the force to become," where the former reflects the search for meaning, and the latter, the "formation" of meaning, which occurs by elaborating the Self via the transference (1989; 2019, p. 20). Therefore, I think it is of vital importance in these situations to constantly maintain the connections between feelings, affects, images and thoughts, within the emotional vortex. The constant, and initially silent, examination of the transference and countertransference will provide the basis on which the subsequent analytic work can be organized.

I shall draw on my clinical material to shed light on various factors that contribute to the structuring of a negative sense of destiny.

DOI: 10.4324/9781003261872-2

1.1 The play of powers that bend life to their own design

The Indo-European etymological root of the word destiny is *stha* (standing), from which derives the Latin *statuere*, to set up, to establish;[1] the prefix "de" means down from, a movement from above to below. Thus, we may define destiny as "what is established above for below": a design that originates from superior entities, institutes an order, and establishes the course of individual human lives. A person in therapy once told me: "It seems as if every time I try to lift my head and catch my breath, a hand crushes me and forces me to stay down." This conjures the image, typical of an infantile fantasy, of a shadow cone that descends from above, investing and eclipsing the human being. In fact, many people picture various powers of a human or a superhuman nature, but characterized by a personal intentionality, which dominate the Ego and force life to comply with their irrevocable decisions. Circumstances, chance and the very actions that the individual could take to free himself from this design extraneous to his will, all seem to conspire to make a story develop to its tragic end. From this standpoint destiny, even when foreseen or foretold, is not fully understandable and, above all, cannot be avoided. It is well represented by the third Moira of the Greeks, Atropos, meaning "the inevitable" (Kerenyi 1951/1958), whose task it was to cut the thread of life at the pre-established moment. This goddess was all the more disturbing because she did not decide things out of hatred, but with the cold indifference of necessity that is deaf to any plea. As the totalitarian regimes of the last century have taught us, persecutions become more cold-blooded and ruthless, the more they are depersonalized and entrusted to ideological directives purged of human emotion and feeling, where reason becomes precise calculation and prevents freedom of thought, which, in a certain sense, touches on and contemplates the obscurity of the irrepresentable. The imposed plan thus takes on a persecutory character: it aims to bring ruin and unhappiness to man, as if this were really the result of an evil intentionality. That is why its unfolding inevitably raises questions concerning the problem of blame.[2] As De Santillana writes in *Reflections on Men and Ideas*: "The idea of Fate comes into being when man does not succumb like an animal, but seeks to understand and does not accept the gift of origin, *le grand don de ne rien comprendre a notre sort*.[3]

Who is to blame? Because blame must certainly exist. If the great cosmogonic myths preceded science it is because man sought to understand what concerned him, the most pressing issue being the why and how of his ills." (1968, 1985, 2004, p. 11)

According to De Santillana, the first question man asked himself was: "Are the gods or humans to blame?" The myth of the Original Sin resolves the issue in God's favor. Man takes all the blame and God is in no way responsible (ibid.). In the contemporary era, the horrors of history have caused the question to re-emerge:

How can a good, just, omnipotent and omniscient God tolerate all the evil in the world? Who has decided, and with what right, to bring us into the world and to place us in an overpowering reality, and who has forced us to experience a human condition difficult to bear?

The answer to the question has implied the negation of justice and also of the omnipotence, and even the very existence, of God, who has been supplanted by abstract and superhuman powers, impersonal entities that nonetheless are felt to possess a form of intentionality. The same can be said for the "step-mother nature" of Leopardi, which is configured in the background as a bad mother who tricks and deceives us, in order to rob us of everything; for the concept of "race" in Nazi ideology; and, especially after the advent of neurosciences, for heritability, the sum of genetic factors that curb the evolution of life through the logic of blind determinism, precisely because they are constituted by the body of complex information that shaped us long before consciousness and freedom of choice could be born. This last is also felt to be overpowering, and though without a human face, still possesses an intention that overrides us. As Bruno Callieri was wont to say, one way of conceiving and utilizing science is as the contemporary version of ancient fate. However, our feeling subject to the will of powers that dominate and surround us implies an experience of constriction that prevents self-expression, and the Ego continues to feel itself victim of a persecutory destiny.

In every case, one characteristic of blame is that it is always projected. As we start along our existential path, the first to be incriminated are, of course, our parents, because they have not loved us or seen us as we wished to be seen, they have been too absent or too directive, they have over-organized our life or prevented us from realizing our desires, and so forth. Then, when we begin our experiences of life, blame can be attributed to secondary love objects, especially a partner whom we expect to embody a parental figure (often the mother, also in the case of a male partner, since she is experienced as an inexhaustible source of giving and love). Thus the partner, and naturally the analyst, to whom a salvific power is attributed, are invested with ideal expectations and, in the course of the inevitably delusive experience that follows, they are accused of not having rectified the damage inflicted on us in the past or of not healing a narcissistic wound felt to be intolerable. Needless to say we are victims of self-deception, since our real parents and important figures in our present life have disappointed us mainly because we projected onto them the archetypal image of an ideal and omnipotent parent. As Jung states regarding our relationship with the mother:

> ...all those influences which the literature describes as being exerted on the children do not come from the mother herself, but from the archetype projected upon her, which gives her a mythological background, and invests her with authority and numinosity.
>
> (Jung 1938/1954; 1970, p. 27)

In fact, our historical parents are the 'natural' recipients of our first transference.

At times, blame loses its persecutory connotation and becomes depressive, for example when the individual, seized by drastic self-doubt, inverts the problem and tends to assume all the blame in the world: "perhaps I'm mistaken, perhaps no one has wronged me, and perhaps only I, myself, am to blame for all my troubles and failings." This is also a projection, in this case on the Ego, because the person is unable to recognize the real manipulations, the real errors that have been committed to the detriment of his own individuation or that of others (not coincidentally, the reference is always to blame and not to error). The individual, and thus the real Ego as a historical structure, judges himself severely and accuses himself of ineptitude and wickedness, though not because he has erred or has become conscious of his real responsibilities and of the fact that they have caused harm and suffering to himself and others. But rather because he considers himself unequal to a model of perfection that abolishes all limitations, and borders on an ideal of omnipotence; a model that is clearly a throwback to the primary narcissism, i.e. the experience as a fetus in the womb, or as an infant, of being one with the mother and the whole world. Thus, it would seem easier to identify with the Shadow, or rather to project it onto the Ego, instead of jettisoning the illusion of one day being able to recover one's narcissistic integrity. Responsibility and guilt are radically different. A sense of responsibility implies, first and foremost, freedom of choice and action, even though this kind of freedom must take into account the conditioning imposed by reality, the human environment, and our psychophysical makeup. It is always a limited, and at times even tragic, freedom, therefore requiring tolerance of the relative order within which it can be exercised. That is why a sense of responsibility also suggests the adoption of a compassionate attitude toward what has happened to us, and encourages reparation. Whereas, a sense of guilt (at least in the above-mentioned forms, i.e. that of the human being incapable of reaching perfection and of coinciding with the absolute) derives from the violation of ironclad rules and results from subjection, since it is caused by our diverging from a way of being or a behavior that we feel is imposed by sovereign entities but bow to uncritically, and almost venerate, and which consequently demands punishment and expiation.[4] (In fact, the identification with superior and perfect powers – as happens, for example, in dictatorships in which the Ego sinks into the numberless masses – whether it occurs in the imagination or reality – causes us to feel a kind of triumph in annihilating our individual self when experienced as fragile and dependent, and held in contempt precisely for that reason.) According to Clementina Pavoni, the lot of Eros, of the capacity to love, on which our ethical behavior is founded, depends very much on whether or not we are able to make a crucial transition, i.e., "to transform anger and desperation into pain and compassion," where anger and desperation are to guilt what pain and compassion are to responsibility (Pavoni 2009, p. 61).

It may be said that the Ideal of the Ego and the Super-Ego join forces to persecute the real Ego, the former to set goals for it that are impossible to reach but to which it must conform; the latter to judge it severely when it inevitably fails to achieve them and to inflict on it a whole series of punishments. I am also of the opinion that the Ideal of the Ego and the Super-Ego – which Freud sees as equivalent because they belong to the same psychic formation and result from a process of identification with the object that is admired and, at the same time, experienced as a rival – are diversely nuanced due to the feelings of love and fear aroused simultaneously by the object chosen as a model. For example, a female patient who suffered from panic attacks told me that she was not reassured when she felt people looking at her understandingly, and that it was precisely when she was shown appreciation and respect that an inner judge awoke and appeared before her in the form of a large intransigent, merciless eye. While this eye demanded great things of her, it was sure she could never accomplish them and, since it missed nothing, denounced her for her inadequacy, especially because she was unable to be "whole" without others, and therefore not independent. Its judgment was inexorably translated into condemnation and imprisonment in illness. What is unbearable in such a case is the prospect of having to re-experience the feelings of fragility, incompleteness, need, impotence, ineffectual anger, and guilt (this time linked to the perception and awareness of one's destructive drives), whose denial was one of the causes that determined the structuring of a persecutory vision of destiny. In the final analysis, subjection to destiny implies a previous persecutory experience that is configured as a "grandiose" design and that in some way concerns and is part of us, as well as the rejection of a realistic sense of guilt, since our behavior has been a source of pain for self and others. We may say, therefore, that when dominated by a negative destiny complex we tend to attribute a completely overwhelming power to an entity or factors that are unfathomable, and to identify with that power. So much so that we are able to look down from above on our "Ego," understood as a historical construction, and without batting an eyelash consider it inadequate and unworthy, indeed an actual nullity that is no longer really part of us because our subjectivity has rejected the feeling of uniqueness and fused with the Absolute. On the other hand, assuming responsibility, albeit circumscribed, for negative events that we have even partially caused, implies the tolerance of a realistic sense of guilt, of suffering linked to remorse, and of a desire to make amends that enables us to experience both our partiality and our limitation. As Jung writes: "In an era which has concentrated exclusively upon extension of living space and increase of rational knowledge at all costs, it is a supreme challenge to ask man to become conscious of his uniqueness and his limitation. Uniqueness and limitation are synonymous. Without them, no perception of the unlimited is possible – and, consequently, no coming to consciousness either – merely a delusory identity with it which takes the form of intoxication with large numbers and an avidity for political power" (Jung 1961, 1989, p. 326).

One of my patients, of whom I shall speak more fully below (see, *Marco's case*), said to me during an already advanced stage of the analytic work:

> Once it was my duty to take heroic, "mythological" decisions, a bit like Achilles who "has that destiny." The choices had to be based solely on reason and its certainties, but that is impossible. Trust is needed, and although there is something rational about trust and it is 'reasonable,' it always implies experience and emotion. Today, I would like to act "for" something, for someone, and not "be obliged" to act. Decisions can't be taken without emotion. In the moments of suffering I felt that everything was "written." The pain, the frustration, the feeling that it was impossible to live, the having to repress everything I felt because it was never the right thing, led me to think that destiny was inevitable and seized everything. For example, my shyness and reticence became characteristics that put an end to my having relationships. The only way of confronting this destiny was with the will and prowess of the hero, but that wasn't me. Whereas I am not doomed to a cruel destiny, like a boy born in the favela of a Brazilian metropolis might be. It is he who is heroic, not me.

When I remarked that his experience of being subject to destiny and the heroic response he felt obliged to make seemed to be a fusion of the representations of two extreme states, perfection and nothingness, he replied: *"Yes, but life lies between these two poles."*

The ancient concept of Fate in Greek culture is, as I shall explain later, quite different. The Greek terms ανάγκη, necessity, and ἐιμαρμένη, fate, the portion that is my due, that I merit, from μἐίρομαι, to deserve, do not derive from a negative, or even a personal, power, but from a cosmic order superior to both humans and gods. Necessity is a law that the entire universe must obey, not because it is imposed arbitrarily, but because it constitutes its very fabric. Thus we find ourselves dealing with a force that is not persecutory, that does not hate or violate, but rather brings the human being into harmony with his existence and his becoming in relation to the cosmos. This force is called necessity, also because it marks the limit of the human condition, the space-time boundary within which life unfolds, and, far from coercing life, makes it possible and real. Fate, in this sense, never becomes guilt.

1.2 Paralysis of becoming

The sense of time presents specific characteristics in what I call the "negative destiny complex," and the configuration of these characteristics is one of the principal forces that goes to make up this complex. With respect to the temporal component of life, it causes the individual to experience a feeling of stasis, as if the flow of becoming had stopped. Time seems to have ceased to be a dimension of being and of place in transformation within which our existential plan can be inscribed and where our various potentialities will gradually be expressed and realized. Our decisions and our choices will no longer mark the rhythms of time that becomes "our" time in which there exists a measurable "chronological" dimension along with a "kairological" dimension, so to speak, consisting in intensely experienced moments that cannot be divided into hours, minutes and seconds because they are pervaded by a sense of eternity and endowed with a precise meaning. As Panikkar so aptly puts it, the magic of the "moment" in which we immerse ourselves lies in its both marking time, and, paradoxically, opening the door to eternity: the present is "tempiternal." But in the aforesaid situation, time – like a series of other factors of nature and life – is felt as a force that overpowers the Ego and its capacity for self-determination, and is thus automatically configured as a characteristic trait of the terrible fate that has been reserved for us on high, which we can only submit to in a state of complete impotence and passivity. It is as if time, which as a cosmic event exists, passes and determines situations and events, passed over our head, alien and ungraspable, without being able to influence what truly concerns us. In this case events in our story happen "to us," but never actually become a real experience, i.e., a process through which we can learn from life and change our behavior and our inner structures, in order to be able to establish ever-new relationships with reality. It is as if the most intimate and essential part of a person had been reduced to a larval state and withdrawn into a hidden corner, perhaps in the hope of preserving all its options, but even more so to avoid experiencing the fear that coming out into the open and expressing oneself would mean remaining empty or being annihilated, instead of delineating the essential traits of one's personality and defining one's life (even by taking risks and making mistakes). A female patient with various autistic components once told me: *"It is as if I wanted to remain enclosed in a transparent egg, in a fetal position."* When I suggested that she imagine the shell breaking, a birth, she replied:

> I see birth as falling into the void, or maybe into a hostile, cold place. Everything that is new and unknown frightens me; the other is a threat for me, which could hurt me, offend me. I must have allowed the barest minimum to filter in from the environment, that which does not concern real things, but can be recognized from within and is like a kind of 'nebulous atmosphere' where there are no real experiences. I have the feeling that if I broke the shell that has contained and protected me, my being would be dispersed in the air, as if I had been nebulized.

The patient and I had often made reference to the fairytale *The Sleeping Beauty*, because we had understood that she felt as if she were living in an atemporal state, eternally waiting for a powerful and heroic act, performed from the outside and without her participation – like the prince's kiss – to break the spell. She would say:

For me, the years of my life or my analysis are not measurable, they could be ten, one hundred or one thousand, and it would be the same thing because I feel out of time. Everything is frozen. It is as if I had not really lived because, from inside the shell, everything seems the same. Things have happened, events have taken place, it's true, but it is as if they hadn't touched me.

It seemed here that a state of "non-birth," or a state that could be likened to "anticipated death" while remaining alive, was unconsciously assimilated to a state of immortality, so that "stopping time," in the symbolic sense, could offer the illusion of obtaining a form of absolute power. At a later stage, when the analysis reached a turning point, she said,

I felt immortal, and, paradoxically, it is as if I were starting to live now, precisely when I feel mortal and I'm seized by this terrible sense of loss. The years that have passed will never come back, but the sadness and nostalgia I'm experiencing are bringing me out of the shell.

Another woman patient was subject to violent panic attacks when she suddenly realized that her interlocutor might judge her as not being up to a situation. These panic attacks grew on themselves, since her first thought was rapidly followed by a second, namely that the other person might notice her state and consider her 'abnormal.' When this happened all the muscles of her body contracted, her face went rigid, and she felt encased in a kind of armor. It also seemed that the living part of her had withdrawn to unreachable depths and that only a mechanical, dead part was left to act and speak. *"I often have to clutch my body to contain myself, because I feel as if I could lose my confines and drain away like a liquid,"* she commented. She frequently expressed doubts about the outcome of the analysis: it was not possible to say how many years it would last, and experience had shown her that the usual symptoms and constraints recurred in time. There was no hope, therefore, that one day she would be able to express herself freely and spontaneously.

This vital stasis can also manifest itself as the feeling of being forced to make a repeated effort that never produces change and always leads back to square one. This situation is often compared to a Sisyphean task. A female patient, of whom I shall speak later, told me: *"I feel like a scratched disk with the needle stuck in a groove, which plays the same motif over and over again. But how can one change?"* Then she added: *"Like my father used to say, I pedal furiously on a bicycle that is fixed to the spot."* Another patient, on this occasion a man, told me about an accident he had on his motorbike and explained that he was afraid of meeting the same fate as his father, who died after being hit by a motorcycle at around his son's age. He went on to describe the following active imagination:

There is a huge motionless wave, the water does not flow. Little men try to climb up the wave, but are seized by a witch's hand. The wave folds in on itself, like me: no matter what I do I always end up back where I started ... Now I would like to block the images, but something prevents me ... I see horses galloping, but always remaining in the same place.

We find a similar situation in Althusser's description of himself in his auto-biography, where he says that he is incapable of using his resources, his abilities, his things. The overriding need to secure reserves of every kind had obliged him to live constantly "in the same present, never having the courage or rather the simple freedom to face the future [...] other than as an accumulation of the past" (Althusser 1992, p. 106).

In all these experiences, time is unusable because it becomes the prison of repetition, where nothing new can begin and nothing can really end. Time, as a cosmic power, seems to have abandoned the human being and kept to itself the mystery of transformation.

1.3 The future as a specular copy of a failed past

The alteration of the sense of time also implies what we might call the expropriation of our own future, which we are unable to imagine as material to be shaped or as the work of our subjectivity, capable of utilizing the exchanges stemming from interaction with others, with reality and with the inner world. The future is not only decided by the powers that also manage time, but actually predetermined in times immemorial, prior to the advent of a space-time dimension. Destiny becomes predestination, as confirmed by the oracle.

Here it is a case of "The stars determine; they do not incline," to reverse the maxim of Thomas Aquinas. The characteristics of a person's past, experienced as unhappy and marked by failures, are faithfully reflected in the future. Hence, if the past can rightly be defined as non-modifiable, irreversible and definitively lost, the future literally seems to mirror it, thus becoming "what is inevitably destined to fail." Then, if the analyst points out that feelings which may be appropriate for the past, are not apposite for the future, the patient often replies: "History has shown me that things have always gone that way and there is no plausible reason to think that they can go any differently." This makes it difficult to introduce the idea that it is worth revisiting one's past through memory and the emotions because, while the events themselves are not modifiable, they are not only objective data but also have a meaning that can always be rediscovered and reinterpreted by our psyche, leading us to change our attitude toward life. The enormous resistance to change and the undermining of hope – the belief of being able to express in the future the potentialities specific to one's own nature, and even the ability to "see the invisible" in the here and now (Panikkar, 1993, pp. 188, 190) – seem to possess the characteristics of an activity that is too organized to be anything other than an expression of the unconscious intentions of a psyche that submits to the aims of the illness.

The healthy part of the person wants authentic change, brought about by a creative impetus that initiates a new dimension of existence; but the sick part conceives transformation as being worked by magic, performed from the outside and implying neither effort nor subjective participation. If the analyst were to go along with the patient's grandiose but destructive fantasy, he would have to possess omnipotent salvific capacities to prevent himself from being sucked into the whirlpool of a destiny doomed to failure! By contrast, since failure can only affect goals inscribed in the relative order of life, i.e. the achievements made in our historical and circumscribed time, we may suppose that our expectation of an ever-impending catastrophe acts as a guarantee of our being able to insert ourselves in an absolute order. If the relative leads to failure, the illusory dream of rediscovering Eden and the promise of an eternal and happy life can triumph, since desire is sovereign in the dream, and its expansion will no longer be hindered by the resistance of reality. It would seem as if the dark face of a nefarious destiny is preserved in such a fantasy due to its characteristics of omnipotence; in fact, since everything is possible within the absolute, destructiveness can always be reversed into unlimited creativity. Indeed, people often escape from the prison to which their image of destiny has confined them, through daydreaming, simulation or other devices, which are all illusory, but nevertheless seem suitable for pursuing goals of power through which to dominate reality. *"It's like I was faced with an irrefutable destiny,"* a woman patient once said to me, *"you can struggle all you want, but then everything goes to the dogs again."* During a session in which she was talking about her suffering, she said: *"Suffering was my only bridge to reality. If I had discovered that my parents had not really been that nasty, how could I have communicated with others? What could I have said about myself?"* She was afraid that if she relinquished her persecutory thoughts she would have found that she had no positive aspects, no elements of worth, only emptiness and a pitiful lack of substance. In a certain sense, she found it more tolerable to be oppressed by an invasive sense of negativity, which pervaded the whole world and completely occupied her mental space, than to contemplate the existence of a positive dimension that had to be recognized, constructed and incorporated in a measurable world. In other words a reality that, having boundaries, cannot eliminate uncertainty, but within which it is possible to receive what life offers and to be active and creative.

1.4 Prison and anxiety of freedom

I have seen that people undergoing therapy are often assailed by images of themselves imprisoned in cramped and ominous places: a prison where they are condemned to death; a cellar occupied by extraterrestrials; a greenhouse; or a family environment composed of parallel tunnels in which communication is by tacit understanding only, without the possibility of distinguishing between what is said and what is thought. This last instance denotes a state in which each member of the family mentally controls all the others, and in which no one can be sure of their own individuality and separateness, because there can be no secrecy. A similar situation was described to me by a patient, who spoke of the "law of the witness," in the sense that only the presence of an outsider could give meaning to the words spoken by a member of the family and void the implicit agreement to which the whole family were bound. These places of imprisonment evoke the ancient myth of Plato's cave as a primordial place where man is confined and isolated by a reality, at the beginning of time, which is irredeemably removed from his sight; in fact, he can only see the shadows of things, simulacra of reality projected on the cave walls, but not things in their essence, as they actually are.

In the context of every prison there are, of course, jailers and judges, who may be embodied by parents or authoritarian figures, but also by an over-whelming reality or invisible, anonymous entities such as a system, an organ-ization or a collective process. In other words, we are dealing with a body of factors that clearly represent the power of destiny.

What may seem surprising, however, is that although the negative destiny complex may be configured as a prison from which there is no escape, a close alliance between the prisoner and his jailers is often established within its walls. Hence, the anxiety of prison is superseded by an even greater anxiety of freedom.[5] Probably, the individual unconsciously forms an alliance with what he senses as the power of destiny. In so doing, he contributes to his own downfall by identifying with the strength and invincibility that this power seemingly offers him, and thus experiencing a kind of triumph in working to annihilate his fragile and dependent parts. What is so important and irresist-ibly seductive to him is the omnipotent nature of this destiny complex, which it promises to bestow on whomsoever obeys it, since omnipotence makes everything possible, including the inversion of the "totally negative" in "totally positive," through an act of magic that excludes time, gradualness, evaluation and effort. And since all creations are necessarily inscribed within a limit, because they do not belong to an absolute but to a relative and partial order, megalomanic omnipotence cannot but coincide with destructiveness: omnipotence becomes impotence, and the "all" that one wishes to attain is inverted into a "nothing." The young male patient, to whom I referred earlier, told me in another session that he preferred not to show anything of himself, to remain completely invisible, because he was terrified that unpleasant, inad-equate or improper parts of himself would emerge, and to wait in his hiding place for the person who would magically restore everything to him and guar-antee a perfect state of fusion. Vanishing into nothingness was like a guaran-tee that the individual would not have to make any compromises or be content with partial realities, in the quest for perfection. In the case of this patient, negation, closure and the urge to self-destruct became the necessary condi-tions for maintaining the aspiration to the absolute. *"But,"* he added, *"com-promise is the space of life!"* Many years later, he and I would talk about real strength, which is not violence, destructiveness, victory and dominion over others, nor a sense of complete self-sufficiency that denies any request for help. Rather, it is "capacity of soul," the ability to accommodate our own experience and that of others, and even to tolerate suffering which, if we question rather than deny it, enables us to experience its transformative power. He would later say:

> The illusory power of "no" is extremely fascinating, it doesn't just make you act wrongly, but possesses you entirely when you are still too ill to be able to see your fragility as an opening, as a you tending toward becoming. I could not even distinguish between a relative "no" that, albeit reluctantly, you are prompted to say to something, to someone, in order to respect your limits, and the absolute "no" that negates any form of communication, familiarity and intimacy. I refused to understand all messages from others or from the depths of my being, until my capacity to feel was completely paralyzed. I still hadn't realized that the "no" was my last anguished cry.

It should be stressed, in fact, that the prospect of liberation does not bring relief, but terror, as if one had to pass between Scylla and Charybdis and risked being swallowed up forever.

In this configuration of mental contents, the figure of the judge likely represents a shadow aspect of the aforesaid attitude, namely the desire to reach perfection and to believe in the mirage of temptation: "You shall be as gods." In Freudian terms, as I have already mentioned, the ideal of the Ego and the Super-Ego would ally themselves, the former to drive the Ego toward unreachable goals, the latter to condemn it for its failures. Once again, rather than renouncing omnipotence and participating in his own human condition, the individual would choose to remain constrained and to hold external impediments responsible for this.

A direct consequence of this situation is that the suffering person experiences anguish whenever life requires him to exercise freedom; for example, when he needs to choose, to adopt a personal stance toward conflicts or complex problems, to express his opinion, to exercise his skills, or to undergo trials. If one has to be perfect and infallible, any initiative, any necessarily partial accomplishment, will be inadequate. The unconscious law of all or nothing will paralyze movement (this is the drama in Ibsen's *Rosmersholm*). A patient of whom I shall speak later said:

> I feel incapable of orienting myself and of choosing, because I am sure that whatever I do will be wrong. I feel like an octopus that tries to grab hundreds of objects at the same time, but at least the octopus has a center that coordinates its tentacles, while I have no center… it is as if it's not me who grabs the things, but the things that grab me, shattering my unity.

Moreover, the invitation to be free often unleashes fury, because the difficulty faced by the Ego is experienced as an abuse. Perhaps the patient feels like the defendant in a fake trial staged in the interests of political power in dictatorial regimes, who is forced to admit to crimes he did not commit, and knows that his words, actions and behaviors will be used against him. We can imagine his internal debate with an unknown and hostile interlocutor: "If you, power of fate, hold my life in check, why do you mock me with the charade of freedom? Whatever I do I will always be a helpless puppet in your hands. I am already a victim of your design, do you also want to attribute to me the responsibility for my troubles, and so ease your conscience?" One of my patients confessed: *"I feel cheated and wronged, besides being unhappy and feeling unjustly treated, must I also take the blame for everything that has happened to me?"* Even the encouragement of well-intentioned people, who express their esteem and are optimistic about the success of a project or a work, can provoke indignation: *"What do they expect of me? I can't be taken into consideration and loved without paying a price. When I don't come up to expectations, everyone will turn their backs on me."*

The isolation and one-sidedness of Ego-consciousness also renders freedom tragic in our contemporary society. The difficulty in reconnecting with dimensions that transcend, while also contemplating, individuality, distances us from the meaning of life. If not being able to decide one's own destiny is tragic, being free in the desert, i.e., in a void without motivations that endow choices with a value, is equally tragic. An Ego that is no longer connected to humanity's soul will not know what to do with its freedom. Jung intuited that a true project of individual life comes from our innermost depths, from a form of consciousness that springs from the unconscious, and that the Ego is simultaneously the creator, interpreter and witness of a work requiring close collaboration with the Self. For Jung, in fact, the dimensions of Ego and Self are inextricably bound together: while the Ego gives the Self the possibility to tell its story, to inscribe itself in space and time, to trace its history, and to incorporate itself in the concreteness of a body, the Self gives the Ego the nascent light of the origins and the unfathomable depth of the mystery that pervades reality. In the words of Jung:

> It is important not to confuse the Self that we must love, with our little being, with our Ego… The "Self" we must love, which manifests itself in us through our individual existence, is different from the Ego. The Self is our psychic totality, made up of my consciousness and the boundless ocean of the soul on which it floats: *My soul and my consciousness, that is my Self, in which I am contained like an island in the waters, like a star in the sky.* Thus, the Self is infinitely more vast than the Ego. Loving oneself should mean loving this totality, through which we would love all of humanity.
>
> (Jung 1943/1987; 2015, pp. 198–199)

Elsewhere, he writes:

> … the individuation process is confused with the coming of the ego into consciousness and that the ego is in consequence identified with the self, which naturally produces a hopeless conceptual muddle. Individuation is then nothing but ego-centeredness and autoeroticism. But the self comprises infinitely more than a mere ego, as the symbolism has shown from of old. It is as much one's self, and all other selves, as the Ego. Individuation does not shut one out from the world, but gathers the world to oneself.
>
> (Jung 1947/1954; 2014, p. 226)

In the first passage from Jung, the emphasis is placed on the Self as psychic totality, while in the second, it is placed on external reality, on the world "other than us" that becomes part of our existential process through relation. Thus, we could see the Self through a double prism, especially if we consider its analogy with the image of God, which, for Jung, is inseparable from the image of the Self. On the one hand, it is the depths, the foundation and the origin of the psyche, i.e., its "immanent" dimension; on the other, it is the world outside me, the entire reality that may be seen as its "transcendent" dimension. In this way, the intra-psychic dialogue cannot but be completed through the inter-personal dialogue, namely the exchange with the other than oneself, and also through a profound interaction with the concrete needs of the community in which one lives, with matter, with nature as a whole and with the dimension of the universe. Thus, the Self would be both my innermost self and that which embodies absolute otherness, and the realization of the Self – the goal of the Jungian individuation process – would fully express the capacity to be free.[6]

In the absence of the network of relationships that enables the Ego to communicate with others, with the unconscious, the world and cosmological time, the exercise of freedom risks becoming sterile voluntarism and enslaving man to a greater degree than the yoke of ancient αναγκη. Sartre seems to have thoroughly understood the malaise of modern times, perceptively rendering the new face of our imprisonment:

> His freedom as a perpetual choice is a perpetual going downhill, all the way to "Minos whom everyone seizes upon." Every moment of life is a moment of freedom manqué within the ambit of a "project" doomed from the start, a nauseous pilgrimage that hammers home the theme of *Huis Clos*, no exit.
>
> (De Santillana, 1968, 1985, 2004, p. 44)

True freedom, on the other hand, pertains to the inner dimension and no one can destroy it, not even by putting us in chains. Chiara Tozzi's lecture *Dall'orrore alla responsabilità etica* (From Horror to Moral Responsibility) included some striking sequences from the film *The Shawshank Redemption*, based on a novella by Stephen King. A young male prisoner challenges his guards by playing a beautiful piece of music on a phonograph and increasing the volume to full blast. After telling him repeatedly to switch the music off, the prison guards break down the door and put him for two weeks in the "hole": a room without light, objects or windows, where he is given very little food and water. When he is brought back to the cell block, his prison mates ask him how he was able to stand the torture, and he replies: "I had Mr Mozart to keep me company." Amazed, they ask him if the guards had let him take his phonograph with him, and he replies, tapping his heart and head: "No, the music was here... and here.... there are things in this world not carved out of gray stone.... There's a small place inside of us they can never lock away, and that place is called hope." And if hope, as Panikkar eloquently states, is a vision of the invisible, it leads us to see in the heart of reality what cannot be perceived through the senses, i.e., the symbolic dimension of things that nothing can ever obscure and that makes inner freedom inviolable. From this standpoint I think that, according to Christian myth, the resurrection of Christ symbolizes this inviolability. The son of God, who is man, but also God himself, does not use his omnipotence to avoid or defeat evil, the torture inflicted on him by his executioners, or death on the cross. He suffers the annihilation of his body to the bitter end and experiences human despair when faced with the inevitable, and the infinite sadness of solitude. Nonetheless, his resurrection reveals the living reality of the true essence of freedom, which not even the most evil force in the world can annihilate.

1.5 Identity theft

The film *Toto le héros* (*Toto the Hero*) opens with an extremely significant image: a meteorite, "a small piece of nothing," separates from the stars and, after passing through the mist surrounding a caravel, plunges into one of our oceans. The beginnings of a new life abandon cosmic space to become part of the history of the Earth. The protagonist of the film, now an elderly man, recalls his past and tells us: "I am someone who has never lived, a person to whom nothing has ever happened." When he was a child, Toto (a name he invents for himself when he fantasizes about performing heroic deeds) was told that, shortly after his birth, a fire broke out in the hospital where he was delivered and that mothers had rushed to the nursery to save their newborn babies. The audience does not know whether he was told this directly or if he himself imagined that, in the confusion, two women had taken each other's baby boy. In any event, Toto grows up with the idea that his neighbor has usurped his place in life. "You have stolen everything from me, my parents, my things, my loves, my story," Toto says later to his hated "alter ego," while thinking about the existence of which he has been deprived. Throughout his whole life, he will search for his beloved sister, whose death he unwittingly caused to prevent his "rival" from taking her. However, a series of events lead Toto and his "double" to cross paths repeatedly, forcing him to abandon the field to avoid re-experiencing the tragedy of someone commandeering his existential place and his specificity as a person. The fabric of events is dotted with apparently insignificant details, like an image, a phrase uttered by a rare interlocutor, or an episode, which replicate, almost identically, something already experienced. Thus, Toto is blocked by the similitude of a memory that constantly reappears and disturbs him, since it could pertain to his "alter ego." It is a kind of *déjà vécu*, a specter that always reawakens and can never become memory of the past. This is probably because Toto is not the master of his own time and cannot make his life a story that is his alone, since he is plagued by the belief that the architect of the events is his double, and possessing a history and an identity is therefore the double's exclusive prerogative. Here, one really has the feeling that an inevitable destiny has done everything to make the protagonist's life a repeated failure. It is as if Toto (who could not but have given himself the name of an invented hero) had been robbed of his identity and condemned to occupy a void, in which is projected the Shadow of his fantasy alter ego (which perhaps can be compared to the figure of the enemy twin in mythology) who has grabbed all the substance of life for himself.

I have mentioned this film because I see in it a series of analogies with the experiences that many people in therapy communicate. For example, patients often talk about feeling alienated from themselves, and therefore having difficulty in considering themselves responsible for their own destiny. Although we do not always encounter the actual fantasy of having a double, who has appropriated the gifts of nature and the evolutionary potentialities to which one has an inalienable right, we often find that an initial condition of life has prevented an individual from drawing on his unique and authentic Self. This is exemplified by feeling that one has to cease to be true and sincere in order to exist, and constructing one's being on the basis of a fiction, especially by adopting a false image that can be recognized and approved by the family. A patient of mine, who suffered from a feeling of inner emptiness and was obsessed by the idea of falling off a balcony, once dreamed that a lump of flesh, a tumor, fell out of his mother's breast, then unrolled and turned into a sheet of carbon paper. This young man felt that all his mother's love was concentrated on his elder brother and, in a different way, on his younger sister. Once he told me:

> To make my mother love me, I adapted, becoming everything: boy, girl, servant, accomplice. I was like those animals that camouflage themselves as a defense against aggressors, taking on the color and features of their surroundings. More than anything else, I tried to be as much like my brother as possible, competing with him in playing the little hero who saved his mother from the violence inflicted on her by our father, but I succeeded only in my imagination. In reality, I could not become my brother, so I tried to keep as low a profile as possible.

One could describe his illness as a form of "modeling," since he could only exist by imitating others. The dream clearly shows that the tumor was actually eating away at him: the lump that came out of his mother's breast instead of the milk that should have nourished him, and was therefore linked to the need to maintain a symbiotic state with her, represented his feeling of being a mere copy. The "cancerous" nourishment of his mother was translated into the obsession with resembling his brother as much as possible, but, no matter how hard he tried, always remaining a "poor copy" of him.

In such a situation, destiny becomes a force that radically exiles and prevents us from rediscovering the state of belonging to ourselves, the place that truly corresponds to us and that only we can occupy. This same alienation is probably experienced by K., the protagonist of Kafka's *The Trial*. In the parable told by the priest, where he speaks of "delusion" in relation to the court, the man from the country does not dare to cross the threshold of the Law, because he is obeying (or thinks he is) what sounds like an order from the doorkeeper: "not now." But the doorkeeper probably represents the person on whom all his impediments to living are projected at that particular moment, and an embodiment of a persecutory destiny. The peasant does not understand that "not now" does not mean "never" and that only a transgression, in the etymological sense of *transgredior*, i.e., "I go beyond" (meaning beyond his self-deception), would have allowed him to change the balance of the psychic forces at play and to enter his life. In fact, just before he dies, the doorkeeper tells him: "Nobody else could have got in this way, as this entrance was meant only for you. Now I'll go and close it" (Kafka 1924; p. 157).

1.6 Possible escape mechanisms

The constellation of impossibility created by these various configurations of a negative destiny is so oppressive that the person affected feels compelled to escape it, but often without being able to truly dissolve his complex. One possible escape mechanism is recourse to grandiose but illusory self-images, i.e., the adoption of a species of manic mode that temporarily stems depression. This is a stratagem for attributing to ourselves impressive and prestigious qualities that are not in keeping with the nature of our personality, and result in our losing contact with the reality of life. Another ruse is reverie, in the sense of inventing a series of stories applicable to our past or projected onto our future that would or could change the course of events. This is a mental ploy, a simulation of change, in which everything becomes different immediately and miraculously, but cannot constitute a life project because there are no identifiable transitions through which we would gradually learn, by means of experience, to construct our personality and relationship with reality. There is no revisitation of one's past through memory, which would enable a completely new understanding of previous events, obviously without changing what are irreversible data, and would give a different meaning to our story and a new direction to our future, which would cease to be repetition of the past. In this case life is not transformed through patient thinking, feeling, intention and action, but is simply invented. A distinction must be made, of course, between imagination and reverie: in the former the Ego relinquishes the role of sole protagonist on the inner stage and allows images to emerge from the unconscious, in the sense that they are evoked by an "other" who speaks in the depths of its self and with whom it establishes a continuous dialogue; whereas in the latter, the Ego alone creates the images. Lastly, there is a defense mechanism that I would call taking refuge in "as if." Here, a series of events, such as studies, projects or emotional relationships, which one is unable to experience, are not only imagined, but actually "acted out" within a simulation. However, the real protagonist of the stories does not seem to be the individual but his simulacrum, a "cover" that could lawlessly create or destroy, modify or replace everything, due to the false belief that it would not irreversibly affect reality and it would grant him immunity to pain and grief.

Whether imagined or acted out, reverie may reflect an irrepressible need to eliminate the gap between the thinkable and the real, between the actual and the probable, and to avoid the need to be true in exercising reason and true to one's whole being, and thus to accept one's own limits. Thus, the power of thought, reduced to rationality and calculation, and able to create an "as if" world, would present itself as a force capable of fighting the persecutory power of destiny on equal terms. This is the source of its fascination but also its defeat, since two absolute powers cannot coexist. In any event, we find ourselves faced with the overriding need to preserve some form of absolute power, even at the cost of identifying with the overwhelming forces of destiny and accepting the defeat of our vulnerable historical Ego. The following reflections of some patients are significant in this regard: *"I don't know what I've learned from life, I've done many things, but it is as if nothing had taken root in me," "I was always convinced that I could not preserve what I was constructing because I knew it was a bluff, even if others didn't realize this," "It's as if I were always somewhere other than the place where I am,"* and *"I feel as if I were speaking from a dream."*

All these situations, in which one resorts to a form of artifice in order to live, contribute to the creation of a series of binomials, which I have already mentioned, composed of two terms that cancel each other out, such as: "Impotence–Illusory omnipotence," "Stasis–Magical metamorphosis," "Sense of non-existence or falseness–Existing everywhere and in anyone's place." I think that these binomials represent the opposite aspects of those paradoxical formulations that would give rise to a negative destiny complex, which is also paradoxical. In the light of all these considerations, in fact, I think we may say that destiny becomes, and is experienced as, "inevitable" because it makes life a tragedy, but also because it represents the absolute power in which the Ego, which does not tolerate its relativity, desires to founder.

1.7 Desire and reality: a clinical case

I would like to speak briefly about a patient whom I will call V, whose problems presented various aspects of the existential situations outlined above, especially those in which a mental defense mechanism against anguish, which I have called escaping into the "as if," predominates. Since birth V had lived in a family that he himself described as "double," being composed of his parents and his paternal aunt and uncle; the ambiguity of the communications between the members of this family left him feeling so confused that he was unable to determine who represented parental authority for him. Moreover, during adolescence he discovered that his uncle, a much-admired figure with whom he identified to cope with the conflicts with his father, was leading a double life, since as well as his regular family, he had an "unofficial" one in South America. V felt that he was neither seen nor loved for what he was, and thus felt betrayed and abandoned. Although rigorous in educating their children, his parents mainly focused on imparting formal rules of behavior – which stifle the life of the soul. His family environment offered him no way of expressing his inner world and prevented him from conveying his anger, desolation and disappointment, since he was afraid it would produce no change in his relationships, and would further chill interpersonal communications. Thus he discovered the power of imagination, which offers the possibility of inventing the world in which one wishes to live. *"History is not made up of actual facts, but by the way they are told,"* he pronounced, then pursued the thought further: *"Everything of which one is able to convince others is 'true.'"*

He recounted a dream in which he was on trial with other people. One of the defendants had two silver pins on his forehead that could be launched as weapons simply by an act of will. *"The power of the mind is precious and terrible,"* V commented.

> In science fiction movies such devices can be used to control thoughts. The rules of life imposed in my family were so rigid, I think I defended myself with lies (I had discovered that not even actual evidence can make us confess what we don't want to admit) and with imagination. In the world of imagination I was stronger than everyone, if only because it is a secret realm that no one else can enter. My father would get angry when I shut myself in my room, but he couldn't force me to do anything.

Evidently, the family's "duplicity" had left its mark on V's destiny. In another dream he had assumed a military rank and position that were not his. Nonetheless, he was wearing an impeccable uniform, and the general did not realize that he was faking it. While recounting the dream, he exclaimed: *"Instead of 'impeccable' I was about to say 'ineluctable' or 'inexorable.'"* For V, "ineluctable impeccability" was a prison created by complicity with family rules, against which he could only rebel by escaping into the "as if," where "trials of life" were organized that could never become part of his true story. By renouncing his authenticity, he made obedience the instrument of a destiny sensed as "imposed will." In fact, as an adult V was unable to experience the dimension of desire together with that of reality. On the one hand, he entered into a marriage with a woman acceptable to his family, which was devoid of passion, and any possible renewal was paralyzed by the boredom of habit; on the other, he sought, as if in a hidden pocket of life, experiences that could rekindle the inner fire of rapture, almost as if he wanted to permanently experience the sublime state of being in love. One cannot but think that the uncle's double life not only disappointed V, but also secretly fascinated him. *"There is something magic about every beginning,"* V commented. *"What matters is the dreams we interweave with the image of the other person. The spell that is cast reveals a hidden part of ourselves."* What is evident in such experiences, however, is that to preserve the quality and boundlessness of the "ahistorical" nature of desire, one ends up sacrificing the real relationship, which has, instead, a history and is subject to change and limitation. The actual relationship with the partner (which can never be equal to desire) is secretly terminated, so that the idea of love will not die.

V had to keep his second world, often more imagined than experienced, hidden and illicit, completely separate from the rest of his life; otherwise, as he himself said, it would have been all-out war. In such a segregated place, the illusion that no loss was real and irreversible could be nurtured, since the intensity of desire would have permitted the substitution of anything or any person, generating a new beginning – indeed an interminable series of beginnings. *"In the 'as if' game,"* V pointed out, when, to his amazement, the analytic process had rendered this defense mechanism unusable,

> success bears the seed of defeat because, sooner or later, desire detaches from things and then the story ends. This didn't worry me before, because I knew I was able to reactivate desire in a new place and in a new time, whereas now I can no longer do it. This troubles me; it is "as if" I were faced with a world whose rules I still have to learn.

In the final analysis, I think it is the capacity to freely face the difficulty of combining incommensurable dimensions of existence which truly orientates our sense of destiny in a new direction, that is toward faith in being able to constructively interact with what life and the world also impose on us, and enables us to creatively establish the new conditions for the development of our personal story. On the one side, there is the unquenchable desire to rediscover the happy, never-ending and perfect union with the loved one that we feel we once experienced, even though all traces of it seem to have vanished from memory; on the other, there is the knowledge that our life, swept up in a constant state of becoming, is transitory, interwoven with relative qualities, and subject to the necessary though not blameworthy separation from our first love objects, namely our parents and, in particular, the mother. Moreover, no matter what we have constructed or what ties we have established, we all have to face death, which definitively separates us from everything and everybody. While our feelings touch on the sublime and draw on unfathomable mystery, the real world requires us to respect its laws and confines, and while ideas can play with large numbers and span endless millennia, the works of life have to be completed within a limited time. We can deny neither the boundless breadth of the soul nor the contingent demands of existence, since the opening up of our being to the infinite can only give quality to life if we are there for actual people and do not forget to be compassionate, thus adhering to the chronological dimension of time. Ultimately, to prevent our need to constitute a unity with the loved one from turning into violence, it must always be accompanied by respect for the inalienable diversity of the "Other." As Vittorio Lingiardi poetically writes: "… we must … learn to swim in the music of otherness, where wonder at similarity can replace obsession with identity."[7]

It may well be that destiny becomes catastrophe when we confuse desire with relationship, or when we seek to make the measurable aspect of the love object coincide with the "beyond" that transcends it: "Because what they call the eternal proceeds from the one and the many and implies both the finite and the infinite" (*Philebus*, quoted by Galimberti 1984, p. 32). For the Guaraní people (who like to be called, emblematically, the "last men"), as Galimberti also reminds us, the land without evil will be the one that will host the language in which nothing that exists can be defined according to the one, but according to the one and the other together. In fact, they are seeking a place where there are not gods on one side and men on the other, but only equal beings: "god-men" or "men-gods." "The way indicated by the Guaraní does not separate man from the divinity or absolutize one language ..., it is the dual (*amfi*) way 'of the one and the other together'" (ivi, pp. 27–28).

Since there is no closed formula that can fully represent the meaning of our experiences, the disorder that obscures our sense of destiny likely originates from the desire to bring two irreducible dimensions together. Finite and infinite cannot overlap because this would mean fatal collusion, but perhaps they can meet at significant points and moments. "Symbolic conjunctions," one might say, which create a true synthesis between the speakable and the unspeakable, between the known contents of consciousness and the still unknown potential of the unconscious.

1.8 The double

Returning to the theme of the film *Toto le Héros*, the protagonist finds himself having to deal with various vicissitudes deriving from a negative destiny complex. One of these is particularly fraught with consequences, since this type of destiny often proposes a kind of stand-in to imitate, a "double" in the form of an "ideal model," which possesses every desirable quality and embodies the perfection to be achieved. This "double" does not symbolically represent the existential striving for a goal, which enhances our transformative potential without negating our worth in the present moment, and from which standpoint every step, every moment of the journey is part of the goal. Instead, it is an unreal, unattainable "double," in the face of which our being cringes with shame because it cancels the value of our uniqueness and does not offer an enriching relationship. Our Self would be completely voided when occupied by this image that contemplates neither time nor otherness and that makes us become an "other," which embodies absolute perfection but also represents what we can never be, trapping us in an unresolvable paradox. In fact, the existential striving for a goal or what we aspire to does not abolish the sense of limitation and of the gradualness of achievements, or the value of each step that does not claim to be exhaustive because we are aware of our itinerancy and our contingency, and therefore of the fact that we are constantly faced with a transcendent dimension. By contrast, an aspiration to the absolute draws on a grandiose fantasy that invokes a magic solution to all problems and withdrawal to an unreal "all" where we are perfect but closed to every need, desire and vital encounter with the other than us. From this perspective, perfection is in opposition to completeness, since it is like a closed circle, *per-fectum*, meaning finished, while completeness, *cum-plenum*, means being full "with" something or someone. Existential striving, which stems from an awareness of our finitude coupled with the desire to go beyond it, disposes us toward change and the new, which transforms, in a certain sense, our lack into richness, precisely because it allows us to be completed by the other than us. Whereas, aspiring to the absolute encloses us in an inaccessible space, which should contain the entire universe but in reality isolates us from everything and everyone. Ultimately, we may say that existential striving is the principal driving force behind evolution, precisely because it draws on all the phases of our being, each of which provides the impetus for the next. By contrast, aiming for the absolute closes us in a world without time and without becoming (the Latin *ab-solutus* means "loosened from").

In fact, returning to the theme of the double, this fantasy "alter ego" is not really an "alter" because it does not reflect any principle of inner otherness or represent an objectively reliable image of another actual person or an internal object, although its constellation can be projected onto figures that one actually meets in life and who, thus, momentarily become bearers of an *imago*.[8] The double cannot have corporeal roots like the instance of the Ego, the psychic entity of the Self, or feeling-toned complexes, and in this respect does not derive from reality. It is a purely mental formation, an abstract idea, which could be likened to our image in the mirror when we mistake it for our real self, without realizing that it is only an icon of that self. Then the image would be reduced to a mere outline, devoid of depth and substance, since the mirror is not the eyes of the mother, or the eyes of the other, or our own. Only an observant subject possesses the psychic resonance that permits access to a symbolic attitude of consciousness, thus enabling us to penetrate the shadow and embrace the invisible and unknowable dimension of our being. Likewise, only an observant subject can flesh out our image with the creative and affective factors deriving from the inner world, linking in a single chain representation and the consciousness it symbolizes, obscure instinctual movement, and the light of its meaning and purpose. I do not think that Narcissus perishes because he loves himself too much and only himself, but precisely because he takes his image reflected in the water for his real self, and thus his identity collapses in the concrete dimension which has neither substance, depth, nor future. In actual fact, Narcissus is unable to know and love himself. Hence, our double could be fantasized as a concrete, specular and reversed image of ourselves that detaches from the mirror and occupies a parallel world that pretends to be real and presumes to possess our originality, making us feel like a mere copy of ourselves. The problem with this crazy proposition is that one cannot regain one's self-respect and the recognition of others simply by resembling the model. Indeed, one actually has to "become" the model, to occupy the entire space in which it has installed itself, and to "be there" in its place, because the path of imitation will never lead us to repossess our original self. This is obviously an impossible undertaking, since it would see us catapulted into the orbit of a virtual world where our real substance would be annihilated. And so precisely the fate designated by inexorable destiny since time immemorial would come to pass: "You will come to a bad end!" /"You are doomed!" A metaphor of this catastrophe can be found in physics: if a particle of matter were to meet an anti-matter particle, i.e., if it were possible for the image of the particle reflected in the mirror to materialize and thus rotate in the opposite direction, and its charge and its direction in time were also reversed, it would result in the simultaneous destruction of both particles, which is technically known as "annihilation."

Between the Ego and its model there can be neither dialogue, nor the tension of opposite poles that could trigger a process of existential transformation. Instead, there is a kind of psychic short-circuit that leads to the paralysis of life. Understandably, when the theme of the double appears – as happens, for example, in *Toto le héros* and as I have already mentioned – the person feels robbed of his identity and condemned to occupy a void, a place in the shadow of his fantasy stand-in who has grabbed all the substance of life for himself. The feeling of self-alienation is frequently experienced, which makes it difficult for the subject to consider himself the architect of his destiny, as if an initial condition of life prevented him from drawing on his unique and authentic Self.

People in treatment often say things like: *"I feel as if I were speaking and acting in a different place from where I am."*

Perhaps it would be helpful to ask ourselves the following questions: Where and how is the aforesaid model configured? Is it a universal configuration or does it have individual characteristics? I believe that this dramatic condition is liable to affect children who have been the object of a narcissistic investment by their parents or whose existential reality has been ignored because the family's attention was focused elsewhere. In these situations the child feels that it exists in the mind of at least one parent as the substitute for another much-loved person who is no longer available; for example, a dead brother or sister, a lost love, or another admired family member. Or simply as possessing needs that are not its own, but must be satisfied to realize a much-desired family plan. The fantasy of the alter ego is then configured as a kind of ideal model, be it concrete or abstract, present or absent, that we must reproduce, despite its being a paradoxical and impossible task. Indeed, it is madness to try to be that other figure of reference we can never be and also ourselves, simultaneously. What parents propose that the child embody is not so much the "reality" of another, as, in Jungian terms, their *imago* of the other; i.e., the sum of the ideal qualities the other is presumed to possess but which are, instead, the product of the parents' projections, or a project of perfection with an almost universal character, because the real object of their desire is their own narcissistic completion. For its part, the child can choose a bearer of the parental projections from among the various figures of reference in its life, such as a childhood friend, a family member, a teacher or a historical figure, who becomes the model to imitate. In this case, the body of exceptional qualities projected onto the chosen object is not only formed on the basis of the parents' mental processes, but is also colored by the child's specific psychological characteristics.

One of the possible developments arising from the constellation of the model is the creation of situations that appear to be triangular, but are in fact false triangulations. For instance, the person invested with the projection of the model can be admired yet deeply envied at the same time, because he has an erotic relationship that the subject himself would like to have. This can trigger the need to possess the love object of the model, which is not a true desire because it does not arise from the instinctual sphere and is not directed at the object itself. Instead, to quote Girard (1990, 2000), it is a "mimetic" desire, being induced by the need to resemble the model by actually penetrating the very nerve center of its being. According to Girard, the tendency to imitate is not limited to the reproduction of the ideas, behaviors and tastes of the person taken as a model, but even reproduces what is considered the essential part of its being: the impulse of desire. Imitating the desire of the other signifies desiring the same things that it does, to which are attributed a specific value of existential completion. Girard sees mimetic desire as ontological because: "Envy covets the superior being who neither the person desired, nor the person who desires him/her, but only the conjunction of the two seems to possess" (Girard 1990, 2000, p. 4). Girard speaks of envy rather than desire because the laws of Eros imply that sharing the object of desire is impossible. Mimetic desire is ambivalent from the start, because the same impulse that has produced feelings of admiration, veneration and impassioned tenderness toward the model, then produces rivalry, envy and hatred. One passes from the basic need to resemble the model, to the desire to occupy its existential place, annihilating it. There is never a true reciprocity between two persons who assume the character of specular doubles, because they both imitate each other and are incapable of perceiving the difference that distinguishes them. Moreover, in my clinical experience I have found that it is precisely because the model seems to possess the existential completeness that stems from the union with a person of the opposite sex, that it also has androgynous characteristics. This figure contains everything in itself, as in the paradise of a primary (or rather originary, since it precedes any encounter with the object) situation, in which one fantasizes possessing a total adherence to things before the difference and separation between beings is possible.

As I have already said, another feature of the model is to condense within itself extreme and opposite characteristics. It is protector and persecutor, good and evil; it promises to offer narcissistic perfection if one adopts a mimetic behavior, but it is also the one who must keep everything for itself and annihilate its rival. Its command is: "Imitate me but do not imitate me: You must be identical to me to exist, but in that case you would not exist anyway, because you would lose your originality." The same ambivalence can be seen in the feelings aroused by the model: love and hate, admiration and envy, attraction and repulsion, fascination and anguish. However, this ambivalence does not derive from the mental process of splitting the object into "good" and "bad" or "loved" and "hated" of which Klein speaks (1957, 1969), which introduces an initial and necessary organization of psychic life, as well as permitting, in a second phase, the reunification of separate aspects. Here, the ambivalence is much more primordial, because we are not dealing with the alternation or integration of opposite situations, but rather their paradoxical convergence. An object is not good a/o bad, loved a/o hated, but is good "because" it is bad, loved "because" it is hated. It is impossible, therefore, to choose a position without canceling it out immediately with the opposite one, precisely because we are not dealing with polarities that possess a potential difference, which would enable the transmission of energy and trigger a process of psychic transformation. As Girard writes, in the constellation of the double there is not a "coincidence of opposites," but an "opposition of 'coincidents'" (ivi, p. 56): the encounter between the Ego and the model always causes a psychic short-circuit and paralysis of life. This way nothing can ever really change and conflicts always reemerge in identical form. One cannot coexist with a double; it always entails a fight to the death.

For other aspects, the formation of the model could be likened to the emergence of the archetypal figure of the "protector/persecutor," of which Kalsched speaks, which serves to protect the vital nucleus of the Self from intolerable precocious traumas by encapsulating it and removing it from life, while also being a source of new and continuous traumatizations. Rather than expose the psyche to the risk of being torn apart by any direct experience, which may also be negative, the archetypal defenses prefer its extinction (Kalsched 1996). Kalsched does not see this diabolical inner figure as the internalized version of the outer perpetrator, since it is far more sadistic and brutal than an actual aggressor. This suggests that it comes into being when a psychological factor, an "archetypal traumatogenic agency" (ibid., p. 31), is set loose in the internal landscape of trauma. On the other hand, the protector/persecutor is the bearer of a monstrous ambivalence, because its function seems to be to protect "the traumatized remainder of the personal spirit and its *isolation from reality*" (ibid.). It is as if, as Kalsched affirms, this tyrannical caretaker functioned as a kind of inner "Jewish Defense League," whose logic leads it to say:

> Never again ... will the traumatized personal spirit of this child suffer this badly! Never again will it be this helpless in the face of cruel reality.... Before this can happen, I will disperse it into fragments [dissociation], or encapsulate it and soothe it with fantasy [schizoid withdrawal], or numb it with intoxicating substances [addiction], or persecute it to keep it from hoping for life in this world [depression].... In this way I will preserve what is left of this prematurely amputated childhood – of an innocence that has suffered too much, too soon!
>
> (ivi, p. 5)

Interestingly, Kalsched's interpretation also offers a therapeutic suggestion that I would later find invaluable in treating Marco, of whom I have already spoken. By grasping also the positive aspect of this archetypal figure – which in this case was equivalent to the "model," and, as we shall see, would almost personify itself in Marco's stories, becoming an essential interlocutor – and refraining from attacking it head-on, all the vital energies it bore could be converted in favor of the Ego. And this precisely because the figure had represented the receptacle in which the nascent Self had placed its last, constantly threatened hope and its most profound values.

Notes

1 Other words deriving from this root are, in Greek, ιστημι, "to erect," "to put in the scales," "to weigh;"; in Sanskrit: *tisthati* "stands;" in Latin: *stare, stabilire*, "to make stable;" *stativus*, "immobile" and *status*, "attitude," "state," "statue."

2 This viewpoint derives from a modern re-reading of Greek mythology, which misinterprets the spirit of the ancient world, for which *necessity* was a "datum" of the cosmic order and not an "intention" to abandon or to destroy the human race.

3 The great gift of understanding nothing of our fate.

4 These concepts have been explored in depth by Clementina Pavoni in her excellent paper: 'Dalla colpa alla responsabilità,' presented in Pistoia in November 2007 and published in *La vita psichica. Percorsi dell'Eros*, Edizioni Magi, June, Rome 2009.

5 Stockholm Syndrome is also interpreted as the captive seeing his captor as an ally against a society believed to be responsible for the monotony of his own life or for failing to recognize his merits: better to find oneself in a condition of "perverse excitement" than to be invisible.

6 Some thoughts expressed in this comment of mine appear in my afterword to the book: *Orizzonti di coppia. Individuarsi con il partner. Un percorso analitico junghiano* by Fulvia De Benedittis, Sandra Fersurella and Silvia Presciuttini. Moretti e Vitali, Bergamo 2019 (p. 245).

7 In *Venerdì di Repubblica* of November 11, 2019 V. Lingiardi wrote about the film *Manta Rey* by Thai director Phuttiphong Aroonpheng, who described the tragedy of the Rohingya people, a persecuted ethnic/religious minority in Myanmar.

8 For Jung the *imago* is the sum of the representations of a particular person, which derive mainly from subjective sources. For this reason, the image of the other does not truly mirror the object because it is steeped in projected elements. In particular reference to the *imago* of the father and mother, Jung states that in these fantasies we are not dealing with the actual father and mother, but solely their subjective and often completely distorted images, which in the mind of the mentally ill lead an existence that is schematic, but not at all devoid of influences.

Chapter 2

The weight of the Shadow

It is difficult to give a precise picture of the pathologies that determine the appearance of a negative sense of destiny in the terms stated above. Indeed, we are looking at various clinical configurations, such as depressive or hypomanic disorders, paranoid manifestations, narcissistic or autistic nuclei, and hysterical elements. However, in my opinion, the characteristic datum common to each is an identity disorder. The sense of one's own existence, authenticity or gender orientation is altered to varying degrees; likewise, the sense and scope of one's life is generally uncertain, and one's belief in being able to give a meaning to the world is undermined.

2.1 The Absolute Shadow

One specific question we can ask ourselves is: Which is the Shadow that structures the negative destiny complex? To what depths of the psyche can it be traced? On the basis of analyzed data, and to sum up what I have said above, it may be defined as a Shadow formed by persecutory fantasies, i.e., projected blame, since our parents, God, nature, or our hereditary genetic constitution are considered responsible for our being fated to submit to an unfavorable destiny. In every case, supra-egoic and super-egoic entities dominating the Ego, which have made, and still make, us feel impotent, have imposed their unjust law on our life. And even when the blame is attributed to the Ego, it is still a projection and not a reliable evaluation, because the Ego is required to attain an impossible state of perfection.[1] In this event, I think we can speak of an "absolute" Shadow, in the etymological sense of the Latin term *ab-solutus*, meaning "loosened from." Not only because the connections between the different psychic instances, and between psyche and reality, would be severed within this type of Shadow, but also because its negative characteristics enable it to assume a power whose exercise knows no limits, and which is all the more fascinating, the more incontestable and invincible it seems. The Ego will have difficulty in carrying out the process of recognition and integration of its true personal and collective Shadow, because more totalizing and invasive Shadow aspects will tend to contaminate the field of its relations with unconscious contents and objects of reality. This will obstruct the psyche's capacity

DOI: 10.4324/9781003261872-3

to introduce unconscious processes in the operative modalities of conscious thought, and to withdraw the projections from its own image of the world.

From a dynamic and a phenomenological standpoint, the Shadow becomes absolute when it is acted upon by defenses more archaic than removal, e.g. splitting or negation, thus acquiring a much greater autonomy than the Ego-complex and, consequently, a strong capacity to possess and engulf it. This does not mean that removal cannot also be a prodromal stage in the construction of an absolute Shadow, since it produces the phenomenon of projection. At a clinical level, and without confining ourselves to a diagnostic or strictly nosographic discourse, I believe we are dealing with situations in which the suffering is more typical of the psychotic than the neurotic experience. Indeed, psychopathological conditions of varying severity can be observed, including: split personality; projection of the Shadow; so-called loss of the Shadow; possession of the Ego by part of the Shadow; and inflation of the Shadow. In every case, the relationship with the Shadow, understood as a healthy and essential component of the human being, is inevitably sacrificed.

2.1.1 Loss of the Shadow

When the projection of the Shadow is the result not simply of removal, but primarily of splitting and negation, the Ego can put up insurmountable resistance to its recognition and more or less totally reject its own Shadow. This results in a loss of the Shadow, which is drastically expelled from the personality. Thus, the individual will have lost an important part of himself, and will be reduced to a single dimension of light; but since a part can never be passed off for the whole, he will find himself existing in a deceptive atmosphere, uprooted from his natural milieu. "The living form needs deep shadow if it is to appear plastic. Without the shadow it remains a two-dimensional phantom, a more or less well brought-up child" (Jung 1928, 2014, pp. 238–9). In fact, loss of the Shadow causes an impoverishment of the Ego, which then identifies with the figure that Jung calls the "persona"; i.e., with the social role or with the characteristic and behavioral traits deemed moral and acceptable by a collective canon. Man is reduced to a mask, to a species of puppet worked by abstract rules, and thus incapable of drawing on his vitality and originality.

An example of the splitting or loss of the Shadow is to be found in a story based on the novel *The Student of Prague* by Hanns Heinz Ewers, recounted by Jung (1943/1987, 2015, pp. 188–189): a poor student agrees to offer the devil everything in his room in exchange for a large sum of money. However, the only thing the devil takes is the image of the young man reflected in the mirror and, from that moment on, the student is unable to see his reflection. Psychologically, the loss of the mirror image symbolizes the loss of contact with the corporeal self and the unconscious psyche that permeates our biological dynamism. The image of oneself that can be represented mentally is made up of the uppermost layers of the psyche and responds to the norms that an isolated consciousness has arbitrarily invented, borrowing them from ideal expectations. It is actually an image without Shadow, which represents the betrayal of one's own truth.

2.1.2 Projection of the Shadow

Since, as Jung states, it is not the conscious subject but the unconscious that does the projecting, one "meets with projections, one does not make them" (1951, 2014, p. 9). Hence, insofar as the Shadow is unconscious, it is projected.[2] If we do not know our Shadow, it will most likely be projected onto an individual who can easily constellate the projection, that is whose unconscious possesses characteristics that will act like a magnet on our unconscious. This person thus becomes our personal enemy,

> whom we denigrate and in whom we criticize all the faults, all the baseness and all the vices that we ourselves possess. We should apply the majority of the criticisms we rain down on others to ourselves ... it is the same old story of the mote and the beam.
> (Jung 1934/1954, 1943/1987, pp. 184–185)

The disastrous consequence of projection is that the outside world, to which the subject lends his face (which is unknown because it is unconscious), will seem increasingly incomprehensible and distant. The individual will find himself gradually enveloped by a web of illusions that veil his world, and the more he reacts suspiciously to an environment he sees as hostile, the more that environment will recede, leaving him isolated and with a devastating sense of incompleteness (1951, 2014, pp. 9–10).

2.1.3 Possession of the Ego by the Shadow

In clinical practice the loss of the Shadow does more than make the personality sterile and reduce it to an automaton manipulated by the demands of the collective, although this in itself may create human beings who live a makeshift and impersonal life, but are well adapted to the rules of society and the prevailing cultural canons. However, since the psyche that undergoes violence sooner or later rebels, the psychic energies rejected by the sphere of consciousness and compressed in the unconscious follow a regressive path and become unrelentingly destructive. The scotomized Shadow becomes autonomous and tends to subjugate the Ego, making it slave to its dynamics and goals. In this case we may also speak of a phenomenon of unconscious identification with one's own Shadow.

In the story about the Prague student, for example, an unforeseen incident takes place on the occasion of a duel with a relative of the woman the student loves, which he could not have avoided, but decides to engage in as a mere formality, without harming his rival in any way. The student is late in arriving; as he nears the place where they have arranged to hold the duel, he sees his double wielding a bloody sword: he has killed the other man in his place! The "himself" he could no longer see was the bearer of potentialities for evil of which he had remained ignorant, and thus they had been realized. Yet again the Ego was used like a mannequin. In this case, not by a conformist society but precisely by the Shadow, by those primitive instinctual forces that had taken their revenge with a vengeance because they had been ignored. "It is always best to know what is in our Shadow, to prevent the 'devil' from taking possession of it" (ivi, p. 189).

2.1.4 Inflation of Shadow

There also exists a process in which the Ego consciously identifies with its Shadow, that is when it is under the impression of gaining power from the negative or violent tendencies of its nature, and thus experiences the inflation of the Shadow. As Augusto Romano states (M. Trevi and A. Romano 1975, p. 63), the Ego merges with the Shadow and remains fascinated by it, choosing, in a certain sense, to be what it cannot and does not wish to avoid: "when the Shadow is in a state of removal the individual 'sinks' into evil; whereas in the case of inflation it is a question of 'wanting to be as much as finding oneself in' evil" (ivi). In the state of possession, the dialectic between the opposites is abolished because the Ego renounces itself when confronted by the inner antagonist, while in the state of inflation the dialectic is abolished because the Ego engulfs its antagonist. In the first instance, it is as if the Ego were claiming falsely: "There is no Shadow in me," only to be subjugated by it; in the second, as if it were asserting, equally falsely: "I am my Shadow, and this gives me power and authority."

I use the term Absolute Shadow rather than archetypal Shadow, or archetypal image of the Shadow, because the latter embraces the fathomless possibility of evil, but only as one pole of an antithesis. Thus, it does not abolish, per se, the relationship that the conscious Ego can establish with evil – be it the one recognized in reality or the imagined one – which is thus containable within certain limits and does not flood the entire personality. This also occurs because the conscious contemplation of a principle of evil enables it to be placed in relation to a principle of good, and both principles can engage in a process of reciprocal integration in which they are radically transformed, acquiring a new meaning. By contrast, in the Absolute Shadow there exists a form of unconscious or conscious identification with a negative power that seeks to conquer everything that resists it. The Shadow is also a vital and healthy part of the psyche, whereas the Absolute Shadow is inevitably a product of pathological processes and, being an artifice of the mind, a falsifying and unreal configuration.

However paradoxical it may seem, fusion with the Absolute Shadow provides access to enormous power, which is sought, above all, when the sense of one's own fragility and finiteness becomes unbearable. In the first place, illness makes one feel authorized to make any request to others, as well as demands and impositions: "everyone must care for me, give me attention and be there for me, because the suffering I'm going through and the risk I'm running give me a right to it." In the second place, a show of unhappiness can also indicate a feeling of vengeful satisfaction:

> I'll play your game, you hurt me, but I'll make you pay, by showing everyone how miserable I am and making you take the blame for it. What's more, I'll make you feel as impotent as I once felt, because I won't accept your help. Whatever you do, you'll never reach me.

As I have already said, an unconscious alliance with the negative forces of a destiny that can destroy all hope of salvation paradoxically creates the feeling of being able to participate in the triumph over reality implicit in the destructive act, even though the harm is inflicted on one's own being. In addition, there is inevitably the accompanying fantasy that, if the force of destiny is omnipotent, it can always transform itself from "totally negative" into "totally positive," and thus give us everything to which we narcissistically aspire: overnight success and exemption from failure; the admiration of all; and the definitive and complete liberation from every need. So, the very aspiration to the absolute is a Shadow, because it deprives the Ego of its dimension of radical relativity, and therefore of the whole network of intra-psychic and interpersonal relationships from which life evolves. In other words, the Shadow tends to absolutize itself and to invade the psychic field every time the relation between the Ego and the different parts of the psyche, the Ego and others, and the Ego and reality, is severed or stultifies.

At times, the configuration of the Absolute Shadow can assume a different connotation while still pursuing the same power objectives; for instance, when it abandons the role of victim and becomes the opponent of destiny, embodying the figure of the hero who is able to challenge and vanquish fate. In this case revenge is taken not by flaunting defeat, but through a fantasmatic victory over everything and everybody, while the feeling of envy is reversed, becoming an irrepressible need to be envied. As Marco, of whom I spoke earlier, told me:

> my need for heroism involved revenge and getting my own back. I wanted to make others pay what I was paying. Anger and envy completely smothered my regret for not having lived, and the desire to live. It was as if I were saying to the other: what I will achieve will be so great that it will make you suffer like I am suffering now because I don't have what you have.

Ultimately, the most harmful and insidious aspect of the Absolute Shadow is that it deprives the Ego of the relationship with its true Shadow, more commonly understood as "the negative and inferior part of the personality" – a knowledge of which nevertheless humanizes us and makes us more humble – and as a source of values. In the Jungian conception of the psyche, in fact, the encounter with the personal and with the collective Shadow are crucial stages in the individuation process that leads to the realization of the Self. We should not forget that for Jung the Shadow is also the true wellspring of renewal and, therefore, of the future. I would sum up the positive aspects of the Shadow by defining it as a principle of reality, a principle of relation, the storehouse of possibilities, and the generative element of the symbol.

2.2 Shadow as principle of reality

In a certain respect the Shadow can be considered a principle of reality, for three reasons. Firstly, as "the negative and inferior part of the personality," as it is most commonly understood, it shows us who we really are in our entirety and not who we would like to be. In so doing, it leads us to seek the truth about ourselves, thus fostering the development of an ethical attitude of consciousness, which humanizes us and encourages humility. As Jung states:

> True, whoever looks into the mirror of the water will see first of all his own face. Whoever goes to himself risks a confrontation with himself. The mirror does not flatter, it faithfully shows whatever looks into it; namely, the face we never show to the world ... This confrontation is the first test of courage on the inner way, a test sufficient to frighten off most people.
>
> (Jung 1934/1954, 2014, p. 20)

Secondly, the Shadow originates from the material and biological substratum of a human being. Not coincidentally, Jung considers the "realization of the Shadow" an essential stage in the individuation process and that, first and foremost, this puts us in contact with our body and makes us aware of our sensations and emotions. In fact, in the early phase of this process, the Shadow embodies the object that is most intimately a part of us, but also the most enigmatic in our existence:

> there are many members of our civilized society who have in some way got rid of their shadow and have lost it; ... they are human beings, then, with two dimensions, lacking the third: depth, corporeality, body. The *body* is a most doubtful friend because it produces things we do not like; we are wary of it, because there are too many things about the body that cannot be mentioned. The body often helps us to personify our Shadow.
>
> (*Le conferenze di Basilea 1934*. 1943/1987, 2015, p. 68)

A consideration that may be made in this regard is that the image of the Shadow transcends the epistemological order and puts us in direct contact with the intimate essence of things. Without Shadow, we would not only be deprived of a part of ourselves and, therefore, not be whole, but we could not actually exist. Apropos of this Jung points out that a solely luminous representation characterized by perfection and absolute coherence (i.e., one equatable with the Platonic idea) can be hypothesized as a mental, but not an ontological, phenomenon. From this standpoint the Shadow would be the very principle that enables the transition from the thinkable to the real. Thus, we may suppose that a hypothetical spiritual world of origins would have had to have included an antithetical element, i.e. matter, to have generated the event of the cosmos. In this event, the Shadow, as a factor whose generative nucleus lies in matter, would actually represent the inexplicable, opaque and contradictory element that can never be completely assimilated and that destroys the unity of an abstract context, while at the same time endowing it with depth and the movement of life. In this sense, and since life and reality are not abstract principles but concern single things and individual living beings, the Shadow also embodies the principle of our uniqueness, while at the same time expressing the mystery of nature that opposes reason's presuming to dominate reality by knowing it.[3]

Thirdly, the Shadow is the bearer of precious elements to be discovered, as well as potentialities of our becoming. In this regard, Jung states that the Shadow "even contains childish or primitive qualities which would in a way vitalize and embellish human existence, but – convention forbids!" (Jung 1938/1940, 2014, p. 100). He also observes that the "Shadow, although by definition a negative figure, sometimes has certain clearly discernible traits and associations that point to quite a different background. It is as though he were hiding meaningful contents under an unprepossessing exterior" (Jung 1954, 2014, p. 270). And with even greater insight, he writes:

> We are eternally incomplete, we grow, and we change. The future personality we will be is already in us, but still hidden in the shadow. In a certain sense the Ego is like a crack that gradually extends across a surface. The future potentialities of the Ego depend on its present shadow. We know what we have been, but not what we will be.
>
> (Jung 1943/1987, 2015, p. 64)

From this perspective, the Shadow is also the seat of creative ideas that are still obscure, simply because they are unknown to the Ego. A content is Shadow because it is "in the shade," but the not-known of today corresponds to the known of the future, just as the unevolved elements of the present correspond to future development. The complex formations of the unconscious and the actual organizing principles of its structure, are the seat of a "paraconscious" activity, as Jung defines it, of a preliminary "luminosity" (present, to some degree, in the roots of a subjectivity that precedes the birth of the Ego), which is interpenetrated with, and indissolubly linked to, unconsciousness. This ties in with the notion that perceptual sensory activity is not, as Freud supposed, the only source of knowledge, and that the unconscious has a kind of pre-consciousness or "unconscious consciousness" which precedes and helps to form the subsequent consciousness of the Ego. In particular, it is also held to be the seat of many small luminosities of consciousness which, at the right moment, are able to expand into the upper psychic layers and merge with Ego consciousness, thus broadening its horizons (Jung 1947/1954, 2014, pp. 189/90). Paradoxically, therefore, the Shadow is the source of light. This brings to mind a poetic image conjured by the profound intuition of a little girl who, perhaps to overcome the anxiety of being separated from the family and their affections when she fell asleep, said to her mother as she tucked her in: "Mom, don't tell me you're switching off the light, tell me you're turning on the dark!"

Ultimately, it is not only consciousness that illuminates the unconscious, enabling us to know its contents, but also the unconscious that illuminates consciousness by thrusting upward and rendering intuitable profound psychic realities. These realities either precede the birth of consciousness or lie outside its perceptual area, and enrich it with new and complex representations.

We represent reality to ourselves through perceptual sensory activity and rational thought, which, understandably and inevitably, gives us a partial vision of things. Though indispensable to our evolution, this partial vision should never be taken for absolute, otherwise we would produce idols and all the dangerous "ideologies." However, it is precisely through the activation of the subjectivity of the Self, which is able to see in the Shadow what the Ego does not see, that we can tap into reality through a direct means which, in religious terms, may be called contemplation, revelation, grace, faith (in the sense in which it is understood by Panikkar, i.e., as a vision of the invisible, or the opening of the third eye of the mystics), and, in psychological terms, is definable as an immediate experience that may be called intuitive. For Jung, intuition is an unconscious faculty of perception, but here, though this may seem paradoxical, it would be "used consciously." In fact, intuition seems to be rooted in the deepest layers of the unconscious and to spring from the faculty of "unconscious consciousness" of which Jung speaks, where the psyche

> reaches down from the daylight of mentally and morally lucid consciousness into the nervous system that for ages has been known as "sympathetic." This does not govern perception and muscular activity like the cerebrospinal system, and thus control the environment; *but, though functioning without sense-organs, it maintains the balance of life and, through the mysterious paths of sympathetic excitation, not only gives us knowledge of the innermost life of other beings but also has an inner effect on them*.... The cerebrospinal function ... experiences everything as an outside, whereas the sympathetic system experiences everything as an inside.
> (Jung 1934/1954, 2014, pp. 39–40. My italics)

It is interesting to note that these intuitive concepts of Jung find confirmation today in the most recent neuroscientific research. For example, Panksepp's research on the emotional brain of animals and humans shows that the real matrix of consciousness does not reside in the cerebral cortex, the receptor of all sensory stimuli, but in the brainstem, and, more specifically, the peri-aqueductal area – a much older part of the nervous system, phylogenetically speaking – where the life of the emotions is also articulated. In fact, if an individual were to suffer grave damage to the cerebral cortex he would, in any event, remain conscious of himself; whereas, if the more profound area of the brain were to be damaged, he would be reduced to a vegetative state.[4]

2.3 Shadow as a principle of relation

From another standpoint, the Shadow may be defined as a principle of relation. Indeed, the Shadow is not just a part of the psyche, but also a relation between some of its parts, which is exemplified in physics by a beam of light striking an object which casts a shadow that may be considered an expression of the relationship between the light, the object, and the part of it that cannot be lit. The Shadow emerges from the relation between consciousness and the knowable and unknowable aspects of the unconscious. I believe, in fact, that the relational dimension has been a constitutive part of the psyche since its origin, precisely because it is interwoven with any number of interactive relationships: between conscious and unconscious, between the different aspects of the personality, between the Ego and the objects in the outside world, between the Ego and the You – even though this last will only be activated through an encounter with a principle of inner "otherness" and with the "other" than us in the outer reality.

From this perspective, the Shadow may be considered as the archetypal background that throws the opposites into relief. For Jung, the latter are constitutive elements of the psyche, because they organize its structure and guarantee its expression at the dynamic level. Just as in physics an electric current can only pass between poles of a different voltage, the psyche can only evolve if the energetic flow on which it relies is guaranteed by a field of antagonistic charges (Jung 1928, 2014). The light–shadow dichotomy is a metaphor of its unconscious–consciousness counterpart, which may be considered the first division to have arisen in the psyche, and which, in the Jungian sense, should more accurately be termed a "polarity." All the other pairs of opposites – heaven and earth, above and below, right and left, in and out, before and after, good and evil, and so forth – would only be defined later; in fact, the formulation of differences was only made possible by the activity of consciousness which extracted them from the undifferentiated, unconscious primitive magma.

In this regard, it is not coincidental that, as Neumann notes, all the world creation myths speak of the birth of light: light is born because the eyes that can see it come into being; the world is created because its image is represented in the soul (1949a, 1954). Shadow delimits light and, in turn, is delimited by it, thus representing the contrast between, but also the radical interdependence of, the two factors: "[...] for what is light without shadow? What is high without low?" (Jung 2020, p. 231). Similarly, consciousness can only arise within an inexhaustible dialectic with its unconscious matrix.

2.4 Shadow as generative element of the symbol

The Shadow also stimulates the symbolic capacity of consciousness, since it enables us to embrace what is not immediately visible and knowable.

In *Psychological Types*, Jung states: "A symbol always presupposes that the chosen expression is the best possible description or formulation of a relatively unknown fact, which is none the less known to exist or postulated as existing" (Jung 1921/2014, p. 474). He also emphasizes that symbols are not produced without a particular orientation of consciousness. In *Symbols of Transformation*, Jung refers to the Gospel passage in which Christ invites Nicodemus to be reborn from water and spirit and, when the Pharisee objects that it is impossible to enter the mother's womb a second time to be born, points out how much trouble Christ took "to make the symbolic view of things acceptable to Nicodemus, *as if throwing a veil over the crude reality*" (Jung 1912/1952, 2014. My italics). The necessarily unsaturated, and consequently relative, aspect of a formulation containing the unknown, and the veil that covers the concreteness of things, may be seen as metaphors of the Shadow. Here, the enigma and the veil do not conceal the truth, but rather "reveal" it, when truth is understood as our representation of things in a way that betrays neither their intimate and objective fabric, nor our relationship with them. However, the Latin root of reveal is *re-* "back," "again" + *velare* "to cover," which in this case means laying a new – symbolic – veil over the factual, or empirical, aspect of reality; in other words, bracketing it, in the sense of phenomenological epoché. This would allow us to see, precisely through the veil, the "states of things" that make up life, which constantly supersede each other, inevitably putting us in new situations. Without Shadow we would stop at a solely rational, and thus an absolutely clear, complete and definitive, vision of reality. But reason does not see reality in all its transparency, and thus prevents us from accepting its infinite character, its aura of possibility, its endless renewal, or the sense of its mystery; whereas a symbolic attitude of consciousness enables us to do this. Only the symbol, with its interweaving of light and shadow, allows us, in a certain sense, to "see" the invisible, precisely because it provides us with an "other" gaze that can see beyond the concrete aspect of things. From this standpoint, symbolic consciousness is also the form of consciousness that allows us to create the new, precisely because it does not remain anchored in facts as they stand, and in their ineluctable concatenation of causes and effects. As Panikkar states, human consciousness cannot be reduced to historical consciousness. In his opinion, time is also made up of moments that he defines as "tempiternal," meaning that eternity is not time that lasts forever but the non-temporal root of time and, in a certain sense, *kairòs*, the time of meaning, which is more qualitative than quantitative and signals the arrival of the new as a beginning instead of a consequence. Since eternity can only be grasped through a symbolic formulation it exists in the "here" and "now," in the intensely experienced present, which penetrates the flow of becoming and thus pertains to a trans-historical dimension.

> Reality is basically discontinuous. We create time. Time does not sustain us like a mother. It is our child. The creative moment is the only reality. History is woven from the detritus, as it were, of authentic human activity, and of any activity.
>
> (Panikkar 1981/1984, p. 81)

I think Jung captures the essence of Panikkar's profound intuition when he states that to make history man has to be, in certain sense, anti-historical, and also in the following passage:

> Life has always seemed to me like a plant that lives on its rhizome. Its true life is invisible, hidden in the rhizome. The part that appears above ground lasts only a single summer. Then it withers away – an ephemeral apparition. When we think of the unending growth and decay of life and civilizations, we cannot escape the impression of absolute nullity. Yet I have never lost a sense of something that lives and endures underneath the eternal flux. What we see is the blossom, which passes. The rhizome remains ... In the end the only events in my life worth telling are those when the imperishable world erupted into this transitory one.
>
> (Jung 1961, 1989, p. 4)

It may thus be concluded that the pathological configuration of the Absolute Shadow can only be overcome if the therapy helps the patient to re-establish the relationship with his true Shadow – understood in the manifold senses of which Jung speaks – that has been lost.

2.4.1 Mental mechanisms that result in the loss of the relationship with the true Shadow and imprisonment in the Absolute Shadow

There are various ways in which the Ego can rid itself of its Shadow. For instance, it can absolutize the horizon of its consciousness so that it becomes one-sided and dogmatic – a risk inherent in the developments of Western culture – thus forfeiting its relation with the unconscious, with its personal Shadow and with the totality of the soul. Said relations can only be established by cultivating a form of consciousness that does not presume to occupy the entire space of the real, and is able to confront mystery and the complexity of things: "because only a consciousness that denies its totality can be receptive to totality" (Galimberti; 1984, p. 187). Paradoxically, the loss of the Shadow, understood as the "inferior part of the personality" and "the combined contents of the personal unconscious" (Jung 1917/1943, 2014), i.e., a relative and easily integrated Shadow, generates a Shadow that is far more difficult to unmask. This latter could be termed a "Shadow of falsification" and identified as the driving force of one of the defense mechanisms that generate the negative destiny complex. "The 'man without Shadow' is statistically the commonest human type, one who imagines he is only what he cares to know about himself" (Jung 1947/1954, 2014, p. 208). Hence the order of reason, based on the principle of identity and the law of cause and effect, imposes itself on consciousness, paralyzing its symbolic capacity and thus preventing it from being receptive to the unknown element, to the ulteriority of meaning contained exclusively in the symbol. As a result, the evolutive potentialities of the psyche become atrophied.

> In the final analysis, causal determinism has the same characteristics as destiny. It is blind and does not realize plans; it neither hates nor favors human beings; it has no future aims, bypassing the past and future in a present that repeats itself, obeying a law that permits no waivers or exceptions.
>
> (Galimberti, 1984, p. 113)

With regard to the sense of destiny, I think that the law of cause and effect is configured as a temporal sequence of crime-punishment that cannot be interrupted by the generation gap, since "The sins of the fathers will be visited upon their children." This is echoed in the gospel story of the Passion. When Christ is condemned to death and Barabbas is released, the people exclaim: "His blood be on us and on our children" (Matthew, 27–30).

As already mentioned, two other paths open to the Ego are conscious identification with the Shadow, which becomes an element of strength and is present above all in maniacal pathologies, and unconscious identification with the Shadow, characteristic of depressive syndromes. Jung writes:

> A man who is possessed by his shadow is always standing in his own light and falling into his own traps. Whenever possible, he prefers to make an unfavorable impression on others. In the long run luck is always against him, because he is living below his own level and at best only attains what does not suit him. And if there is no doorstep for him to stumble over, he manufactures one himself and then fondly believes he has done something useful.
>
> (Jung 1940/1950, 2014, p. 123)

Though it may seem paradoxical, this path also enables the individual to draw power from the Shadow – here configured as a state of inferiority – when he is unable to tolerate the sense of his fragility, and especially the feeling of impotent rage. In fact, in refusing the current of empathy from another human who offers help, the individual becomes vindictive and is thus condemned to failure and impotence. For example, a patient once told me that she had succumbed again to her depressive thoughts when she saw a beggar who had passed out on the street: *"I had the feeling that I could become like that man whom the passersby were unable to help. It was as if I were going to fall into a well so deep that no hand could reach me."* Moreover, the masochistic position clearly hides an identification with the aggressor, and in such a case I think we may speak of a kind of "projective identification" with the power of destiny.

2.4.2 Origins and possible evolutions of the Absolute Shadow

2.4.2.1 The originary Self

My notion of the "Absolute Shadow" can be better defined by drawing on the Jungian concept of the originary Self, the mysterious *prima materia* that the alchemists perceived as an impenetrable chaos and personified as the contradictory figure of the god Mercurius. "It is like a fragment of primeval psyche into which no consciousness has yet penetrated to create division and order, a 'united dual nature,' as Goethe says – an abyss of ambiguities" (Jung 1946, 2014, p. 27). We are not therefore dealing with a Self at the dynamic level, i.e., as an organizing center of the individuation process, but with the structure of the psyche at the beginning of its phylogenetic and ontogenetic history. In the most profound and archaic depths of the psyche there still exists the matrix that once generated all the differences, and continues to generate them in the *hic et nunc* of our life. In other words, every time a new orientation of consciousness, and hence a new vision of the world and of ourselves, comes into being, there will always be a psychic area that has not been able to go along completely with the renewal. Apropos of this, Jung stresses that the capacity of consciousness to distance itself from the undifferentiated is an expression of its need to be freed "from any excessive attachment to the 'spirit of gravity'" (1942/1948, 2014, p. 165). He also points out that every change, even when regenerative, is actually a relative change, because otherwise there would be a completely split personality and a loss of the memory of past experiences. According to Jung, when a new orientation of consciousness is formed, "The connection with the earlier attitude is maintained because part of the personality remains behind in the previous situation; that is to say it lapses into unconsciousness and starts building up the shadow" (ivi, p. 166). Moreover, this shows that unconsciousness and the Shadow are essential parts of the totality of the psyche, and that, together, they are functions which permit a continuity to be maintained in the course of its evolution. We may therefore deduce, if we go back in time both in individual life and human history – which always repeat themselves – that a part of the personality may also have remain entangled and, consequently, engulfed in the primordial (uroboric, according to Neumann, 1949, 1954) psyche; in other words, in the "before" any differentiation, when the Shadow was not yet the opposite of light or – dynamically speaking – a pole generating energy, but still a combination of shadow and light, i.e., shadow that "can" but "has yet" to give birth to light. This explains the difficulty confrontation with the Shadow poses for the Ego. This difficulty may consist in a feeling of inferiority to be corrected and overcome or a state of unconsciousness to be illuminated, but it may also hide a magma of elements that become increasingly enigmatic and confused as one approaches the deepest levels of the collective unconscious. Furthermore, these elements can exert a strong and dangerous fascination since, just as they can enrich the Ego by enabling it to contemplate mystery, they can also trap it in the illusion of having merged with an "all," indeed to have become "the all." In this event, as Jung states in *Symbols of Transformation* (1912/1952, 1967), the work that ushered in analytical psychology, the Shadow can represent the danger of regressive incest which, for the son, does not consist so much in erotically investing the mother (an aspiration that obviously also concerns the daughter), as aspiring to be one with her again, as if the physical, and later psychic, separation caused by birth, had never occurred. At the intrapsychic level, it is a question of the attraction that the unconscious (collective) – the place equated with the maternal experience – exerts on the adult Ego, threatening its individual differentiation. The mistletoe that kills Balder, the hero of a Germanic mythological cycle, is a parasite of the tree and represents the Shadow brother, i.e., a weak Ego dependent on the maternal world. Immersion in the unconscious is required to renew the personality, but "The shadow becomes fatal when there is too little vitality or too little consciousness in the hero for him to complete his heroic task" (ivi, p. 259).

Only such configurations, which reconnect with the originary self and the primordial uroboric psyche, can be identified as an "Absolute Shadow," since its power is stronger, the greater the attraction it exerts on the developing personality and the larger the part of the psyche that has remained embedded in its primary structure or tends to regress toward that structure. Thus, it exerts a possessive effect on the Ego, almost creating the illusion that it has immersed itself in "pure light."

In anthropological terms, this Shadow may be said to coincide with the sacred place (sacred having the same etymological root as execrable) with the violence exercised by the sacred when it floods the psyche, abolishing individual differences: "The night of the Self is an unimaginable night that is not even the opposite of day, because it is night *and* day, light *and* darkness. It is a faceless night ..." since "its face is every face" (Galimberti 1984, p. 172). The Absolute Shadow is a paradoxical Shadow, because its construction implies the negation of the Shadow as part of the psyche; it tends to abolish any form of dialectic and, with it, the capacity to become aware, to see: a dazzling light is as blinding as the deepest darkness.

2.4.2.2 The integrated primary Self

A concept similar to the "originary Self" is referred to by Fordham, when he states that the Shadow can be seen as the part of the Self that integrates the

opposites. The background to this activity is the originary condition in which
the opposites "were united in the self before consciousness began to emerge"
(Fordham 1973, 1994, p. 105). According to Fordham, in healthy development the integrated originary Self moves toward a process of de-integration
through which the psyche is divided into various parts that establish a relationship with reality (thus making it possible, for example, to constitute
and then go beyond the state of physiological fusion with the mother) and
maintain the attributes of totality belonging to the originary Self from which
they derive. The phases of de-integration are followed by phases of stability in which the various forms of progress achieved are welded together to
strengthen an ever-more complex totality of the psyche. Hence, for Fordham,
the Shadow is a manifestation of the Self striving to achieve totality not
through the progressive means referred to above, but the regressive return to
the integrated originary Self. (ivi, pp. 41, 46). At this level the Shadow does
not, as yet, indicate the opposition of "good" and "bad" associated with the
paranoid-schizoid phase described by Klein, nor, obviously, their integration
as partial aspects of a single reality, in the subsequent depressive phase (Klein
1946). Rather, it signals a collusion between the images of good and bad and
the feelings of love and hate, which is manifest through a form of ambiguity
(more than of ambivalence) that is still not conflictual for the Ego. Clearly,
this would render impossible both the act of choice that would set the Ego
on a viable path, and the embrace and visualization of the real, with its chia-
roscuros and complex totality.

In this regard, I found illuminating a comment made by a patient who
was striving for unity: *"Before the division between good and bad there must
have been a more primordial division, between everything and nothing."* It
seemed evident to me that a division between everything and nothing
implied a paradox, since neither a total volume nor a total void can exist in
reality. That is why I speak of "Absolute Shadow," which in clinical terms
signifies "when the idea of absolute becomes Shadow," rather than of an
"archetype of the Shadow," a principle that already refers to a sense of the
negative, of the inferior and of evil, and therefore presupposes the existence
of a sense of the positive, of value, and of good. The Ego is fascinated,
subjugated and persecuted by the image of totality in which everything is
contrary to everything else, as in the ideograms of primitive languages in
which each sign embraces opposite meanings. Perhaps the concept of
Absolute Shadow could be more relevantly compared to the archetypal
image of the parent (rather than parents, since the idea of perfection, which
is projected as much on the mother as the father, implies the coexistence of
both sexes) or to the archetypal image of God, the principle held to be the
sole creator of the world and the generator of man, the Son. The opposites
coexist within this tendency to fuse with an element sensed as omnipotent,
and are either equivalent to each other or abruptly change into one another
other – as happens, for example, in the transition from an idealizing to a
negative transference – or their meanings are inverted, the negative

becoming positive and vice versa. For the suffering individual it is of the utmost importance to preserve the nearly always unconscious illusion of being able to participate in a form of omnipotence, be it constructive or destructive. "A total incapacity to be equals total omnipotence," as Althusser writes. "We are constantly faced with the same terrible ambivalence, the equivalent of which is found in medieval Christian mysticism: *totum = nihil*" (Althusser 1993, p. 278).[5] Thus the Shadow becomes a kind of negative pathway to existence: the void, the lack of sense, and the refusal to give a meaning to things, to expand indefinitely, merging with a volume, an "all" that occupies the place of the lost feeling of belonging to oneself. Without the sense of destiny as the antagonist and absolute master of existence, the terror of annihilation would explode anew.

2.4.2.3 The paradox

We may therefore hypothesize that the nature of the pathological nucleus which forms the negative destiny complex is more psychotic than neurotic. Indeed, it is the bearer of a paradox which, as Racamier writes, is a mechanism typical of psychosis: "A paradox is a mental formation that indissolubly binds two propositions or directives that are irreconcilable and yet not contradictory" (Racamier 1980, 1983, p. 145).[6] In particular, the paradox of clinical interest, because it is an expression of madness or induces madness, is actually a mental and relational strategy, and takes the form of "a closed pragmatic paradox." In other words, it is a paradoxical proposition that also requires a response implying action from the person to whom it is directed and, being a paradox, leaves no possibility of his avoiding this, even simply via thought (ivi). While listening to patients, we often detect typically paradoxical positions which are sometimes explicit and, at others, perceivable as implicit. For instance, a female patient, of whom I shall speak later, told me: *"If my parents had asked my permission to have me, I would have refused it. I did not choose this unjust life filled with suffering. The only thing I am still free to do is to die."* It is almost as if she had said: "I can only exist by not existing, because to be me I would have to create my own life myself, and therefore self-generate (which is also paradoxical because one would have to exist before existing)", or "I can live only by dying, because I would then enter the life I want, a life with neither suffering nor separation, and therefore an immortal life."

Another patient remarked: *"Analysis makes me feel better but this scares me because it means I'll never be able to become independent because I'll always need someone, and so I'll never get better."* Here, too, it is as if a severe inner judge had said: "To be well, you must be able to do without all relationships, but you are not 'whole' without others, so you must preserve their love at all costs." This was clearly a case of the patient's mistakenly equating independence with isolation, and relation with illness, and her paradoxical proposition was more or less the following: "To be independent you have to be dependent, therefore to be healthy you have to remain ill."

The analyst is, of course, also involved in the paradox, which would require him/her to heal without healing, to employ therapy that would only be successful if it failed, to help the patient to live by helping him/her to die, or to make it possible to end the analysis without needing to work through any form of separation. I think the only way to deal with such a situation is to identify the paradox, to spell it out in words as soon as the therapy has progressed to a point where this is permissible, and to help the patient to become conscious of the way in which s/he uses the paradox. "I wanted at all costs to destroy myself because I had never existed," writes Althusser, who, on several other occasions, states that he felt he existed only through "artifice and deception" (Althusser 1993, p. 278). In fact, it would seem that he wanted to destroy his "non-existence," but this "destroying oneself to exist," which was taken literally by his unconscious fantasies and translated into compulsory and unconscious behavior that engendered tragedy, could have been transformed by consciously working through the mourning of the false self and of false relationships, in order to be reborn to his own truth. In other words, it was a question of shifting the paradox from a concrete to a symbolic level, which would have permitted the transition from acted-out madness, which, by forgetting reason, becomes psychosis, to creative frenzy in the psychic depths, which can unite contradictory realities in a multifaceted global context pervaded by complexities, and without which reason can never become wisdom, i.e., the expression of freedom. It is only through this approach that the analytical process has some hope of escaping from the trap of a destiny that is felt, or willed, to be catastrophic, and of emerging from the stasis of an unfavorable psychic constellation capable of exerting its destructive effect on everything that approaches or dares to challenge it.

I shall elucidate on this brief theoretical excursus by summarizing various stages of different case histories, already cited briefly above, which are certainly more eloquent than any theory.

Notes

1 Following the advent of psychoanalysis as a science, we may say that the unconscious itself became chiefly responsible for our negative destiny, being experienced as an entity extraneous to the Ego and a source of alienation, instead of as a sense of belonging, and thus being able to oppose, or even overturn, a person's real intentions.

2 One could say that the whole knowledge process took place through a gradual withdrawal of the projections. In the primitive state, the image of the world was steeped in characteristics of the soul, and only slowly was the capacity developed to distinguish between mental representations of things and the things themselves.

3 Here I am speaking of cognitive activity that utilizes solely scientific method and experimental verification, and which interprets data on the basis of its own theoretical presuppositions. The meaning of knowledge, understood on a phenomenological level, is different, because it is seen as an action that captures the flow of experience and events as they occur.

4 From a lecture given at the AIPA in 2013.

5 On the basis of what has already been stated, here ambivalence should be understood as that form of primordial ambiguity that does not yet require the Ego to make a choice or to effect a synthesis.

6 In effect, this means that it is impossible to arrive at a compromise that preserves both positions of the paradox, or to opt for one of the two.

Chapter 3

Journeys of life and therapy
Five clinical cases

3.1 Marco's case:[1] The model: fascination and damnation

3.1.1 Anamnestic details

Marco is now almost 40. He began depth analysis with me, which is still ongoing, around 17 years ago, with three sessions a week. He was referred to me by a psychiatrist colleague who had been treating him for a few years and supporting him with pharmacological therapy. The colleague told me that at first he had thought it might have been a case of a difficult and delayed adolescent transition, but that he now believed that the situation was more serious and that analytical treatment could be beneficial. After a long period of analysis with me, his former psychiatrist said that we could finally speak of an "avoided psychosis."

In the first therapeutic phase Marco confided to me that he had not left the house for many months: he no longer saw his friends; he had given up sports; he was unable to take exams. In addition, he was plagued by terrible anxieties, such as being seized by an irrepressible urge to jump out of a window he found open or to throw himself off a bridge. He was obsessed with the idea that he would wet himself when he was with people, so he would always make sure he was near a bathroom. He was also tormented by the fear that he might hurt children. My first thought was that, without knowing it, he was talking about a sadistic instinct of which he was particularly afraid, because he might not be able to control it. Reflecting on this today, and in the light of various considerations made during therapy, I am sure that the particular form of sadism he defended himself from was not an originary datum of his nature, an instinctual component (although I believe that real sadism does not derive from instinct but from distorted or interrupted psychic development), but, rather, the energetic form of a feeling-toned complex that had split and developed a considerable autonomy with respect to his Ego. From a post-Freudian perspective, we would say that Marco had incorporated a very powerful and destructive object with which he had identified, possibly because he had once been invaded by forms of identification projected onto him by his parents. In particular, I think that Marco's fear stemmed from the rejection of the fragile and dependent aspects that he perceived in himself but wanted to destroy, in

DOI: 10.4324/9781003261872-4

order to preserve only the image of perfection that was required of him, especially by his mother, since a little boy clearly evokes the idea of vulnerability. It was as if his imaginal world had been parasitized by what Marco would one day describe as "dominating thoughts" or "dead thoughts." Countertransferentially, I also picked up a feeling of alarm and, although his disorder had the characteristics of a serious obsessive neurosis, it seemed to me that the nature of his suffering was closer to that experienced in psychosis.

This young patient had been unable to express his emotions as a child, because his parents, and principally his mother, who were frightened by anything that could be neither foreseen nor controlled, had not recognized them. During the analytic exchange we reconstructed that they had probably transmitted to him an image of himself that had nothing to do with the characteristics of his true nature but was rather an ideal image of what he should have been: a perfect, fully realized person, without tensions, without needs, without faults and desires, and this primarily to placate their anxieties and reassure them as to their infallibility as parents. It is likely, in fact, that they nurtured the unconscious desire that their son would be completely fulfilled by their mere presence and thus would not experience feelings of fear or states of lack, nor even, at a later age, the desire for completion in a relationship with a life companion, since this would have implied accepting his diversity and independence from them.

Such a turning point, in fact, would have irreversibly marked the end of the state of fusion between parents and child (and especially between mother and son) typical of early childhood, which offers the illusion of possessing a narcissistic form of omnipotence. Indeed, when an adolescent Marco confided to his mother that he liked a particular girl and intended to ask her out, she replied: *"No, don't even think about it, not now. I'll tell you when the moment has come."* During one of our most recent sessions Marco spoke to me about the importance of being able to betray, then added: *"Betrayal is a gateway to truth."* He was obviously referring to his mother's expectations and plans for him, which falsified the true essence of his being.

For his part, Marco experienced his parents as a closed, self-sufficient couple who, while never showing any signs of mutual affectivity, seemed to have resolved all the contradictions and problems of life within their relationship. Hence they formed a united front that their children could not penetrate in the slightest. In a certain sense, this young patient found himself in a paradoxical double bind: "To exist you must not feel anything, but if you don't feel anything you don't exist." Then, as he so meaningfully put it: *"My parents were absent, but their shadow hung over me..."*

Since the patient's archaic experiences had never been mirrored in the mind of an adult who could have restored them to him through a form of shared representation warmed by affection, they could not be configured as an expressible experience; hence, as he grew up Marco had let his emotions die. While he was talking to me during one of our sessions, I realized that those emotions had nearly always been ignored by his parents, and if, by chance, they had been perceived, had met with drastic disapproval.

Consequently, Marco had been confronted with a blank, blind gaze which, by not seeing him, prevented him not only from seeing himself, but even from feeling that he existed as a whole, since it is through parental mirroring that the child is able to perceive itself and its reality. When Marco had to deal with a situation that required affective involvement he was seized by a panic attack that obliged him to flee and then to falsify or deny the demands of reality and of his own desire. *"If I express an emotion, that emotion is me, and if I am unable to do it, or if that emotion does not materialize because it is not accepted and recognized, then I am annihilated."* In order to protect his identity that he felt was *"like a tiny flame that could be extinguished by the slightest puff of wind,"* he had confined it to what he described as *"an idea of self,"* and it was as if his entire affective sphere, and even his corporeal sensibility, had atrophied. When, after a certain period of analysis, he realized that he was beginning to experience sensations again, he confided to me that he had not felt heat or cold for some time. He had increasingly reduced his contacts with the outside world and had taken refuge in a deep niche of his being, seeking to live as little as possible. Once he said to me: *"When you can't say things because they're not understood, you reach a point where you can't think them and, in the end, you can't even feel them."* On another occasion he explained just how removed he felt from his emotions: *"A smell was enough to trigger an angry reaction. As soon as I was touched by an emotion I rejected it and the rejection became emptiness… but the rejection lasted a moment and the emptiness forever."* In fact, he experienced emotion as something that originated outside himself; indeed, in a dream it had taken the form of a thief who threatened to ransack his house.

During many years of our work together, Marco had brought me dreams with a recurring theme: pursued or threatened by enemies, he was forced either to engage in an endless fight with them, or to make an escape fraught with danger. Also in this case we may speak of the amputation of his Shadow (here I am referring above all to the Shadow's positive aspects), understood both as a principle of reality and corporeality and also as one of relation. His mother, in particular, had not known how to mirror an image of him that also contained the profound and invisible aspects of his person, which sprang from his own corporeal root and, above all, from his subjectivity. Instead, she had wanted him to be identical to an abstract ideal of perfection in which things were fixed beforehand, where everything was accomplished in a completely self-sufficient universe in which there was no time and no measurement. A universe that did not offer the possibility of contemplating the need for effort, error, transformation, limitation or otherness, understood both as "the other part of us," of our inner space, and "the other than us" that we encounter in the world, both of which are essential and founding elements of our wholeness. Looking back after a long period of therapy, Marco said: *"At the beginning, it's our parents' acceptance that gives us the frame of reference within which we are situated, and also our time. If you are told: 'You're like this and you must stay that way,' time never begins."* By entering into collusion with his parents' pathological mental processes, Marco had set himself an unattainable and perfect model of self, which was both what he should have been and what he could never be. It was a double, in fact, that, on the one hand, seductively promised him salvation by solving all his problems by magic, and, on the other, ruthlessly stole beforehand everything that could have been his. Thus, it condemned him to an insurmountable feeling of inadequacy, to defeat and, indeed, to annihilation, since its victory implied the destruction of everything imperfect and hence his reality in the making which, inscribed in space and time, was inexhaustible but unfinished. In fact, an awareness of being in a space/time context is indispensable to accepting the gradualness and limitation of achievable conquests and to shattering the state of illusory omnipotence in which one is "all" in a dimension of "achronicity."[2] In such a dimension time does not yet exist, since it is not perceived by consciousness as a series of successive moments, but is an eternal time, the time of myth, so to speak, which is also the temporal modality experienced during the state of primary fusion between mother and infant. Once Marco said to me: *"I aspired to becoming someone I could not be, and had I been him he would have annihilated me. I must go beyond the enduring skepticism toward me!"* Clearly, he was referring to his skeptical attitude toward himself.

As the sessions progressed, we personified this mental formation and called it the "model." This helped us, on the one hand, to gradually dissolve Marco's identification with the above fantasy, and, on the other, to restore to him his initiative and freedom of choice regarding the evolution of psychic processes that are neither predictable nor ineluctable, as they would have been had his destiny been decided by extraneous superhuman powers. In a certain sense, it was a question of also restoring to Marco the responsibility for having offered to this unhealthy psychic formation the healthy mental energies it fed on, expropriating them precisely from him. At one point I said to him:

> If the model were to cease exerting such a fascination on you, if you were to reclaim the seed of hope that you felt you had to entrust to it, then it would melt like snow in the sun, or, who knows, change into something else that would not be so hostile toward your life.

One of the model's "promises" was the fantasy of meeting a woman with whom he could achieve a perfect union, which would have saved him and solved all his problems. However, it was as if the plan for the future was not prepared by the present, but imploded in a timeless place. It was impossible, in fact, to imagine a love affair, a growth phase in the relationship, gradually-won achievements, a physicality of the encounter, and a real setting in which the event could unfold. Everything would have been realized immediately and to perfection, without any break between fantasy and reality and without any trial or error. Consequently, Marco always found himself on the threshold of life but could not cross it, because if he had made even the smallest mistake he would have failed, and been exposed to the model's reprisals:

> To succeed in doing anything, to express myself in some way without failing, I would have had to have been "another." But expressing anything: an emotion, a feeling, a desire, meant losing substance for me, distancing myself from the absolute perfection of the model and abandoning a safe place in which I was everything.

Then he added: *"I had to silence my anxieties by being remarkable to a degree that was not human. I wanted the woman to see me as exceptional and provide me with a certificate."* Much later, Marco would tell me that the invincibility promised him by the model was not a real strength, but only "an old cape" in which he enveloped himself, like the kids' hero Superman. Only now was he able to perceive a different strength that he described as *"the expression of self, freed from the monster of the model."* But it would be several years before Marco was able to see that the "perfection" he had miraculously acquired by rigorously complying with the model, was absolutely unreal, and he would say to me:

> Perfection does not come into being, it has always existed. There is not a time in which it is acquired, as there is for life, wisdom or experience. Only now can I say that a thing is "perfect" in a non-literal sense, simply because it is beautiful and gives me joy. It is as if I used to need perfection without feeling, but that kind of perfection lacked everything!

Conversely, Marco would gain an increasing sense of the importance of the limitation inherent to the human condition: *"I experienced limitation as something that cut off existence, whereas it is a horizon."* He would later comment on the importance for him of our discussion in analysis about the concept of "partiality" as an order in which life is inscribed, as opposed to that of "absolute," which is placed in the register of illusion and belongs to our most archaic imaginary world, saying:

> being able to accept a minor loss, a lack, is one of the most important things I have achieved here, and it marks the beginning of my improvement. It has signified being able to access a partiality that is profound, rich, infinite ...

This paradoxical thought of Marco's brought to mind *The Infinite* by Giacomo Leopardi and his having intuited the indissoluble link between the limit and the unlimited: without the "solitary hill," which prevented the poet's gaze from embracing the whole horizon, Leopardi would not have been able to contemplate in his imagination the "endless spaces ... and unearthly silences" beyond it. Without limit, which is also a *confine* (con-fine, from the

Latin *cum-finis*), in other words an opportunity to share one's own finitude with someone or something, one cannot make contact with what is beyond yet is part of us, since it expands our network of relations and inhabits our interiority as representation.

Marco's Shadow, understood as a metaphor of one pole of the symbol, had been amputated; that is, the unknown, and unknowable, part of his reality, which cannot contain the "clear and distinct" idea formulated by Descartes (philosophically premised on Parmenides's concept of the equivalence of being and thinking). As I have already mentioned, only the symbol and the symbolic activity of consciousness are able to represent reality without falsifying it or reducing it to a concrete profile. The Shadow may also be considered as a pole of the symbol that surrounds the unknown, which indicates but does not define it and intuits the potentialities of becoming and the presence of an active subjectivity. This subjectivity is the bearer of what is not yet given, but is created step by step, and hence of freedom. The appearance of the symbol could also be considered a fortunate coincidence that opens a breach in the sense of destiny that rises up like a "wall of the inevitable": *"I was subjugated by a destiny that had become my nature."*

Once a small boy pointed his finger at the starry sky, and said to his father: "You can't imagine or not imagine it." The child's amazing insight showed that a truly profound thought, capable of expressing itself symbolically, also contains the shadow of the unthinkable and enables us to embrace reality in its entirety, without betraying its mystery.

A dream that Marco had a few months into the therapy showed me a way to recover the wholeness of his personality. In the dream Marco was going back to his high school to do a Greek translation, but he did not have his dictionary and when he asked the various people belonging to the school if they had one to lend him, they all said no. The dream could be interpreted as representing the risk of repeating in the transference the desperate impossibility of expressing his emotions, which he had experienced as a child. Marco's fantasy, which was so pregnant with meaning that it aroused a similar fear in me, could have implied that he would not have been given a dictionary – symbol of an interpretive code that would have enabled him to decipher the enigmas of his life and discover their meaning – even in the place where he was receiving treatment, that is by his therapist, in whom he had placed his last hope of salvation. But the analysis of the transference and of the countertransference are not the only means of therapy: hand in hand with this goes the encounter between two people who accompany each other along the path of ordinary life, reciprocally engaged in unraveling knots that concern them both.

As Bruno Callieri writes in the book entitled *Io e Tu, Fenomenologia dell'incontro* (2008, pp. 31–32), published to celebrate his 85th year, the analysis of the transference and its resolution are of fundamental importance, since the transference

> ...represents the abreaction (akin to reflection) onto the analyst of behavioral models of early infancy.... But it is only when the patient becomes

open to encounter (granted that the therapist is both inwardly disposed and capable of this) that it begins to have a true capacity for relation, which is always enriched at a practical and emotional level to a surprising degree, and in fact inherent to the dimension of *reciprocity*. Thus it is necessary (and in recent years this has become an ethical dimension for me) to lift the transference out of its narrow naturalistic, and almost mechanistic, setting and make it open to encounter, i.e. to the *we*.

(pp. 31–32)

In his preface to the above volume, Gilberto Di Petta conveys the magic of encounter through the poet so beloved of Binswanger, Elizabeth Barrett Browning, who saw her beloved as the only place where she could exist (ivi, p. 16). Also for Giuseppe Maffei (2002, p. 135 and ff.), in remarkable accord with Callieri's insights, the course of treatment, which runs from a beginning to an end, is deeply rooted in the extra-analytic space of interpersonal relationship. To understand when a therapy is arriving at its conclusion the analyst must listen not only analytically but also "phenomenologically," which will enable him to gauge how the analysand is facing life and how, although conscious of the many ways in which his environment and his unconscious itself have conditioned him, he has nevertheless acquired a sense that everything that has happened to him is a part of himself and that he has become the subject of choices and free actions, i.e., the subject of his *story*. Maffei describes this analytic listening as subterranean listening:

> The analyst reverberates at deep levels, he listens to himself listening, and if he speaks, it is only after listening at these levels. But in a section of his psyche, which is also deep but somewhat separate, a particular observing Ego listens and senses how the analysand is, step by step, confronting existence itself. It glimpses his approach to life and his ethos. The analyst most certainly cannot dispense with the technique of suspicion: his specificity consists precisely in this, he must know the fantasies and deceptions of the psyche. But in his own psyche he will find, if he is attentive, that next to this analytic place there is often another, a place of listening that could perhaps be described as phenomenological, i.e. concerned with understanding the analysand's way of "being there." It is a place of listening where what is listened to is, so to speak, the primary approach to life, the way in which the analysand is open to the world.

(ivi, pp. 135–6)

Returning to Marco's dream, and my fear that it might have foretold therapy coming to a halt in the future, I had necessarily to admit that, as the analyst, I did not have a dictionary, or rather a tool able to translate unknown and incomprehensible signs into known and comprehensible ones. But I also had to recognize that this was only right, precisely because it is the nature of analysis to arrive at the "symbol" that embraces multiple meanings and unites the known with the unknown, rather than to stop at the "sign" that designates a univocal content and leads from known to other known things. Like a dictionary, in fact, which is consulted at the level of logic and thought, and does not draw on the depths of our being, which is invisible to our senses. Moreover, I was able to recognize myself in various figures in the oneiric context, such as the severe, unbending headmistress; the underrated and unassuming female janitor; the teacher who was friendly with the mother and led a monotonous conventional existence devoid of values; the people in the dream who certainly did not have a dictionary to lend Marco; or, more benignly, the girl who greeted him with a smile. I could have seen all these figures as representing the premature appearance of a negative transference, and deduced that the analytic couple did not have enough resources to interpret and to heal Marco's suffering. Instead I made, in a certain sense, a brief incursion into the extra-analytic space and, drawing on the dimension of encounter, empathized spontaneously with Marco's sense of bewilderment and his feeling disoriented by a text that he did not have the means to translate. However, since the lack of understanding he had suffered as a child was actually configured as his parents' false security about his feelings – since they "knew" exactly what he felt, or rather what he should have felt, as if they were only able to offer him a preestablished emotional grid that matched their expectations and view of life – I realized, and told him, that although we did not have a dictionary we had the text, and we knew that it was the bearer of significant content. At that moment, in fact, it seemed to me that the Greek text really was untranslatable, like the Jungian "symbol," whose meaning is already contained in the expressive form, but which cannot be definitively defined because it also contains the unknown. The necessarily incomplete formulation of the symbol, its enigma and, in a certain sense, its shadow, enable us to embrace reality in its entirety, without betraying its depth and its mystery. The young man had an epiphany and, visibly moved, responded: *"But … I am the text!"*

Many years later, Marco thought again about that first dream – which throughout this long period he had remembered as the dream about the dictionary but which would have been more precisely described as the "dream about the text," since the text also represented his identity and his uniqueness – and he said to me:

> The terror of being swept away and my sense of emptiness were so great that I had to fill out the text with the dictionary. I had to be capable of a simultaneous translation, I had to know everything at once, and the text disappeared. Whereas, the text is patient, it offers itself bit by bit, it doesn't necessarily have to be translated, but to be made to speak, made to live, you must feel it, and today, as I do this, I'm all of a quiver. … The text is the acceptance of ourselves, it consists of matter, it has a physicality, it can be touched, it occupies a space, it is form and the time in which we live. I was terrified of being present, of assuming a form, of leaving

traces behind me. I could not show my feelings, unique though imperfect. ... Uniqueness and perfection are poles apart! So I fled, leaving only a sense of loss and emptiness in myself. ... Now I concentrate on the text and not on the dictionary that is missing, and the text is there anyhow, even if I don't talk, even if the book in which it is written is no longer there. If we are present, if we have substance, space, essence, soul, spirit, it takes a lot to annihilate us, maybe it would take an atomic bomb, but, who knows, maybe even in this case something of us would remain ...!

Reflecting on his words, I think that Marco wished to distinguish the text not only from the dictionary, and hence his interpretation of it in another language, which can explain it without necessarily understanding it, but also from the book, the paper support on which it was printed. We may also say that the book corresponds to our *Körper*, our organism, our anatomical, physiological and biochemical body, whereas the text is our *Leib*, our living body, bearer of all our humanity, and which, in the course of our existence, can change its material substratum to express itself while always remaining itself. But here, surprisingly, Marco poses a question about the essence of our very being and does more than consider the possible significance of the annihilation of the mental illness, the state of *"being dead while alive"* that had encapsulated him in a period he described as of the *"deepest darkness."* A time when he could no longer transcend in the world, in the other than self or in the future, and it was as if his Ego had curled up in the depths of a cave, which gave him that *"sense of emptiness ... so great that I had to fill out the text with the dictionary."* In his response Marco "enters" the border zone between life and death (destruction by the atomic bomb), pushing his imagination beyond the limit of our earthly journey. The existential question is shifted to the metaphysical sphere and to our possible transcendence in another world, touching on religious themes. Perhaps distinguishing between text and book is also like asking: Will something of us remain after death? And what form will it take?

At this level, if we cannot draw on faith, or rather the contents of a belief (because actual faith does not have an object and is, rather, an unconditional openness to mystery), we have no choice but to stay with our questions and images, which do, however, give depth to life. I obviously did not express these thoughts to Marco, because his most urgent problem was certainly not having to face death, but his fear of life, and I was most grateful to him for having sparked reflections in me that broadened the base of our therapeutic alliance. This brings to mind two considerations and a metaphor presented by Raimundo Panikkar during a series of seminars at Città di Castello in Italy. The considerations were: *"Death does not lie in front of me but just behind me, because the longer I live the farther I move away from that mortal non-being of 'before' that I was."* And *"Time cannot stand still in us, but we cannot stand still in time either."* I think that here Panikkar goes beyond the idea of "life" as duration and is speaking, above all, of its meaning and of our capacity to capture it, which are contained in a single action. As I have already mentioned, there exists alongside *Chronos*, measurable time, *Kairos*, the time of meaning, which makes *Dasein*, "being there," qualitatively unique. Although conscious of the transitory nature of life, we can entertain the sense of an eternal dimension of existence, which does not stem from the representation of life that lasts forever, nor even of a reality that begins after we die, but from the possibility of tapping into a non-temporal root of time and into the richness, the depth, the magic and, in a certain sense, the eternal aspect of an intensely experienced present. Moreover, in the metaphor referred to earlier, Panikkar compares our lives to drops of water that return to the ocean:

> If we identify with the drop of water, then death is the end of everything, because the drop disappears into the ocean, but if we identify with the water of the drop, then that water, with its specific qualities, which are unique, will remain intact, united with all the other waters.

In Jungian terms, we may say that the drop represents the Ego as restricted individuality that does not establish a relation with its Self and thus is isolated from others and from the world; while the water of the drop represents the Self that comprises the Ego and the whole of reality. I think we might draw a parallel between the drop and the book and the water and the text, in Marco's dream. The book could also represent our individuality, our Ego, while the text could correspond to our entire person. As Callieri states, there is a radical heterogeneity between the Ego and the alter-Ego, the I and You, "one receives from the other only to remain other-than-it, but our true identity, a heterogeneous identity if you will, can only be drawn from the 'we,' since the feeling of belonging, as an essential category of the human being, springs from the dimension of reciprocity" (ivi, pp. 27–28). Furthermore, without the Alter, without the You – and in Jungian terms we might add without the Self, bearer of a subjectivity that precedes the birth of the Ego and transcends its horizon because it comprises also the others and all of reality – our very Ego would wither and die like a plant without roots.

3.1.2 Some therapeutic turning points

Returning to Marco's case, I would now like to concentrate on various transitions and dreams in a specific stage of the therapy that occurred in the sixth or seventh year of analysis, since they make it possible to delineate some turning points that were particularly transformative in my patient's psychic life.

Marco had just finished describing three different modalities he had adopted in his habit of reverie. We had already distinguished the latter from imagination, because it was not a mental striving to represent reality or even the capacity to let the unconscious express itself through its images, but rather the prospect of an alternative world that omnipotently replaced reality.

In the "daydream" he would only have started to live when he was perfect. Marco described it thus

> At the beginning I was guided by what I call "dead thoughts," which led me to prefigure everything I would have done or said. Next, I stepped into reality but quickly stepped back, because reality does not correspond to fantasy and is therefore disappointing. In so doing I took refuge in fantasy again. But now I have entered reality and I say to myself: "Why on earth are you picturing things down to the last detail beforehand, when you know perfectly well that they'll go differently from how you imagined them?"

I think that Marco was also taking up a suggestion made by his psychiatrist when he asked him: *"Tell me how one can live?"* And the psychiatrist answered, *"You'll know that when you get to my age. In the meantime, start living, and then think about 'how!'"* I had the feeling that, in the past, Marco had existed completely in his fantasy, and did not even sense that reality was something different. Now he had begun to discover reality and he was taking the risk of living, but it seemed that the clash between the contradictions stemming from the irreconcilability of the two worlds was making him suffer and he was scared of having to abandon a state in which he felt safe. At the next session, he recounted the following dream:

> I think I'm with my family. In any case, I'm in a place that seems familiar and protective. Different events occur one after the other, which I can't reconstruct, then suddenly I find myself in a dangerous situation. Someone wants to harm me and I must escape. I know I have the power to go back. It is as if I were able to travel through space and time and return to the familiar situation. I try to perform a kind of magic ritual, like looking at the clock and doing other things required by the practice, but this time I'm unable to use my power. The ritual doesn't work and I wake up in a state of anguish.

I thought that to enter reality Marco had to abandon the talisman of omnipotence promised to him by the model. But if he escaped its dominion, it was as if he had to suffer its reprisal. The model's revenge essentially consisted in making him see reality as a hostile place. So I told Marco that abandoning his former magic power was a condition for encountering reality: we leave one world and find another. He replied that reality was distressing in itself, but when he came into contact with it *"far worse"* anxieties reared their heads: *"I have the sensation that I have to cut away a piece of myself."*

I sensed that Marco was talking about an originary anxiety, an anxiety of birth, and I told him that perhaps he felt like a child coming into the world, who leaves behind one condition to acquire another. In the mother's womb, the child may not yet have had any disturbing sensations; it is enveloped by a universe with which it merges, because it has not yet been separated from the maternal container. Birth brings the experience of cold and hunger, the perception of gravity, the fear of falling, and, since one begins to feel, anxiety, but there are the mother's arms to hold one, her whisper, her song, her rocking and cradling. The mother's affection, her "touch," makes that child special and gives it an identity, by recognizing it as existing. After a pause for reflection, which I sensed was filled with anxiety, Marco told me: *"While you were talking I felt a terrible anger."* I asked him to try and remember when the anger first arose and what provoked it, and he replied:

> Maybe I'm envious of that child because I didn't have those arms? Maybe I didn't have that affection?... No... no..., that's not it, the anger is actually for that child, it is aroused by it, because it should not have needed everything, it should not have been so helpless. **I am disturbed by the idea that I exist because I am touched...**

He was obviously referring to the support given by the mother's arms, and we talked about how difficult it was for him to accept his vulnerability, his dependence and his needs, and about how he found it intolerable to have to rely on and accept help from others, since the model commanded him to be absolutely self-sufficient and invulnerable. At the end of the session Marco confessed, *"it's true, anxiety and anger cover my humanity."* As he was leaving, he said *"thank you"* to me and, without thinking, I said to him: *"thank you."* I realized it was a mistake, a kind of acting out on my part, although I knew I had given this unconventional response because I was so grateful to Marco for having the courage and generosity to communicate such an archaic psychic experience in words. While he was putting on his overcoat with his back to me, I heard him mutter to himself in annoyance: *"yes ... goodnight ... thanks for what?"* ... even though he had just told me he could not tolerate gratitude or a bond. I thought in dismay that his anger would soon pour forth in the transference as well, which is exactly what happened, though luckily it gave us another opportunity for growth!

At a subsequent session he recounted the following dream that seemed to have a high transformative value:

> There is a young man who is not me but who at the same time is me, because I experience things in person, while also being a spectator. He has very long hair and he gradually starts to lose it, a lot of it, more and more, like the leaves of a tree in autumn. I realize that it is an event that cannot be controlled and which one cannot oppose; an event that changes a person's image. I experience an enormous sadness, the pain of a radical change and a loss. The young man is also suffering, like someone who is approaching old age.

Marco reminded me that we had spoken of the need to depotentiate the image of the model, to make it lose its fascination, step down from its pedestal.

Abandoning the model makes me suffer, it's true. One feels lost without a guide! Yet today I feel that losing something is not the same as nullifying oneself. The passing of time is part of life. Today it seems as if I am able to combine the possibility of suffering, sacrifice and compassion. I feel compassion for that young man and I know that I am beginning to exist and to experience my feelings.

I could not help but think of the myth of rebirth of which Jung speaks in *Symbols of Transformation* and of the hero's nocturnal journey through the belly of the whale. One of the stages in the myth is the lighting of a fire in the bowels of the mammal and the hero losing his hair due to the fierce heat. Jung states: "Fire-making is a pre-eminently conscious act and therefore 'kills' the dark state of union with the mother" (Jung 1912/1952, 2014, p. 211). In Marco's fantasy, becoming one with the model also meant remaining enclosed in the prehistoric mother, that is in the original Eden, where one has the illusion of being everything and everyone through a kind of total adherence to things. During analysis we had followed the path of reverie, not passively, as happens during the construction of unhealthy mental mechanisms, but actively and consciously, as was Jung's approach:

> He [the patient] is like a man who has unintentionally fallen into the water and sunk, whereas psychoanalysis wants him to act like a diver [...] In reality, however, they [his fantasies] exert their great influence just because they are of such great importance. They are sunken treasures which can only be recovered by a diver; in other words the patient, contrary to his wont, must now deliberately turn his attention to his inner life. Where formerly he dreamed, he must now think, consciously and intentionally.

Jung then explains: "psychoanalysis follows the false tracks of fantasy in order to restore the libido, the valuable part of the fantasies, to consciousness and apply it to the duties of the present" (Jung 1913/1954, 2014, pp. 186–187). After my patient and I had discussed the myth of Jonah and the Whale for a while, he said to me that he was beginning to see that "changing" did not necessary imply laceration, catastrophic separation, or severing a part of oneself. *"Maybe I can take with me a piece of previous experience, of an earlier state ... who knows ... maybe a piece of the whale's heart!"*

After a few more sessions, Marco brought me the following dream:

> I have an appointment with a very important client of my uncle's, to whom I am to bring some documents. I have to arrive at a bar or a restaurant in the open air. It is difficult to reach. I hurry, but I'm still late. When I get there there's no client, and I realize anxiously that I've missed the appointment. Then I find myself in your office. We are in a session and I realize that there is a girl I don't know behind me, perhaps my age.

I am a bit embarrassed to speak in front of her. The girl says: "This is not just therapy, it's much more." You are not sitting in the armchair in front of me but at the desk. A little girl of about five and an adolescent boy, perhaps between twelve and fifteen, appear at my side, between you and me. I watch the scene and would like to speak, but I can't because I get emotional, so I just think: "These are my problems." You are waiting for me to say something, but you smile at me, as if you had read my mind, and I realize that this understanding between us is the reason I became emotional.

The uncle's client was a powerful man. The typical example of someone who has made it: wealthy, respected, dynamic, incredibly strong and able to impose himself. A man who could be considered in the collective imagination as the perfect model of masculinity. So Marco actually allowed himself to abandon the path of the model and to engage with himself and his therapy. The unfamiliar girl behind him expressed what he was really thinking. When he started analysis he imagined that it was a bit like having surgery that would remove a diseased part of him, but he also thought that he was going to find all the answers to his problems by following a script. Instead, he found a world that was extremely rich, multifaceted, and filled with feelings and emotions with which he was not familiar: *"There's not only being well or being ill. A whole world exists between suffering and joy."* When he was about five, his second sister was born. He remembered feeling a gentleness and tenderness toward her as a little girl and joking with her, even though at nursery school he no longer played with "girls" because he felt they were different from boys and he was a bit disdainful of them: *"Little girls seemed to belong to another world."* A few months later, Marco explained to me that the birth of his sisters had also meant that he was faced with something he himself did not have, precisely because it belonged to the different female world, and that he felt indelibly marked by this lack. Marco remembered feeling the first stirrings for girls when he was an adolescent in high school. Attracted to one in particular, he was never able to show her he was interested – until she started going out with one of his schoolmates, and he experienced a burning sense of defeat. This theme also recurred in Marco's dreams: a woman, known and desired, or unknown and often beautiful, approached a friend or neighbor instead of him, and he witnessed their passionate embraces and kisses, experiencing both a lacerating anguish and tremendous anger. Marco realized that he was attracted to the girl at school when he dreamed he was kissing her, but immediately afterward he had to spit out something very bitter, and so the attraction turned into disgust. In the dream his father came into the room and said to him: "You don't even know how to kiss a girl!" It seemed to me that in this dream the father took on the semblance of the model, its mocking attitude that humiliated Marco. I told him that the two moments, experienced in reality and in the dream, marked the birth of an emotion, of a possibility of living and loving, but were aborted moments.

His sensibility had reawakened, but was immediately quashed. The dream indicated, therefore, that we had to go back precisely to that point, in order to retrieve his former "feeling." Sometime later, Marco would tell me that he felt most desperate when he came close to the possibility of being happy, because that possibility was always transformed into failure in one form or another. Consequently, he had kept well away from that unbearable pain. *"Looking back was like looking at a graveyard, the graveyard of attempts, or rather of dreams, because I didn't even make an attempt."* I believe, in fact, that Marco attacked his feeling of hope to avoid the anguish connected with the real possibilities of life, because hope does not promise the magic fulfillment of desires, but implies trusting one's intuition and tolerating uncertainty. In so doing, Marco inevitably brought about the paralysis of his life, because hope, as Panikkar observes, is the opposite pole of anxiety and the only feeling that can alleviate it, by allowing us to arrive at the profound truth of things that neither the senses nor the intellect, alone, can grasp.

We also explored what had happened five years, and twelve to fourteen years, previously (the ages of the two youngsters in the dream) and he reconstructed that they were times of inner darkness. After graduating from high school he withdrew into himself. He remembered the sense of gloom, unspeakable suffering, anger and resentment he experienced. During the session important memories emerged, like that of a dream he had had at the beginning of the analysis (which I do not remember, so I don't think he ever recounted it to me) in which he was armed with a pistol and was facing someone, also armed with a pistol. It was not clear who shot at whom. I was struck by the dream because it heralded the theme of the double early on. As I have already mentioned, it is not possible for an individual to coexist with a double, because each tends to occupy completely the space of the other. Other significant memories surfaced. For instance, Marco told me that he played a game with his little sister, in which he would look at her in a really nasty way until she started to cry, and then hug her and say: "I'm only playing, I'm only playing." We commented that the episode revealed the same dynamic that came into play while I was telling him about the helplessness of a newborn baby, and that the anger directed at his sister may have been aroused precisely by the intolerance of own vulnerability, which the model ordered him to get rid of. Then again, he may also have been testing his power while, at the same time, seeking to banish the fear aroused by the model's sadism. I told him: "It is as if the model had repeatedly commanded you: *"Turn to stone, freeze, put your life on hold. Only the dead are immune to harm."* We then reconstructed an important earlier dream pivoting on the same theme:

I'm opening the front door of my house and the key gets stuck. There is a young man beside me and he touches me with an ironic air, as if to say: you can't even open a door! I look at him, then remain terrorstruck: behind his gaze there is absolute emptiness, nothingness, but, at the same time, a terrible malice. I rush into the house and pile furniture up against the door to make it safer, but I fear he has the power to enter through the walls. So I try to leave, but I realize that I'm a prisoner, because the young man has barricaded the door from the outside. I wake up filled with anxiety.

In this dream the double definitely abandoned the guise of protective and admired model, showing itself as a ruthless enemy who displayed his terrifying power through the annihilation of sensibility and of the capacity to suffer and feel compassion for oneself and for others, as is evident from the emptiness of the gaze. Marco would later say to me: *"There is a difference between feeling awful and experiencing pain. I lived in the grip of a nameless anxiety because something in me was messed up, but it is as if I no longer felt my suffering."* In fact, Marco could no longer empathize either with his own suffering or that of others, indeed the latter bothered him and he needed to distance himself from it, just as he had to detach from positive emotions; for example, if a couple were kissing in a movie, he immediately had to prevent himself from participating in that emotion.

When Marco came to me, he brought me a note from the psychiatrist who had been treating him; the envelope was not sealed, and Marco had read the following sentence: "You do not have ice-cold eyes." He saw the phrase as referring to him, as if the colleague were telling me: "Everything is not lost for him. In his eyes there is still a glimmer of life, and the hope that he can make it." I explained to Marco that the words were addressed to me, because my colleague was referring to a text of mine that I had given him to read, so that we might exchange ideas on a clinical case. Marco thanked me for explaining; however, it seemed evident to me that the image had constellated his fantasy, superimposing itself on the figure of the model, which really was like a man with ice-cold eyes, but from which my patient could finally hope to depart.

As the therapy progressed, Marco not only obtained his degree and began a steady job in his uncle's office, but also engaged in various recreational activities. These included a wine tasting course where he met a girl who had aroused his interest and whom he liked. They had got on well together, laughed and joked, and he recalled that they had been close, they had had an understanding. Once he said punningly: *"Do you remember that 'di-vine' moment?"* At the end of the course he had been able to ask the girl for her phone number, and had called and invited her to dinner. She had told him she was very busy that week, but they exchanged various text messages. So Marco had to deal with the frustration of a temporary refusal, and he admitted that he had felt a bit disappointed. I pointed out to him that the girl had not said "no," but rather "wait," "perhaps," and that he still had the possibility to make a conquest. He also recognized that previously he would have interpreted the girl's answer as: "You're a jerk. … I never want to see you again!" Both of these expressions would have plunged him into despair, and made him back off. We then reflected on the fact that an enthusiastic "yes" would also have sent him running, because the model would have immediately instilled a feeling of inadequacy in him, and nipped the relationship in the bud with negative considerations and doubts like: "well... maybe... she's not that attractive or likeable after all ... perhaps she's not the right woman for me ... maybe I'm not really that interested in her ...." I believed that his doubts were a cover for his absolute dread of living a relationship, but now he was experiencing a variety of emotions and was able to recognize what he feels, to give it a form and contain it. I commented that giving up the absolute world of the model implied dealing with contradictions and imperfections. Reality has a measure, it can excite or disappoint, and we are never immune to loss. (I thought of Eros as the son of πόρος and πενία, and thus as an arc spanning fullness and emptiness.) The obstacles Marco encountered in embarking on a love relationship were mostly of an inner nature, as is clearly illustrated by the following dream.

> I'm in a bar or a restaurant in the open air. I see two women: one is the girl from the "di-vine" course whom I was attracted to, the other is a stranger. A man arrives and embraces both of them, then takes them away. I feel really bad. The scene is repeated: I am there again with the two women. I would like to talk to the girl I know, but the other one butts in. I am held back and distracted by this other woman who fascinates and attracts me because she's very good-looking.

Marco observed that there was a connection between the two scenes in the dream. In the first he does not feel like a real man because another male appears (the one that he should be if he is to correspond to the model, I thought), who takes everything away from him. In the second, the imaginary girl takes the real woman away. We reflected that the other man and the imaginary girl are perhaps both part of the model, of his double, who presumes to be the original element, while Marco feels that he is only a copy. The model is both man and woman, because it represents the absolute state in which nothing is lacking. This dream enabled us to experience first-hand the fascination exerted by the model, but also its bullying, because it forces one to sacrifice the possibilities of life in the name of abstract perfection.

> The model demanded that I be complete, but without living. I had the feeling that if I had expressed myself I would have lost substance, I would no longer have had everything in me, and I would have been annihilated.

Marco described the unknown woman thus: *"She has blonde hair, she's pretty, seductive, determined, arrogant; she knows what she wants, and especially how to attract a man. She's terribly attractive."* I said that we had to expose this enticing world that set such treacherous traps for him for what it was, and he replied: *"I'm beginning to see what I'm losing, what I deny myself when I say: 'Stop, don't do anything, you won't be happy, but you won't suffer or run risks.'"*

Now, as I reconstruct this stage of the analytic path, a dream Marco had recounted to me some time earlier and which, at the time, I couldn't fathom, comes back to me. In this dream he saw a woman's genitals, but noticed that they were anatomically different. Between her legs there were three small aligned openings, three holes that resembled craters of the moon. This image reminded him of the photos of a series of planets that his uncle had downloaded from the internet, and which included an image of the moon and its craters. Marco was cheered, and also a little amused, by the fact that his uncle's enthusiasm had led him to contemplate things so remote from their daily concerns. In the dream he had been filled with dismay, and had said to himself: *"How can I not even know what a woman's body is like? Yet I know it isn't like this."*

She was therefore a "lunar" woman, and it brought back to me Plato's description of the ancient nature of man in the *Symposium*:

> In the first place ... The sexes were not two as there are now, but originally three in number; there was man, woman, and the union of the two, having a name corresponding to this double nature, which had once a real existence, but is now lost, and the word "Androgynous" is only preserved as a term of reproach. In the second place, the primeval man was round, his back and sides forming a circle; and he had four hands and four feet, one head with two faces, looking opposite ways, set on a round neck and precisely alike; also four ears, two privy members and the remainder to correspond.

Hence, these primitive humans had a "double" conformation and were divided into three sexes. Plato describes them as being so proud and arrogant that Zeus decided to cut them in two to depotentiate them and to punish their insolence.

So I saw the three lunar craters in the dream as an image of the third sex, as an hermaphrodite, metaphor of a human nature that is fully complete, lacking nothing and lacking tension, and close to a state of divine omnipotence. In fact, a dream of many years later featured a woman with a penis and a vagina, thus representing the incarnation of a perfect hermaphrodite. In Marco's imagination, the lunar woman could have been a face of the "double" and have represented the model's fanciful faculty of containing everything in itself and its immunity from the "originary castration" – understood as a symbolic transition that allows us to forego the aspiration to the absolute of a paradisiacal state and to enter the human condition, where we are distinguished only by certain characteristics.

I said earlier that I expected Marco's anger to be unleashed on the analyst, and it was indeed, but through a dream:

> You and I are in a room, in a situation similar to that of a session. You say to me: "It's 40,000 euros." I ask for an explanation. I ask if it's a sum

I have to pay in general, or if I owe the money to you. You do not answer and simply repeat with calm detachment: "It's 40,00 euros." So I become irritated and get angry with you. I think your behavior is unheard of. I very nearly insulted you.

Then he remarked: *"While I was on my way to the session I wondered if it were not perhaps the price to be paid for the feelings and the life I have lost so far."* He was unable to relate the sum in the dream to any business he had conducted recently. The only thing that came to him was that it was more or less double the amount of his savings. Together we reconstructed that his anger arose when I had spoken to him about the helplessness of the new-born baby, and how essential loving contact was in calming its anxieties. I pointed out that in analysis he felt dependent on another human being who was helping him to shape his emotions and that this defeated the fantasy of self-sufficiency. I went on to say that his anger could also have been provoked by my description of reality as a place of imperfections, where achievements require time and effort, where there is no guarantee of happiness, which is interwoven with suffering, defeat and loss, and where things have their own measure that is different from ours, and can never belong to us completely. Then I told him:

> At a profound emotional level it is a little as if you had said to me: "Whatever kind of exchange are you proposing to me, that I should abandon the place of the 'model' where everything is perfect and complete (he recalled how many times at the start of therapy he would ask: "Is it perfect?") to enter an order of things that is so disappointing and, what's more, requires so much hard work?"

I then added that since his debt amounted to double the sum he possessed, the dream could have alluded precisely to his "double" and to the amount of money required to liquidate it! Marco looked at me in considerable amusement and replied: *"All things considered, that would be a very good deal!"*

In the last analysis, Marco's anger was also an expression of the movement of the psyche that consisted in blending with the "Absolute Shadow" of the model; a shadow that condemned everything transient to defeat and annihilation, but in doing so gave him the feeling of being victorious and of overcoming his inadequacy, indeed his "nullity," as he himself often described it. This enables us to better understand the paradoxical character of the double that must "annihilate nothingness" to obtain "everything," and which thus actually determines it and renders it absolute. "Everything" and "Nothing" thus become equivalent.

> When I enter a relationship there is always an undercurrent of anger, an immeasurable anger against everyone and against destiny. Perhaps it stems from my feeling small, needy and dependent. The more helpless

I felt the more energy I put into my anger and my appeal to the salvific model, and the model always wants me to impose myself on the other.

Once Marco told me that one of the characteristics he did not like about himself was his being too diplomatic and submissive, his "pusillanimity." *"I change from black to white according to the situation, in order to meet the expectations of others. I would say that I do everything to match them perfectly."* Thus the anger, the pretension of knowing everything and of convincing people at all costs, was always present in his fantasy, even though it had only marginally constellated his behavior due to his repressive defenses, and it functioned as a pseudo-strength that he saw as a source of energy. The model could not be abandoned because it also represented his visibility and his capacity to assert himself. As the son of a patient of whom I shall speak later, said: *"My good part wants to die and my bad part feels strong!"*

All this made me think that the only way the therapy could help Marco to approach life again was to transform the destructive anger encapsulated in the model into the ability to be proactive, courageous and trustful, instead of ignoring or attacking it frontally. Rather than use vengeful weapons against the model, it was necessary to break the infernal vicious circle in which Marco furiously attacked his sense of nullity, further denigrating his image of himself and triggering a new wave of anger that fed on itself: *"Restlessness compresses anger, which leaps through it like a burst of flame,"* as he so eloquently put it. Marco himself would point me in the right direction by saying:

> Resentment will always rise from its own ashes if the original wound from which it has sprung is not healed. You see ... there are times when I am oppressed by anxiety again, because life seems incompatible with the model, and so I think: "What must I do, must I smash this model?," but then I feel that this is not possible, because there's too much of me in it.

I reflected that we really did have to take "a piece of the whale's heart!," as he himself had said. More precisely, we should suppose that the price that Marco would have had to pay, to which his dream alludes, was not really that of liquidating his double, but of "redeeming" it. In fact, it was not a question of destroying or eliminating the model, but of transforming it, which also meant transforming the desire for perfection into a striving to achieve new goals in life and a state of completeness and wholeness, implying a dialogue with "the other than us" and with "the other parts of us" that inhabit our inner world and transcend the Ego complex. The term "Completeness" (from *cum-plenum*), as the etymology explains, means being full of something or together with someone.

Besides this, we had to trace a backward path to retrieve Marco's true Shadow, which after being abandoned seemed to have detached from him and, remaining trapped in the unconscious, had become unrecognizable by constellating the figure of the model.

A few months later, Marco said to me:

> You know … it was as if I had to kill my sense of annihilation and my anxiety about being inadequate, because they made me so angry. I did myself a terrible violence. I had to destroy myself to survive. But then, what sense is there in getting angry about anger that is so warped? I was engaged in an endless struggle with myself. No… I don't think you lose anything by expressing yourself, because my identity goes beyond what I know. I have eliminated the "imperatives" of life and of non-life (which were commands given by the model, when life was a "perfect" life that coincided with non-life) and now I find there is room for possibility. I can feed energy into a vital circuit. It as if a dead part were being poured into a live part.

The following two dreams indicate that Marco was re-establishing contact with his body, with sexuality and with affectivity.

> 1st Dream:
> It's an image: I see a boy's hand playing with his penis, but the penis seems to belong to the body of a man, which is also me, and the penis is that of an adult. It's as if a child's soul were in an adult's body, or as if I felt smaller than the body I have. In the image there is only the penis and the hand.

Marco tells me that during puberty his erect penis embarrassed and distressed him; he felt that his penis was something extraneous, that it did not belong to him and it disturbed him. He would have preferred not to have had instincts, not to have grown up.

> 2nd Dream:
> I was with the "di-vine" girl. We were chatting and laughing, there was a conspiratorial atmosphere. I put my hand in her hair and ruffled it, like you do with a small child.

I thought that both dreams represented the recovery of the body's sense of belonging to itself and of one's sexuality. We passed from autoeroticism to affectionate play with a person of the opposite sex. Feelings, however, have to be retrieved from the infantile soul, because the psyche has remained behind while the body has continued its natural biological growth. So it was a question of recovering and bringing back to the present a lost affectivity that was still buried in childhood.

3.1.3 Turbulence zone

Two dreams experienced in one night show that Marco was not following a clear path but one beset by doubts and hesitations, and thus not exempt from risks of regression.

1st Dream:
I'm with the "di-vine" girl. There are various images, like photos, in which we have our arms around each other or our faces are touching "cheek to cheek." I am surprised and thrilled to experience the physical contact. I think I'm becoming embodied!

2nd Dream:
I'm leaving for Paris and find myself at the airport. I've already checked-in. I realize that I've forgotten my medications and wonder anxiously what I can do. I'm already on the shuttle that's taking me to the plane and I think that at this point it would be best to go to Paris and then get a direct flight back to Rome to pick up the medications.

These were the medications prescribed by his psychiatrist. By then the dosage was so low that he knew they had more of a reassuring and symbolic than a biochemical value. He sometimes forgot to take them for a day, but if he went away he always remembered to bring them with him because he would have had difficulty in obtaining a prescription. Marco remarked: *"I don't know Paris, but I would very much like to go there. It is the city of artists and love."* Regarding the first dream, he told me that he once had a panic fear of contact with another, especially another woman!

Now I feel that I'm present. I can accept or refuse, but I don't flee. If anything, I stop and think. At the moment of contact I have to bring out things with which I'm not familiar in myself, and that scares me a bit. Yesterday I was wondering: What do I do about the girl? Do I call her? And what do I tell her? This didn't happen in the model's world, because the model was timeless.

At first, Marco did not feel as though he belonged to himself. He had the impression that he was never really part of what he was, what he said or what he did. Now he was being prompted by reality on several fronts; for example, his parents had suggested that he leave home because they could help him to buy a house. I thought that, faced with his present tasks, Marco would be tempted to regress and take refuge again in illness, but I also realized that if his unconscious had led him to forget his medications, it was a sign that he was then able to count on a broad area of healthy equilibrium in his psyche.

3.1.3.1 The analyst's expressing affection: a calculated risk

During one session we reconstructed how difficult it was for Marco to experience love, and especially to feel loved and understood. This had always triggered anger and detachment in him, as if he wished to enact a preventive abandonment and actively provoke what he feared he would suffer. I took the calculated risk of partially revealing to Marco the feelings I had experienced toward him:

> Can you imagine how long I have had to hold back my affection for you? I felt it but I kept it inside because I knew that expressing it would put you in danger. My communicating this may also provoke emotional reactions in you, but then ... we shall deal with them!

Marco told me that he knew I was thinking of him and thanked me for keeping silent, because he was, in fact, always afraid of being invaded by the other.

Marco's profound response to my intervention was not long in coming. The following two dreams, which he had on the same night, are revealing:

1st dream:
There is a party at my house, with lots of children. I'm happy, laughing and joking with everyone. There are a lot of people there, more than I am able to greet, and maybe there are also some strangers.

I go into my parents' bedroom and see my girl cousin lying on their bed. I get really mad at her and threaten to throw her out of the house, pulling her by the legs. Aside from my anger, this girl is out of her head, she's talking nonsense, maybe she's ill. She looks at me and there is hatred in her eyes, resentment, but also the desperation of someone who is losing it. ... Someone cries out. My eyes meet those of my cousin who stops me and makes me reflect. I understand what he wants to tell me in a flash, and follow his suggestion not to treat her so harshly. Then I speak to her with great affection. I try to be convincing and I talk to her about the family, about the people who love her, so that she will feel better and stay with us. Marco commented: "I was struck by the rapid succession of different feelings in the dream. At this point I think I woke up, but then fell asleep again and had another dream."

2nd dream:
I am in a car with you. We are driving along Via Tuscolana [in Rome] and going to your office for a session. At a certain point we park the car, get out and start walking. Suddenly, you are not beside me anymore, instead there is the "di-vine" girl. We laugh and joke together. I get into the elevator of a modern building, where I meet other men a bit younger than me who were all treated by you. I feel slightly embarrassed and you, who are there again, begin to tell me the names of some of my friends. I don't know how you know them because I never tell you the names of people. I call you on my cell and complain about this. I'm nitpicky, but I realize that my complaint has no sense. You say to me: "Only with feelings and love (I don't know if you said "could you have resolved" or "would you have been able to resolve" those four or five critical points.") I get

emotional and close my eyes. I visualize the four or five critical points and I feel as if we had dissolved or shattered them. I actually see them disintegrating in front of me.

The female cousin in the dream was a second cousin who, like his elder sister, was a few years younger than him. He had always seen her as detached, distant, cold and unpleasant. He believed that they had always been indifferent to each other. The male cousin was the son of a sister of his mother's; he was the same age as Marco and they were close, they got on and enjoyed a meaningful dialogue. This young man had had a hard life and had solved many problems. He had an elder sister who suffered from bulimia and was grossly overweight, while the father had contracted a serious form of depression after retiring. This cousin had faced life courageously. He had a job and a solid love relationship. He was sensitive and reflective. What he did in the dream he could have done in real life. Marco also had a sister, born two years after him, who suffered psychologically, and he found it unsettling to meet her gaze filled with desperation and a boundless request that could never be met. In her he was afraid of re-encountering an ancient suffering with which he was familiar, and especially of being dragged back toward a state of psychic devastation; a state in which he could have found himself, but had managed to avoid – also thanks to the progress he had made in analysis – and whose shadow was still threatening him through his sister.

I asked Marco what had aroused his anger when he saw the girl cousin lying on his parents' bed:

> I felt that an ancient wrath had reawakened. Do you remember the fear I had of experiencing it toward small, fragile children? Well, the woman arouses the greatest wrath, because she is as vulnerable as a child with respect to a man, but at the same time she is very powerful. I think my parents abandoned me to my vulnerability and my anger. Once I thought I could solve my problems by taking their place, but in that case I would have had to eliminate them. Now I believe that I can have my own place, and let my parents have theirs. Remember the ice-cold eyes? My female cousin's eyes are not as bad as that, though they come close where absence, anger and violence are concerned. But in her eyes there is also so much suffering and desperation.

I thought about how many things had changed since the beginning of our journey; for example, the children in his dream no longer aroused his anger but were a source of joy. I told Marco that he saw the woman as powerful because he had given her the faculty of deciding his destiny and of decreeing his salvation or his perdition. I also explained that this was foreseeable because the woman was part of the model and hence a part of him, or rather, of what he always thought he had to be to become invincible. I then pointed out a turning point in the dream. The female cousin, who embodied both a part of him and of his sick sister, was aware of her own suffering.

Your sensibility has returned, the ice has melted and, through your cousin, who represents another part of you that is positive and vital, you have recovered all your capacity for compassion and your helpful attitude, both toward your sister, and everyone else who is suffering, and toward yourself.

Marco immediately told me that, in the past few days, his sister had been a little better and had talked more! In fact, I was quite aware of how much Marco had recently been caring for her and had sought to make contact with her at an emotional level.

As far as the Via Tuscolana was concerned, Marco told me that it was a road he had taken the day before to go to Frascati, but he had gone in the opposite direction, toward Rome, by mistake, and had to make a U-turn, arriving a bit late. I then told him that we too had made a U-turn at the beginning of therapy. There was a dangerous window open onto the inner world of his fantasies through which there was a risk of him jumping, but we turned toward the world and his real self. Then it didn't matter much how long it took to move forward, and Marco exclaimed, *"Holy smoke... that was some U-turn!"*

We asked ourselves why he was put out by my knowing the names of his friends, since he actually never refers to them by name but always describes them in a way that enables me to visualize them, with expressions like: "the man who had a baby girl" or "the man who is going out with the ex of another male friend" or, of course, "the girl of the 'di-vine' period." Marco said that the last time he had been to his psychiatrist, he had asked him: "Shall we give these people a name? Otherwise, we don't know who's who." Marco had always thought that the analyst knew more than he did and that he saw things from a perspective that he himself lacked. Marco's slight anger was therefore caused both by my expression of affection and his need to get the analyst's power in the right perspective (since being a woman she could not but attract the projections of omnipotence formerly directed at the mother). In another dream, which he would have at a later date, the figure of the therapist was associated with that of a notary, with whom he lost his temper because he charged him an exorbitant fee. Just as the notary issues a certificate with a public value, the therapist certified what was right or wrong, what was healthy or sick. The fact that I had suggested that I was perhaps wrong in telling him about my feelings for him, possibly helped Marco to see me as fallible and to take his life in his own hands again. Moreover, in the dream Marco's anger was more contained than the panto-clastic destructiveness that would have once erupted and made him shout: *"How dare you know about me, how dare you understand my desperation, enter into my experience of nullity and continue to love me, and thus call me to life without magically changing a condition that I hate?!"* Also, the men I was treating in the dream, whom he encountered, were young, which meant that he was seeking to establish his male identity. I thought it was important for him to feel that he could love a woman without necessarily having to match her perfectly. He could finally enter into an intimate relationship without "being" the other, and thus obeying the model's orders! So my decision to take a calculated risk, so to speak, by touching on the theme of love, paid off.

The end of the dream was a mystery to Marco. He had no idea what four and five might be, but he remembered the powerful emotion he felt when, with closed eyes, he saw those "blocks" disintegrate. I couldn't help but think of the numbers in symbolic terms. The quadripartite division of space has always been associated with the structure of the psyche and the world, as well as the capacity of consciousness to orientate itself. Five brought many things to mind, especially the "fifth essence," or ultimate substance, the synthesis and harmony that brings us into the heart of wholeness.

It was likely, therefore, that the "blocks" that were made to crumble by the expression of feeling, and especially by Marco's communicating in an interpersonal relationship, represented also the overcoming of inhibitions that prevented the organization of the interior order and the relational order. Further light was shed on the sign of five by De Santillana who, when speaking of archaic cosmogonies, writes:

> Five times, in the course of eight years, the star of Venus rose at the moment preceding sunrise (what is known as the heliacal rising, a solemn moment in many civilizations). Then, the five very distinct points on the arc of the constellations, joined by lines according to the order of their sequence, are shown to form a perfect, or almost perfect, pentagram, since the figure rotates through only two degrees every eight years. This seems precisely a gift from the gods to men, a way of revealing themselves. Wherefore the Pythagoreans said: "Aphrodite has revealed herself in the sign of five. And the sign has become magic."
>
> (De Santillana 1968, 1985, 2004, pp. 25–26)

I told Marco something about the image that had constellated in me, and that the critical points of existence could be resolved, metaphorically speaking, through the pentagram of love. After reflecting at length, he said to me: *"When I think of the barren desert in which I lived … and then of this spring…!"*

I would like to conclude my account of this phase of the therapeutic process by quoting from a session that took place in the seventh year of analysis, or thereabouts. A session that both surprised and moved me because Marco spoke to me about shadow, when, of course, I had never discussed the Jungian concept of Shadow with him.

M: … I've emerged from the shadow, or, to be more exact, I've found my shadow.

A: What do you mean? What's the difference between the two shadows?

M: Well … this other shadow I want to describe leads to the light …

I was living with an enormous burden, this "having to be" that loomed over me, this having to resemble an idea of perfection. It was something that was obscuring me ...

It was as if I were obliged to achieve an absolute clarity, to know myself completely, to immediately realize my desires. But that perfect transparency corresponded to total darkness. I was being ordered to be "another," not to change, and everything had to happen right away, almost as if by magic. So I constantly passed from one situation to another, but I was always the same. Now I'm adding new elements to my person ... it's not always the same doubt, the same fear, the same hope. The bar of mood has shifted. There is a dialogue between what I want and what I am.

You see ... I had difficulty in leaving my footprints. It wasn't me who was walking, me who was feeling. I had withdrawn into a corner and there was a huge shadow in my place. ... it was a powerful shadow and I left it to find everyone's shadow: if I talk to someone, or something, they emerge into the light, while other parts of me remain in shadow. In the past, if I sought to make contact with them, I experienced a complete break, now I am rediscovering a unity, a growing sense of complexity and richness. In my dark zones I still find fear, anger, dread and anxiety, but I also find an energy that I can use to illuminate them. The massive shadow is no longer looming over everything, even though it is not easy to illuminate the various parts of ourselves, because it's not an act of magic ... it makes for hard work.

The other day you spoke to me about "structure." That idea helped me a lot. Before, I felt like a wall with a void behind it, now I feel like I have a structure in which there is an organized space.

Today I am sure that my steps are my own, and when you move, and have a certain substance, you also have your own shadow.

At a much more advanced stage of the analytic process it was possible to work through his anxiety in the face of possibility and freedom, and that arising from the question of his identity, as well as his fear of relating with the other than self.

Marco would later clarify that his relationship with his mother was based on an unexpressed bond, whose value and problematic aspects had never been communicated or interpreted:

There was no dialogue between my mother and me, I never told her a single thing I thought. A deafening silence reigned. I lived as if she did not exist, treating her like a ghost, but the less I looked at her, the stronger her presence inside me became. I incorporated her. When I was small she was my mother, now she is faceless and nameless inner angst.

The implicit agreement between them, as I have already mentioned, was that he should correspond to a model of perfection in which complete self-sufficiency reigned, because this model reassured the mother that she was a perfect parent. Obviously the maternal command prohibited him from having any relationship with a woman, and, in a certain sense, any real relationship at all, because it contemplated neither need nor desire. While this model brought anxiety, since he obscurely sensed the divergence between what he should have been and what he probably was, it also exercised a strong fascination because it ensured a perfect dovetailing with his mother, the promise of finding himself in a state of fusion with her and never losing her.

Many years after we had begun the treatment, we were finally able to deal with the last and most enduring obstacle on the path to his individuation: the relationship with a woman. When I asked him what his fear of women consisted in, he replied:

> Everything about a woman scares me. I agonize over my ability to loosen up. I'm scared of feeling attracted and of being attractive; scared of being touched or being loved; scared of having to come up to her expectations; scared of emerging from my state of isolation, and scared of happiness itself. I'm scared of the encounter with the other; scared that someone will accept me and make my experience real. By imagining a relationship with a woman I separate myself from my mother, from a state of fusion with her, from being a son. You do not incorporate a girlfriend and going steady does not mean fusing together but finding completeness in becoming, and so I ask myself: "How come I'm already made and, at the same time, infinite? I'm adult and I evolve?" I considered myself perfect and that was it, and I thought that nothing could be added to my complete being. How is it possible to combine completeness and the infinite? A woman opens you up; she's like a window on a boundless elsewhere. In the relationship you're individual and couple at the same time, and being alone or being together is not, as I had always thought, an irreconcilable alternative. I'm also scared of becoming fond of a person, of recognizing their fundamental importance for me, and then of losing them and of suffering. A mother is always with you, but a woman chooses you and separation is always a possibility. And then to have a relationship you have to open up, to express what you're feeling at the time, and this brings me up against my shortcomings, my weakness, which has always been a source of shame and annoyance. How can you tell a woman you're scared of her? She's bound to run a mile! Pain is easier to share than fear, it is defined and it can be circumscribed, whereas fear makes you uneasy because you don't know if it derives from reality or from your inability to face life. In other words, it's always that image of perfection inside that blocks me, which I had to embody to comply with my mother's prearranged design!

This brings to mind the words of Jung, when he speaks of the secret conspiracy between mother and son and how each helps the other to betray life. The son has

> a desire to touch reality, to embrace the earth and fructify the field of the world. But he makes no more than a series of fitful starts, for his

initiative as well as his staying power are crippled by the secret memory that the world and happiness may be had as a gift – from the mother. The fragment of the world which he [...] must encounter [...] does not fall into his lap, does not meet him half way, but remains resistant, has to be conquered [...] It makes demands on the masculinity of a man, on his ardour, above all on his courage and resolution when it comes to throwing his whole being into the scales. *For this he would need a faithless Eros, one capable of forgetting his mother and undergoing the pain of relinquishing the first love of his life.*

(Jung 1951, 2014, pp. 11–12, my italics)

When I suggested that perhaps this young patient saw a relationship with a woman as a betrayal of his mother, he exclaimed: *"Yes, but even more than a betrayal it would be like killing both her and myself, a real murder."*

On another occasion he said to me:

I find myself in great difficulty when I sense that a woman desires me. But if I am seen and desired as a whole, what could threaten my integrity? If I have been chosen it's because I'm the way I am. Yet I am seized by an unbearable anxiety. I think that my fear has two aspects. The first, perhaps unconscious, is that of being controlled by a woman, like I was controlled by my mother as a boy; the other, which certainly predominates, is that the supply and demand of love may activate in me a profound, unexplored energy and bring out something that goes beyond what I know about myself. I'm scared of being, but even more so of becoming, of being transformed through a process whose evolution may be uncontrollable.

This made it clear to me that he was about to emerge from the paralysis created by the impossibility of choosing between "being" and "having to be," since his "having to be" was an unattainable state of perfection and his "being" was felt to be inadequate and impotent, and hence a shameful place from which to escape. The meeting with a woman, instead, would open up the possibility for an encounter with his deep Self – an endless reservoir of forces – which would trigger a process of change in his Ego. Finally, his existence would be orientated not toward a pre-established, fixed perfection, but toward a "becoming" that would bring unimaginable novelties. I realized that anxiety was the inevitable price to pay for this existential step and that only the encounter with the radically "other than self," with the feminine universe, could be the agent. In fact, not long afterward he told me: *"With a woman I feel receptive to different, unknown depths that only she, as a woman, can illuminate."*

Here I would like to open a theoretical parenthesis on themes that emerged during the period of therapy, whose elaboration enabled me to propose interpretations that often resulted in productive developments in Marco's life and his sense of self.

3.1.3.1.1 ANXIETY AND FREEDOM

In order to realize the capacity to be free one has to deal with anxiety, which may be defined as fear without an object and also as an emotion fundamental to existence – a *Grundstimmung* in phenomenology – because it flares up when we feel the call of possibility and freedom. Although we are free to make ourselves and are able to embrace some desired form of being or life, we cannot be certain of succeeding. Indeed, we could fail and thus fall back into the abyss of nonbeing. As Panikkar writes: "Anxiety is the sentinel of the void; it is what makes us experience the dizzyness of freedom" (Panikkar 1993, 1999, p. 186). I think that one of the ways in which a human being escapes from anxiety is by seeking refuge in the safety of the ineluctable, even if it takes the form of a negative event, as shown by an episode described by Bion, in which he tells of a group of shipwrecked people on a raft who suddenly see a ship appear in the distance. The possibility of being saved combined with the even greater likelihood of the ship's not spotting them and disappearing from their horizon forever, reawakens in the survivors a panic anxiety that was previously sunk in the depths of desperation and resignation (Bion 1977–1983).

This passage in Bion may well explain our resistance to entering a love and erotic relationship that may not ensure lasting happiness, and also the reason for the forced unions and separations that punctuate married life. These, in fact, are expressions of the irrepressible impulse to throw oneself into an "irreparable" situation, in which anxiety vanishes because the possibility to evolve by making free choices in one's own existential context disappears, along with the possibility of "becoming" with its disturbing aura of uncertainty and mystery.

At this point, I wonder if one of the most significant goals of depth analysis might not be to enable a form of freedom that goes well beyond the freedom of choice and which, in line with Panikkar's thought, we may call the "freedom of being." As Panikkar writes:

> The sphere of true freedom lies outside the causal, rational or karmic structure of the world; it does not contradict these earthly structures, but it oversteps them by far. The sphere of freedom is the sphere of hope against all hope, the sphere of impossibility, of the incomprehensible and the nonmanipulable.
>
> (Panikkar 1979, p. 182)

He further observes:

> Man ... on the one hand is part of the universe and on the other the meeting point between the whole cosmos, and all the more human the more the destiny of the universe is realized in him: human freedom is a cosmic force, not a mere psychological capacity to choose.
>
> (Panikkar 1993, 1999, p. 145)

To return to the concept of the nexus between freedom and the sense of anxiety, Panikkar states that true freedom, the freedom of being, knows nothing.

> It is stepping into the void, into what still does not exist, into nothingness. ... Man is anxious because he participates in the expansion of creation, in creation from nothing. Anxiety is this pre-freedom; it is the feeling of pure possibility that does not know what is possible.
>
> (ibid., p. 189)

3.1.3.1.2 ANXIETY AND HOPE

For Panikkar, the opposite pole of anxiety – and therefore feeling – which can allow it to open up to the new, is not courage, since this faculty is too firmly anchored in the willpower and heroic aspirations of the Ego or, one could say, in a male chauvinist mentality that rejects vulnerability and healthy dependence. The opposite pole, as I have already said, is hope as the capacity to see the invisible in the here and now, rather than as a form of consolation in the face of a non-verifiable future, or even the mere anticipation of what will come to pass.

> It is hope that allows us to see in the present a dimension that otherwise we would not see. Hope is the gift of a vision, of an experience that makes us open to transcendence in the immanence of things.
>
> (Panikkar 1993, 1999, p. 188)

I think that in the above excerpts Panikkar is saying that it is necessary to embrace the moments of discontinuity in experience and in our psychophysical constitution itself, in order to gain access to what is really new, and thus unprecedented in the course of history. The new is truly without precedent and is born from the creative act itself, but it asks us to be willing to take the step into the void. Moreover, I believe that anxiety and hope cannot be separated. Anxiety without hope risks becoming depression; hope without anxiety, omnipotent certainty and fanaticism.

Not long ago the young man of whom I'm speaking, and to whom I had communicated some of my reflections, said that he felt greatly relieved by the idea that anxiety is a normal state of mind in life and not, as he had always thought, a pathological condition. Furthermore, he was cheered by the fact that anxiety was simply one pole of feeling, and hence necessarily linked to an opposite pole. He then confided: *"So I can imagine going through anxiety and hoping that the possibility to hope will open up for me!"*

During the therapy that we were obliged to continue online during the coronavirus pandemic, I found there was an astonishing improvement in Marco's mood. The feeling that space and time had been momentarily suspended, even as experienced virtually during lockdown, had in fact allowed him not to feel obliged to respond to environmental stimuli by making choices or taking decisions and actions more or less immediately, and to take a break, which this time was not attributable to a personal failing or inadequacy but required by reality itself. This had enabled him to withdraw into his interiority without feeling guilty and to make emotional contact with it, thus perceiving its depth, its inexhaustibility and its multiple nuances. Precisely during this period of quarantine Marco told me that his reactions were more correct and proportionate, and reflected his more serene inner state. He had less difficulty in listening to others and the periods in which he felt the need to isolate himself were shorter. For some time, he had been able to "be" with others, but now he also felt able to accept the emotions that other people aroused in him. While in quarantine he contacted a lot of friends online and was introduced to new people, to whom he chatted. He told me: *"It's nice to say 'hi' to people you don't know!"* Moreover, a girlfriend of a girlfriend of his suggested that they get to know each other better and, although overcome by emotion, he did not freeze up this time. After collecting his thoughts, he accepted her invitation to meet and chat online. Afterward he said:

> Emotion is hope and also fear; it makes you throb, tremble and is so intense that I feel it carries with it a possibility of life. I experience a feeling and I know I must not repress it. I feel grateful because I am being born to life. And what a paradox: I experienced all this thanks to lockdown! If I had that woman next to me in the flesh ... what a state I would be in, but I feel that the end of the untouchable is nigh! Now I think that if I were alone with a woman I could look at her and feel joy, pleasure, liking that becomes love, interest that becomes relationship.

Then he added:

> I feel that I must live the present moment, that it is not measurable in hours, minutes and seconds, but is the time of beginning. Feeling that one is whole is great and "everything" is already in me. What I still do not know lies in the step I take; a revolution is starting. ... I have always been out of time, I could see others, but not touch them. Emotion neutralizes isolation and you are no longer alone in an ivory tower.

A few sessions later, when friends were permitted to meet up, he said:

> Now I can handle contrasting feelings: you are happy and scared, you expect and fear, you desire and are afraid, you seek and tremble. I realize that it's not doubleness and that I can experience these emotions by remaining open, whereas before I closed up when faced with contrast. ... Yes, the girl's invitation did spark an emotion I could experience, I had more time during the pandemic, and I could accept it! ... Saturday evening I went to dinner with friends and I was more open and honest in talking

about myself, and the others listened to me and asked me things directly. We've become closer. The pandemic was fundamental in making me feel a basic need for others and for contact with them. I was experiencing loneliness that made me suffer, and I gained a better understanding of what loving means. Compared with my past solitude and isolation, those enforced by the coronavirus are a piece of cake! I fell into darkness and now I am emerging from it! I didn't feel overwhelmed by an enforced solitude and I dealt with my inner solitude by seeking others. In the beginning the phone made contacting people easier, but it was a means for being able to be together physically, it became a transition toward meeting. I also needed to talk to other people before, but the capacity to do it came, above all, with the pandemic. I felt that my diversity and uniqueness were recognized – an experience I have never had until now. And then I discovered I was more loving toward my friends, more open, more involved. Before I loved them as much, but now I express and convey it. It's a trait of mine that I have won back and it mirrors my inner self, whereas indifference did not.

It is also significant that, during this period, Marco's friends themselves asked him things about his life, and he took pleasure in confiding in them, which had not happened before because they probably froze up due to his embarrassment and closed attitude.

I would like to conclude this clinical story with some reflections that Marco communicated at an earlier time, when the treatment was already well advanced, since they seem to anticipate the latest conquests he has made thanks to the coronavirus experience:

I think that destiny drew its strength from many of my deepest fears. So destiny was the target of my anger, which thus became ineffectual because you cannot even scratch the surface of destiny. It took away all my responsibility for what happened to me, or rather it gave it all to me, then took it away in a second.

A few sessions later, he elaborated on this:

Heroism was the counterweight of destiny. My identity, or at least the image I had of myself, was caught between these two demands and could not take on light or form. My answer to the question "Who are you?," which terrified me, would have been based on what I wanted or had to be. I had an unbearable feeling of emptiness, failure and inadequacy inside. Whatever I did or said was unacceptable, whoever I was was unacceptable: in actual fact, I should have been "another." Identity was like something proposed from outside that I had to adopt inside. I had to stick to that proposal like a trading card that is glued onto the appropriate image. Now we have given identity another meaning. There is no need for others to give me one, I have my own, I do not necessarily have to possess that absolute knowledge that I once thought would have freed me from all my ills. I don't know everything, yet I can walk and live. The image has changed ... "from being a hero to being myself." And then true identity is a "tension" toward something. I experience a sense of belonging and, at the same time, of being open, which didn't exist before. ... How worthless was the perfection I strove for, and how rich and, in a certain sense, "infinite" is this limit I shunned!

Now I would like to talk about a woman patient I treated in the 1980s, who was also convinced that a negative and inevitable destiny deprived one of the right to exist. The period of therapy helped to change her suffering caused by dark despair, which had structured defenses profoundly hostile to life, into the belief that pain could not only give way to joy but, above all, coexist with hope.

3.2 Giovanna's case: The use of the Shadow to hide one's own light

3.2.1 G.'s story

G. was born at home, in Madrid, with a problematic delivery.

During G.'s childhood, her grandmother told her that the birth was so difficult because she was passive. *"You didn't want to be born,"* she said. In the first days of her life G. experienced considerable suffering – noticed precisely by her grandmother – because she had weak suction and was losing vitality through undernourishment. The fact that she did not cry or become agitated was mistaken for tranquility by her mother: *"Look how good the baby is!"* whereas when her grandmother saw her, she exclaimed: *"But this baby is dying!,"* and she had to be nourished intravenously to survive. When G. was told this story, her emotional reaction was: *"I would have let that newborn die. Why struggle so hard to save a baby who did not want to live?"* When G. was two her baby brother was born and she soon realized that, because he was a boy, he was given more attention by her parents; above all, he was her father's favorite. This was confirmed a few years later when she found out that her father's first reaction to her own birth had been one of disappointment: *"What a pity, it's a girl!"* Some traumatic episodes in her early childhood emerged only after years of analysis. Once she cut off all her curls, which were actually much admired, probably because she wanted to look like her brother whom she felt was more loved. Then, while she was out walking with her mother and younger brother, some flyers fluttered to the ground, her mother picked one up and, when G. asked her what was written on it, she replied: *"It says that G. is a naughty, ugly little girl because she has cut her hair off."* At first she thought that her mother was teasing her, but she wasn't quite sure. Perhaps everyone did know that she had done something really naughty, and she felt terribly humiliated. Another time her little brother, with whom she was playing, picked up one of her hair slides and swallowed it. Her father was so angry that he threatened not to speak to her until the hair slide had appeared in the little boy's potty. On yet another occasion, while in bed in her room, she was suddenly seized by an acute feeling of loneliness and anxiety, and called out to her parents, in tears. Her father appeared in his pajamas, wrenched open the sliding door, and told her to be quiet or else he would make her sleep in the passage. G. wanted to beg him to leave the door slightly open but she didn't even have the strength to speak, and her father abruptly slid it shut, closing her in her room and making her feel excluded. She put her head under the sheet, trembling with fear. Shortly afterward, she thought she had an hallucination: she saw a light go on and felt something brush her head, as if someone had thrown something soft at her, a blanket perhaps; then the light went out and she heard footsteps disappearing along the passage. The next day she asked her mother if someone had come into her room, and she replied: *"No Nena* (an affectionate nickname her mother called her by), *no one at all, you must have dreamt it."* But her grandmother, G.'s sole confidante and only real source of affection throughout her childhood, told her that it was probably her dead grandfather who had come back to give her courage. Instead of calming her down, this explanation conjured the mysterious presence of a ghost, terrifying her still further. At the age of four she was sent to a provincial town near Madrid to stay with a maternal aunt. At the time Spain was ravaged by the Civil War and her father, a militant communist, had been imprisoned. Moreover, the family was going through a period of financial difficulties and G. had contracted tuberculosis. As the disease was still at an early stage, her mother thought that the country air and life in a more affluent environment would enable her to regain her health. G.'s uncle was, in fact, a very well-off forestry engineer, engaged in reforesting the region, and the summer was spent in a house in the country that could only be reached by mule-drawn cart. G. remembered those summers as the happiest of her life because she ran free in the countryside, played with the animals, and came into contact with the peasants. Once she was deeply touched when she saw a peasant woman giving food that she had already chewed to her baby boy, seeing it as an act of tender care, and paying little heed to her grandmother's speaking of "savage" people. Above all, she remembered experiencing being one with nature, and a sense of freedom that she had only felt in the stories she made up in her imagination, and the fairytales her grandmother read to her. She often imagined becoming a fascinating woman, a princess perhaps, or being reborn into a different family. Or having delicate features and blonde hair – in keeping with her criteria of beauty – or her parents, now rich and famous, coming to get her in a limousine and finally taking her to her own house. Otherwise, she remembered her life then as a burden. Her relationships with her uncle and aunt were somewhat oppressive, formal and devoid of any spontaneous affection. Furthermore, she always felt that she was in a strange place, and her grandmother herself would tell her to be sure to be obedient and sensible, because she was a guest. Her entire childhood was also dogged by health problems: as soon she had recovered from tuberculosis, she went down with a very serious case of typhoid, which prevented her from going to elementary school, and she had to study with her grandmother. All this accentuated her permanent feeling of being different from other children, who did go to school, and sometimes made her feel truly inferior and ashamed. She said that it was as if there were something obscure in her that she could not define, as if she herself were adopting a ruse to present a false image to others. She remembered how very uncomfortable she felt when her strict, authoritarian uncle sat beside her bed and sang her a song: "Morena, porque siempre eres mala y nunca eres buena?", in which *mala* and *buena* have the double meaning of "being well" and "being ill" and of "good" and "bad." I think this episode might have aroused or strengthened in her the suspicion that her illnesses were caused by her inadequacy, or that she was to blame for them. Shortly after she arrived at her aunt and uncle's house, a boy cousin of hers, the son of another maternal aunt who had been widowed, came to stay as well. This cousin, like her brother, was two years younger than she was, and G. once again had the feeling that she was being discriminated against because she was a girl. The relationship with her cousin (Raul G.) was important to G. all her life, even though it was always characterized by ambivalent feelings. During this period, she was occasionally seized by a nagging thought: "All little girls should be killed because they are too unhappy, and this way men would be punished because they would remain alone, without women." At the age of four she tried to suffocate a baby girl in a cradle with a pillow, and she remembered her grandmother rushing in to stop her.

G. found herself in a difficult situation at her aunt and uncle's house because the Civil War divided the whole family. These relatives and, indeed, all the family on her mother's side belonged to the upper middle class and were staunch supporters of Franco, while her father was a carpenter, a militant communist, as I have said, and an active member of the Resistance. When he was released from prison he was seldom able to find work, and could rely neither on health insurance nor an old-age pension. The aunt and uncle's judgment of him was very negative, with regard to both his political ideology and his socioeconomic position. His wife was known by everyone as "la pobre Isabellita" (poor Isabellita) because she had entered into a marriage that guaranteed neither a tranquil nor comfortable life. Nevertheless, in those years G. often saw her father as a hero who fought for ideals of freedom.

The return to her family in Madrid, at the age of twelve, was extremely dramatic. Her father, whom she had always idealized, had become a tyrant. He was only capable of giving orders and imposing his will; he was never at home, and showed no interest in his children or his wife. G.'s mother had become very depressed, devoting herself to domestic chores all day long and complaining about the way her husband treated her, about her loneliness and unhappiness. G. often thought her father had not responded properly to the sacrifices his wife had made and to the risks she had taken in supporting his political militancy; in fact, her mother had lost the approval of her own family, but was not compensated by her husband's protection. G. also suffered another, more brutal, disappointment at this time. She had recently discovered books, in which she immersed herself as she had in the imaginative stories of her childhood, hoping that she would be able to go to high school with a girlfriend with whom she had established an affectionate and exclusive friendship. Instead, her father told her that, since his financial means did not permit him to give both of his children higher education, she would go to a commercial school and then work to help the family, while her brother, being a male, would receive a university education. During this period, an episode occurred that offended G.'s dignity: her father found the letters from her best friend and read them out loud to those present, ridiculing their relationship. This was when G. began to go into deep depression, also because she had become fat, she was obliged to wear glasses due to a vision defect, and she felt ugly. Her father commented: *"All you needed was a pair of glasses, my girl, no man will ever want to marry you, that's for sure!"* Another remark made by her father – perhaps because he was annoyed that his daughter had been taken away from him by a family who despised him – stuck in G.'s mind, to the point that she adopted it, actually identifying with her father's description of her: "Eres candil de puerta ajena" (*"You're like a lamp destined to illuminate other people's doors"*). Thus G. introjected this paternal judgment, which she considered negative because she never had any faith in herself, as if she were unable to create a personal place in which to exist, but could only accompany the life of others, experiencing it indirectly. We may say that she was possessed by a projective identification of her father's. *"It was then that I felt lost,"* she told me, *"because I saw all my prospects for the future turn to dust. I was too young to rely on my own strength, too old to hope that my destiny would change."* At the age of fifteen she tried to commit suicide by cutting her wrists, but was saved by her mother who, as she was saying goodnight to her, noticed the blood on the sheets and immediately blocked the hemorrhaging. The day after, her father exclaimed: *"What would people have thought? That we treat you so badly you were driven to commit such an act?"* In the following years she completed her secondary education in five years instead of seven, and immediately began to work as a clerk. She went to London and obtained a master's in economics, then returned to Madrid and signed on at evening school to prepare an integrative exam in Latin and Greek that would enable her to go to university. At the age of twenty-three she enrolled at the department of philosophy and studied productively until she graduated. At university, though, she felt as if she had "entered by the back door," as if she had usurped a privilege to which she was not fully entitled, due to the irregular nature of her studies. Her late teens and university years were marked by positive aspects, however, because in Madrid she also met up again with her cousin R.G., who was much admired for his intellectual prowess and with whom she established an alliance in order to escape from her oppressive family environment. Together with him she frequented cultural societies, met various friends, and devoted herself to clandestine political activities within the communist party. When she was around twenty her cousin expressed his love for her and his desire to marry her in various letters, but these were intercepted by her mother. Their relationship was thwarted by the joint action of her mother and her aunt (R.G.'s mother), who were against the couple's plans because they were related, and also because R.G. was younger than her. Moreover, G. later told me that she would only have accepted an unconsummated marriage with her cousin, since she saw sex with him as incestuous, and the idea of it repulsed her.

On a more profound examination of G.'s relationship with her parents, we may say that the conflicts experienced with her father were more easily identifiable and, in a certain sense, caused her less anxiety than those inherent to the relationship with her mother. In fact, she developed an attitude of challenge and, indeed, open war, toward her father. Her rebellion against his criticisms and her need to contest what she experienced as negative predictions about herself provided part of the energy that fueled her actions; energy that was obviously charged with anger, but which was also a propulsive force that helped her to achieve a series of intellectual conquests. She parried her father's male chauvinist slight that reprised a Spanish saying: "Tu no inventaras nuca la polvora" ("*You will never invent gunpowder*"), meaning you will never become a genius, by completing her university studies and supporting herself financially while she did so. Regarding her mother, instead, G. had no doubt whatsoever that she was the person who loved her the most, and had always accepted her as she was; however, she was equally convinced that she was unable to offer her protection. Her mother was incapable of transmitting strength, courage, a sense of her own worth, and especially of female dignity, to her daughter, as well as love. During early childhood, G. had never felt comforted by her in moments of distress, and when she met up with her during the summers in the country with her aunt and uncle, she always found her distracted. *"If at least she had kept me close to her, as if proudly saying to others: This is my daughter!"* G. once exclaimed. While in her early teens, G. realized that her mother was insecure and was asking her for help, but she was extremely irritated by this. She could not stand her mother's moaning and groaning, nor her adopting the position of the cringing wife who is the victim and submits to the husband's abuse without rebelling. *"If my father makes you suffer so much why don't you leave him?"* G. told her mother repeatedly, irritated by the fact that she was deeply humiliated by her father's behavior, but continued to sleep with him. Her attacks on her mother were often quite merciless: she accused her, she told her off, and she then withdrew like a hedgehog whenever her mother showed affection. *"I could only kiss you when you were sleeping,"* her mother once said. In short, G. tormented her until she made her cry, and then felt unbearably guilty. The danger that G.'s mother seemed to pose for her was that of feeling assimilated by a humiliated, masochistic female figure, a loser, who resigned herself to her destiny with despairing fatalism. As a woman, G. could not be mirrored in her mother, but she could not oppose her because she felt that she was too fragile. *"My father was unjust and one can always fight injustice, but my mother was unhappy and I felt helpless because, whatever I did, I was unable to help her."* So the attack on her mother also became an attack on herself. She neglected personal grooming and always dressed sloppily, to the point that her mother told her: *"It looks like you were dressed by your enemies."* On the other hand, she was unable to benefit from any encouragement or admiration from her mother, precisely because she had been so devalued. *"When my mother told me I was attractive it meant nothing to me. It would have been important if my father had said it."* One day, she explained the emotional tone of her experiences more clearly:

> I did my utmost not to resemble my mother, but she threatened me from within, almost as if she had planted herself inside me. I remember the anguish I felt when she read my correspondence with R.G. It was if she had succeeded in eliminating the distance that I had sought to put between us by having a secret.

Nevertheless, every time G. spoke about her mother, she was moved to tears. As the analysis progressed she became increasingly distressed because she had only been able to be there for her mother for brief periods, for example when she saw that she was seriously ill and close to death. The truth was that she couldn't bear to see her suffer.

After obtaining her degree in philosophy she never managed to take the state exam that would have enabled her to enter public competitions for a job in Spain. Instead, she found work as a translator and accepted a series of temporary contracts, which offered excellent pay but no security, with international organizations. It was as if G. had drawn all her energy to plan from her reactive attitude toward her father, but the inability to recognize herself in her mother prevented her from truly believing in her own worth, especially as a woman, and condemned her to renunciation. She could do something "against" someone, but not "for" someone or for herself. Her identity could not have been built on a love bond of *"us,"* i.e., of *"being together."* Thus G.'s exile began. From that moment on, she always worked abroad: in London, Geneva, Paris, and New York, only occasionally returning to Spain, especially when her parents needed her due to financial or health problems. Her father contracted Buerger's disease, and had to have a leg amputated; he would die from a bowel obstruction a few years later. During that period G. felt great sympathy for her maimed father. Shortly before he died, he begged her forgiveness for not having supported her enough in life, then asked her to do him the favor of going to see his mistress and giving her one last message; a favor that G. granted, although it was difficult for her. G. met this woman with mixed feelings: on the one hand, she was the reason her father had betrayed her mother; on the other, she seemed affectionate and truly attached to G.'s father (she actually had photos of G. and her brother when they were children on her table!). So G. began to feel compassionate toward her father's mistress and invited her to attend his funeral, seeing that no one knew who she was. This episode caused G. to feel terribly humiliated again, due to the female condition. She felt sympathy for her mother who had been deceived, but also for this woman who had been relegated to a clandestine position, and who had not been allowed to fully share the life of the man she loved.

Shortly after G.'s father died, her mother had a mastectomy for breast cancer. A few years later, she suffered an embolism that resulted in hemiparesis on the right side with loss of speech. She died within months, following other cardiovascular complications.

3.2.2 G.'s affective life

G.'s love relationships were difficult and tormented. Following the episode with her cousin, G. married a young man with whom she was not in love, but who gave her the chance of showing her father that a man could find her attractive. Thus, the marriage was one of the challenges issued to her father, and ended in an annulment by the Sacra Rota, after G. had voluntarily had an abortion. During this period G. again felt that she was living inauthentically. She saw all her plans and choices as a sham, as if she was always in a place that was not hers. A part of her organized plans and took decisions, rather like a character in a play who follows a script based on other people's lives, while her true essence remained outside, always elsewhere, always in an "impossible," in a kind of inner exile that had sequestered her.

In the following years G. had an important love relationship with a man who, significantly, had the same name, "Raul," and was the same age as the boy cousin with whom she shared her childhood. After they had been living together for a while, this new partner (whom we shall call R.B.) was arrested after being caught with communist propaganda material. An idea of the political climate in Spain in those years can be had from the fact that R.B. met up with his father in prison, whom he had not seen since he was a child. The father, forced into exile as a result of his political views, had tried to re-enter Spain under a false name, but had been recognized at the border and arrested. At this time G. was expecting a baby boy by R.B., but again decided to have an abortion because she felt that she did not have enough support from her man. In actual fact, R.B. had left her free to choose whether or not to have the baby, because he did not know how long he would be in prison, or if he would be able to give her sufficient financial support when he was released. The truth was that pregnancy caused G. unbearable anguish: *"I could not have a child,"* she once said to me, *"because it would have meant compromising myself with reality, saying 'yes' to an experience from which there is no going back. The bond with a child is the only one in life that, once established, can never be severed."* On the other hand, G. did not even believe that R.B. loved her. This was not because he had given her few demonstrations of his affection, but because the doubt that made her destroy every relationship was so deep-rooted that she could neither believe that she was worthy of being loved, nor that feelings expressed to her were genuine. Her father's attitude, distorted by persecutory fantasies, had become an internal structure of G.'s, who continued to exclude, and not to recognize, herself, in the same way that she had once felt disowned and excluded. In actual fact, G. was backing away from the birth of her Self by identifying herself with a figure that negated her, but made her feel powerful by deluding her that she was protected by the fragile aspects that made her feel similar to her mother. In order not to be abandoned, which for her was a given, she adopted various behaviors that would put an end to her love relationship. While R.B. was in prison she had an affair with a man she met while studying in a European city, she became pregnant again, and had the third and last abortion of her life. After he had been released, R.B. was deeply hurt when he learned about these things, which G. herself told him. Their relationship was irredeemably damaged, and gradually deteriorated until it ended for good. Nonetheless, some time later G. established a solid, warm friendship with this generous-hearted ex, which would last the whole of her life.

Later G., then over forty, settled in Switzerland and fell in love with another man (García), this time older than her, who was able to satisfy her need for tenderness. She put all her hopes in him, as if she had found the person who embodied the idealized characteristics of both of the parents she would have liked to have had, as if he represented the archetype of the parents *"You are everything to me,"* she told him, *"father, mother, friend and lover."* But their relationship was unable to survive the conflicts arising from reality: García lived with his wife and children, which was an insurmountable obstacle for G., who wanted him all for herself.

At this time, G. experienced another failure. In Switzerland she met Maria Zambrano, a well-known Spanish philosopher and writer in exile, who encouraged her to resume her studies for the state exam and to present a thesis on her work, which was still little known in Spain. Despite the commitment and enthusiasm with which G. worked at the beginning and an initial success, she was soon seized again by a lack of self-confidence, and gave up. Her mother also died during this period.

These events plunged G. into very deep depression and, on the advice of her psychotherapist who had followed her for some years, she decided to move to Rome and to begin a process of depth analysis.

3.2.3 The exploratory period

3.2.3.1 The first two meetings

G. first called me just before Christmas 1984, and I was surprised that she spoke to me in Spanish. She told me that she had been given my name by a girlfriend who was in analysis with a colleague of mine, and had been told that I spoke her language and was familiar with various aspects of Spanish culture. She immediately pointed out that this was very important for her, because she had only been in Rome for a short time and did not have a good command of Italian, and above all because she felt it would be impossible for her to speak intimately about herself in a foreign language. I thought about the affective valences that speaking in a language linked to my personal story would have for me, but I knew that it would not prevent me from carefully investigating the real therapeutic needs of the patient.

At the first meeting I noticed that G., who was then forty-nine (a few years older than me at the time), had pronounced and intensely expressive features. She wore pants and a sweater, and would wear sporting clothes in a masculine style throughout the analysis. She moved brusquely, almost impetuously, as if she were already familiar with the space, and had no doubts about what she should do or say. I was struck this attitude that seemed to show not the slightest hesitation. As soon as G. sat down, she told me that she had arrived in Rome with symptoms of severe depression. She also thought that her illness coincided with entering menopause, seeing that her periods were irregular. She felt that she had no enthusiasm, no desires, no plans. For her life was nothing but a burden, and what really disturbed her was the fact that, more and more often lately, she had not had the strength to leave the house, not even to go to work, and was obliged to ask for sick leave. She was terrified by this because she had always thought, even during the most painful moments in her life, that as long as she could maintain her financial independence she would be safe. Therefore, she saw the block about work as a particularly catastrophic sign. She had moved to Rome, where she had accepted the offer of a permanent post as translator with an international organization, also on the advice of her Swiss therapist with whom she had worked for around three years. According to the therapist, in fact, her continually moving from city to city was a way of escaping from her problems; therefore, she should settle in one place and undergo proper analysis, perhaps with a man. The therapist had then given her the name of an Argentinian analyst. The neuropsychiatrist in Rome who treated her with an anti-depressant pharmacological therapy also urged her to enter analysis. She had recently decided to contact the Argentinian, a mature professional who, unable to fit her in, had referred her to a young male colleague of Freudian formation and orientation. She had already talked to him, but was still very confused; she was not sure that she wanted to work with a man, and was also worried because he was only thirty and she was afraid he would not have enough experience to help her. When she told me this I immediately said that it was only right that she work through her doubts with the analyst with whom she had just begun a dialogue. In the event that they should decide not to work together, she could contact me again. At this point, G. told me that she was thinking of conducting a series of interviews with me and with the other analyst, in order to decide with whom to work, and she asked me a series of questions about my professional formation: if I was a doctor, which school I belonged to, and so forth: *"What do you expect,"* she said, *"the analyst is a guide to whom you entrust all your secrets."* I explained to her that initiating an exploratory process with two therapists at once would have falsified the examination of her

Journeys of life and therapy   89

problems, and made it impossible to identify the therapy that would have been helpful to her. Only an agreement between two people would have enabled her to focus on herself and her inner world. It was then that G. offered me a glimpse of her most profound suffering. Her earlier confidence disappeared completely, and it was as if she were paralyzed. For a few seconds, which seemed like an eternity, she remained motionless, staring into space with an anguished expression that was heartrending. I felt my chest tighten and I couldn't breathe. Then she slowly roused herself and looked at me, saying: *"Choice is the crux of my problems. I cannot, do not know how to choose. I feel that I want to work with you, but I am unable to decide."* At this point G. stood up and said goodbye, without uttering another word. I sensed that she was absolutely desperate, and also perceived an inner motion that would have made me try to alleviate her suffering and help her, but she rushed out.

In the minutes that followed, I reflected on the conflicting emotions that this first meeting had aroused in me. At a certain point I had felt as if I were being scrutinized and examined, which irritated me. It also seemed to me that G. sought to avoid making a commitment toward herself by overturning the roles between therapist and patient, and that her fantasy of a triangular situation represented the desire to control the analysts and acquire power over them by means of a system of alliances to be entered into, or abandoned, at will. On the other hand, I had strongly empathized with her when she had enabled me to understand how little her intentions were rooted in a profound conviction, and to perceive what was, instead, her deepest drama; namely, her inability to "be there," to consider herself the creator of her own destiny. She had been overwhelmed when called upon to act for herself, and by the anguish of having to come into being by attributing to something, or someone, an important meaning in her life. Later, when the analysis was well advanced, G. said to me: *"At the beginning I was not even scared of having to depend on the analyst, I simply could not recognize my analysis as an important moment in my life, in the same way that I could not recognize myself."* Even though I felt urged to help her solve the problem of choosing, I knew that this would have meant colluding with the patient's wanting someone else to be responsible for steering her life, and that I would have cheated her out of her freedom. I was sure that standing my ground was the only basis for a possible therapy, even though it troubled me when I intuited that, in this phase, freedom, i.e. the possibility to make a choice, was not a gift for the patient, but a terrible burden that deprived her of initiative and literally left her speechless. In some respects, I had almost hoped that she would resolve her doubts concerning the other analyst. If she had come back to me and we had decided to start the analysis, I knew that I would have found myself dealing with a difficult pathology and terrible suffering.

A few days later G. called me again. She told me that she had seen her therapist, and they had decided not to work together. I fixed an appointment for her and, when we saw each other, she explained that the analyst had said that her reservations could have been overcome, but that there was another matter, which he called a "datum of reality," that was not open to interpretation and would have jeopardized the therapy. The truth of the matter was that he would not have been able to give her the receipts she had requested because she had health insurance that would have refunded 50% of the cost of the analysis. She felt that this justified her earlier rejection of the analyst, even though, as she herself said, a girlfriend of hers was perhaps right in saying that analysis should be paid for in full with one's own strength. *"Let's hope that your Super Ego does not make you pay too high a price for taking care of yourself,"* I reflected. In the meantime, she had consulted her neuropsychiatrist, who was convinced that she was already disposed toward me, but also suggested she to try and understand why she wanted to work with a woman. With hindsight, I think that G. had experienced a profound insight. It was precisely because she, too, had devalued her femininity that facing this pivotal dimension of her nature, which she had always sought to ignore in order not to be like her mother, was fundamental to her being able to determine her own destiny. After providing the above explanations, G. went into her personal story, giving me some essential information about her life: the Civil War in Spain; her father's imprisonment; her childhood far away from her family, in the countryside with her upper middle class aunt and uncle on her mother's side; her marriage to a man in whom she was not interested, but accepted to show her father that she was desirable as a woman, and because she was convinced she would never be loved by a man whom she respected and admired; and her last love affair with García, in Switzerland, the only man by whom she had felt truly appreciated and loved, and the devastating break-up of their relationship.

> My last sparks of life, the hope of realizing myself sentimentally and intellectually, died with García. Spurred by the enthusiasm that this love gave me, I had resumed my philosophy studies and was writing a thesis on Maria Zambrano's thought, but I failed to complete it. During the same period my mother died, and I felt that my roots had been severed at the top and bottom: I had lost my parents and I had not had, nor could I ever have, children.

She also mentioned that she was relieved by the arrival of the menopause, because it signaled the end of the period of love relationships that had always been a source of torment for her. Sexuality was mainly experienced by G. as a humiliating concession made to the male in order to be loved. She once said to me:

> It's tragic that a man and a woman are obliged by nature to have an essential relationship even though they are irreconcilable enemies. I see no possibility of love between them, only a power struggle in which the woman is usually the loser.

Then she spoke of her abortions and a dream that she had had during one of her pregnancies: *"The fetus grew beyond measure in her belly until it caused it to explode."* I thought that G. had probably not been able to experience a "good" symbiosis in which, as Racamier writes (1992), there is no self-sufficient closure in a state of static fusion, but an opening up to the dynamism of the relational dimension, and the experience of recognizing oneself in the other does not preclude the feeling of separateness. The benefits of a good symbiosis will be enjoyed by the psyche throughout a person's life; thus, the other will no longer be solely the external object, the outsider, the totally different from our own Ego, but rather a part of our Self, the *other* part of us that dwells inside and illuminates our unknown side, but without abolishing the consciousness of our wholeness as a person. I supposed that G. had not experienced the transitional space, described by Winnicott, in which the other is found and invented, and reality and imagination are woven from the same material. So, for her, the other was configured as the irreducible enemy, whether parent, lover or child, even though, paradoxically, it would remain essential to her life, as if she had been cursed. Consequently, any form of relation placed her in an unresolvable dilemma: on the one hand, it would result in the invasion, assimilation or complete possession of one by the other; on the other hand, its loss or interruption would result in her annihilation. The image of the dream she had described gave me considerable cause for concern, and I asked myself: *"Will the analytic container withstand the birth of the new parts of G.? Will the bond between analyst and patient be strong enough to deal with the changes that make psychic growth possible?"* The patient also made a dramatic statement that revealed an irreconcilable generational conflict: *"There is no room for both mother and child on this earth, either one dies, or the other."* But in the analytic situation, as in any relationship geared to individual maturation, success or failure always depends on both members of the couple. The analyst is successful if the analysand achieves well-being, individuation and independence – which we should actually call "inter-independence" because it includes relation. Despite the fact that the patient introduced death-related themes and referred to plans to commit suicide over a long period, it was already clear to me that she was not driven by a death wish, but the wish not to be born. G.'s greatest difficulty lay in accepting limitation:

> Better to stay among the non-born, in the shadow of the infinite possibilities of the unconscious, than to determine oneself and enter the order of reality with its spatial demarcation and its temporal scansion. Better to preserve an illusory state of fusion with parents sensed as omnipotent, than to become separate individuals and to experience one's state of incompleteness and imperfection.

For G., death was not the backcloth that provides the setting for the events of life, marking their position in time, but the image of immortality itself, evoked to satisfy a narcissistic need. Once she spoke of a dream she had experienced at the end of her previous therapy: *"I saw my dead body and I thought: I am dead and I was never born."* She added that her not having taken her life was due to a lack of courage, which was proof that she could not see anything through, and this also gave me to understand that she expected the analysis to help her in this regard. It was impossible for her to accept that the need to put an end to this state of death in life did not necessarily mean killing oneself. To be more exact, I would say that G. still had an intense and vital impulse to express herself and to establish affective contacts, and that she did in fact want to be born. But she was terrified of not being able to do it, and assailed by the doubt that the transition toward the new would not signify a beginning for her, but the loss of what she still possessed. Her real problem was the conflict between forces that drove her in opposite directions, with a paralyzing effect, while destructiveness took on a defensive value: better to lose everything than give life to something that could be threatened. *"I would like to go back to Spain to die,"* she once said to me, *"like rabbits that go back to the* madriguera *to die."* (In Spanish *madriguera* means "rabbit hole" and has the same root as *madre*, "mother"). It was as if, in G., the vital fabric had been inverted, and the direction of time overturned. The signs of life were altered and mistaken for threats of death, and death fantasies were assimilated as protective forms. While the theme of death, as a return to the womb, can symbolically allude to psychic rebirth, it clearly seemed to have a regressive meaning in the context in which G. spoke of it. On the basis of this, it was easy to imagine that the work with her could have led me to establish a fusional relationship, which carried the risk of an unconscious identification between analyst and analysand. Therefore, I had to prevent G's desperation from flooding my thought space, and to work constantly on the possible temptations for me to regress. The caution and care I adopted during the exploratory period were like the rope that Ulysses used to combat the Siren song of his unconscious forces.

I suggested to the patient that we work together once a week for around three months to see if the analytic therapy was really suited to her needs.

3.2.3.2 The emerging problems

The exploratory period saw the emergence of some fundamental themes related to G.'s problems, which would reappear in multiple variations during the subsequent years of analysis, and which I shall sum up below.

3.2.3.2.1 A CONSTELLATION OF IMPOSSIBILITY: ILLUSION OR DEATH

G. presented to me a life in which any possibility of change was inconceivable. Everything was closed, static, and repetitive. The only two paths that she considered following to emerge from her suffering were reverie and death. For G., reverie was not a form of imagination, i.e., using representations to bring to light what is hidden in the depths of the unconscious – which implies hard work and, I would almost say, faithfulness to the objective data of one's nature. Instead, it was the creation of grandiose and illusory visions of herself and the world, which reminded her of the fairytales told by her grandmother and of her previous therapy, which she described as a time of giving vent to her feelings. As in her childhood, G. often dreamt that she was another person and invented extremely detailed stories, projecting them onto her past or future. Some of them were so credible that she would tell them to people she occasionally met. G. found a certain relief in pretending to herself and to others that everything was true, but immediately afterward she was ashamed of her deceitfulness. Furthermore, all these inventions were carefully separated from reality and situated in an ideal world, almost to prevent their character of omnipotence from coming into contact with possible, and therefore partial, dimensions. If, by chance, a fantasy element neared the flow of life and thus became realizable, albeit with slight modifications, G. rejected it by devaluing, denying, disowning or paralyzing the activity. She often used expressions like: *"This has no value," "It represents nothing new," "It's not me"* or *"I want it, but I can't have it because I'm too lazy and unable to commit."* So when G. spoke to me of change, she envisioned it as the consequence of an extremely powerful external intervention that would radically and immediately transform her, as if by magic, whereas the idea of constructing something on the basis of her interiority and in collaboration with others, which would gradually produce actual, though limited, results over time, was alien to her. On the other hand, G. presented death to me as the end of suffering and therefore as the cancellation of what she considered to be the supreme injustice of life. I think that for her death and reverie represented two parallel modalities for pursuing the same goal: the establishment of an illusory order in which everything is possible, instead of the order underpinning a reality that she did not like, and viscerally rejected.

3.2.3.2.2 INTERRUPTED TIME

G. felt that it was impossible for her to find a thread that linked the events of her life. It was as if a force constantly interrupted the continuity of her existence.

> I was not able to complete any task, I have always interrupted everything along the way, especially at two moments that are crucial to me: the beginning and the end of something. I feel seized by a terrible anxiety and become paralyzed. I have always met with failure.

G. also fled from places every time she experienced frustrations or disappointments: *"I left everything, imagining I could rebuild on fresh ground"*; but when she went she never left parts of herself with others, nor took parts of others, or experiential baggage, with her. It was as if G. could only experience a total presence of self to things, without any separation, which actually took the form of physical closeness; or a total absence in which she even sought to erase the traces of memory. This modality could also be perceived in the rhythm of the sessions; for example, when the hour had ended and G. had glanced at her watch or noticed that I had intimated that time was up, she jumped to her feet, gathered up her things in a hurry, and rushed down the stairs, without even allowing herself a few seconds to say goodbye to her analyst. At times I found myself thinking: "It is as if G. felt that I were driving her out." Later, after we had clarified the conditions of the therapeutic contract, she would often miss a session without letting me know beforehand and without offering any explanation at our next meeting. I had the feeling that it was impossible for her to conceive of my thinking or being concerned about her. For a long time, the analytic space could not become the place in which, symbolically speaking, one was continuously present, precisely because each component of the therapeutic couple continued to exist in the mind of the other. I told myself that G. must have felt mentally aborted by her parents when she was sent to her aunt and uncle, as if the break in the continuity of her life, though anticipated by very early experiences, had only been confirmed at that moment. That was why the experience of separation, or rather of her separateness, had not led to the discovery of her existential integrity but to the laceration of her psychic experience, inflicting a painful wound that reopened every time she experienced abandonment. The upshot of all this was that G. had absolutely no faith in the ties she established and, overturning the order of early events, she continued to actively inflict on herself the trauma of the loss of affection she had once experienced. Maria Zambrano, who for a long time sought to establish a profound relationship with G., once told her with infinite sadness: "You do not leave, you disappear."

G. described this situation dramatically:

> It is as if I had the power to reduce everything I touch, everything that comes near me, to dust. After a while I find myself surrounded by desert. Then the pain of feeling alone and rejected becomes unbearable and I escape elsewhere, but the place in which I was seems to me like a shadow, a big shadow that I leave behind me.

I came to the conclusion that I had to help G. to make a transition that would bring her out of her desperate situation where there was only rejection, escape and loneliness, which also abolish the possibility of memory; a situation that was the antithesis of the possibility to create the new. The shadow that G. felt she left behind her was, in fact, an "absolute" shadow, since it was totalizing and allowed no room for other than self. I thought, therefore, that I could perhaps use some of the symbols offered by the great cosmogonic myths in which the sacrifice of the absolute dimension generates the cosmos and relationships between beings.

This brought to mind Yahweh's words to Moses:

Thou canst not see my face: for there shall no man see me, and live ... thou shalt stand upon a rock. And it shall come to pass, while my glory passeth by, that I will put thee in a cleft of the rock, and will cover thee with my hand while I pass by. And I will take away mine hand, and thou shalt see my back parts: but my face shall not be seen.

(Exodus 33, 20–23)

I was also reminded of an interesting thought concerning this passage expressed by Galimberti: "We are in the trace of God, in that trace that God leaves of himself when he departs" (*La terra senza il male*. Feltrinelli, Milan 1984, p. 172).

The cosmogonic myth of Prajāpati of which Panikkar speaks (1979, p. 95 ff.), basing himself on the Brihadaranyaka Upanishad, is even more radical. The myth recounts that in the beginning there was the radical solitude of Prajāpati, the One, the primordial God, who was surrounded by absolute voidness. Prajāpati did not experience joy because joy can only come to us from a second entity. Therefore, he decided to create the cosmos and all living beings, forming them from his own body, because he had nothing else with which to create. But after his immolation nothing of the God remains, he dies as God, having created a non-God: absolute and contingent order are incommensurable. It is then that Prajāpati, fearing his death, invokes the help of his creation; thus, the very elements of the universe and all the beings that hear him, renounce the fascinating mirage of their radical independence and join up again with their origin, reconstituting the dismembered body of the God. This myth speaks of the perfect circularity of the gift between creator and creatures. God and man can truly lose each other and be swallowed up by nothingness if the relation of reciprocal belonging that permits them to exist to the full is interrupted. Reality is not made up of beings that are isolated and an end in themselves, and generosity is its essence. The cosmos and man exist because they are in relation to each other and to their divine source.

Returning to G.'s story, we may say that, in a certain sense, life begins in the shadow of God, since it is only possible in a relative space and time, in which the absolute has withdrawn, or actually immolated, enabling the creation of a contingent order. Yet that shadow does not represent the disappearance of God, because it is pervaded by his most intimate essence. Whereas the shadow that G. believed she left behind when fleeing from a particular place was not relative – like the one that, in terms of inner reality, may derive from the original bipartition of the psyche. It was, instead, a totalizing shadow, similar to the obscure part of an omnipotent and terrible God, incapable of sacrificing his absolute dimension for the love of his creature, and with whom the creature, inebriated by the fascination of the absolute, identifies, in order to see itself as an unrelated and unlimited being.

3.2.3.2.3 THE AFFECTIVE DIFFICULTIES

G. was convinced that she had never been and never could be loved, not even in the future. The only emotions she had experienced in relationships were negative, like feeling excluded or rejected. On the other hand, she believed others were right because she did not like herself; she felt ugly, lazy, incapable, nasty, and hence not worthy of being loved. It seemed evident to me that this dynamic could only be modified if it were appropriately interpreted, since G. strenuously resisted recognizing affection when it was offered to her. In fact, if someone showed their respect or liking for her, she immediately thought that they were pretending in order to exploit her, or that they had the wrong image of her (she was very good at presenting herself for what she was not!), and that as soon as they realized their mistake they would ignore her. G.'s suspicion also obscured others or obscured herself, sullying any relationship. On the other hand, she invariably adopted a mechanism that we called her "cover": when she wanted to contact someone in whom she was interested, and since she did not have enough confidence in herself to believe that she could give or receive anything good at a meeting, she had a friend, male or female, go with her, who became the custodian of her positive elements and was supposed to represent her. According to her, however, what tended to happen was that the two people she cared about most regularly established a personal relationship that excluded her. This role was frequently played by R.G., the cousin she admired and transformed into a "shadow brother," after the disappointing experience with him. R.G. represented a kind of narcissistic ideal for G., who felt obliged to denigrate herself in order to preserve it. Significant in this regard is a childhood memory: in the village where her aunt and uncle lived she often went to contemplate the image of a Madonna dressed in black, known as the "Madonna of Solitude," to whom she confessed her unhappiness. According to G., the icon represented a mother mourning her son, but also a woman alone who found the justification for her existence within, without needing to depend on others. This made me realize that G. had turned her isolation into a means of gaining power: *"I challenge you to try and get close to me and help me, I'll show you that I'm better than anyone at destroying relationships. I'll make you feel impotent and alone, like I once felt."* In actual fact, she often had good feelings about others, but when someone approached her and sought to establish a relationship, everything became contaminated.

3.2.3.2.4 REALITY AND VISION OF REALITY

G. was unable to accept that reality does not completely match our image of it; for example, when she told me about something that had happened to her it was as if she were describing a show she had watched without being involved. Then, whenever I sought to elicit a more subjective response (by saying things like: *"That was how you felt it"* or *"That was how you experienced it"*), she often replied aggressively, *"I'm not making it up, it's a 'datum of reality.'"* Her sense of time was also extremely distorted because it had lost its characteristic flow that could accommodate a form of planning. For her, things had gone a certain way and she had no good reason to believe that one day they could go differently. It seemed that G. had let herself be robbed of her future, because she expected it to be a kind of copy of the past and thus a never-ending repetition of the identical. *"I feel like a scratched disk with the needle stuck in a groove, which plays the same motif over and over again."* she once said despairingly, when my interpretations had breached her defensive wall, *"But how can one change?"* When we were working on memories, she would sometimes suddenly intervene in annoyance, as if she had realized that she had allowed me to touch on, and maybe modify, one of her innermost emotions: *"What's the use of evoking the past? You can't remedy it anyway."* To which I would reply – if she let me: *"Remedy it, no, but our way of seeing and feeling it, yes."* Therefore, the reality that G. envisaged for herself consisted in a world of mere objects whose behavior was predictable and which seemed to be independent from her attitudes and her way of feeling. When, instead, she was able to accept that her way of relating to others and of expressing herself might elicit compatible responses from others, she saw it as an unmodifiable characteristic of her nature – almost as if it were solely a biological imprint that was part of an order, dictated by destiny, which differed from that of freedom and personal responsibility. The feeling of guilt was not tolerated, and immediately changed into a feeling of persecution or produced a denigratory attack on herself, whenever it manifested. More often, these two types of response to the perception of guilt were simultaneous: the others had treated her unjustly and she was completely worthless. What she could not accept was that it had, at least in part, actively conditioned the events of her life.

Once I asked her if she had difficulty in interpreting reality. Since she had doubts about everything, how come she had none about the image she had of herself? How come it had not occurred to her that she may have possessed positive parts and potentialities for development that she, too, had rejected? She answered that, in theory, she was also able to accept that her inner orientations had shaped her experiences, but that she was not able to accept it in practice. Then she added:

> The reality that a person experiences dictates the law. It is reality that has put me in a situation from which I don't know that I will be able to emerge. It is like a glove that is so stuck to the hand, you don't know where the glove ends and the hand begins.

This metaphor, to which I shall return later, was extremely helpful to me in perceiving the space in which the analytic action could intervene: "However glued it may be," I thought, "the glove is not the hand."

3.2.3.2.5 HABITS

G. told me about what she called her drug: TV, which she watched for hours, zapping constantly, while eating chocolate. Perhaps, she said, she felt so empty that she had to stuff herself with images and food. I saw this as compulsive behavior that had the same characteristics as her habit of indulging in reverie, because G. was able to identify with the characters in the TV films, as she did with those in her stories; whereas she was unable to become involved in the experiences of real people without being seized with feelings of envy and hatred. *"I can't be in the same space as others: either I'm in the space of fantasy, or I'm left out."* At the level of countertransference, I felt obliged to occupy two extreme positions: either I was totally active and had to move frenetically and to revolve around her, like one of the countless TV images, while she remained completely passive; or I was immobilized, and it was she who conducted the analysis, as if using the remote control. G. was not able to tolerate being jointly active and, at times, it was as if there was a huge boulder in front of me, asking to be lifted up. Indeed, she once said: *"Any undertaking in my life is like a Sisyphean task: everything must always be done from the beginning again,"* where "must" should also be read as "can," since the prospect of inevitable failure probably concealed an omnipotence complex: *"You don't make compromises with life; ruin, which is the counterweight of perfection, is better than partial or short-lived success."*

3.2.3.2.6 DECEPTION

One day G. described her personality with an image:

> It is as if I were composed of concentric layers. On the surface there is a golden layer that corresponds to the guise of sweetness, generosity and willingness that I present to others in order to be accepted, but which is false and serves only to cover the black layer underneath, where my true nature, made up of solely negative feelings, resides. Imagine, a little boy, the son of a girl friend of mine, drowned in a swimming pool, and I went through the motions of rallying round, without feeling any compassion! My life is interwoven with so much underlying pain that all other forms of suffering don't exist for me. Lastly, there is a deep nucleus where a poor, empty being exists, who sends desperate signals, in order to be recognized.

Another time she recounted a dream in which she was abandoned by a group of friends, who told her: *"We've realized you're deceiving us and we can't trust you anymore."* When commenting on it, she compared herself to Cassandra, who was isolated by the people: *"The difference is that Cassandra was not believed but she believed in herself, while I don't even believe in myself."* I thought that G.'s truth was not to be sought in the golden layer or the black one which, equally unreal, was possibly the expression of a scotomized shadow with which she had identified to feel strong. But rather in the fragile and disoriented nucleus where she had a terror of not existing, which, had she been able to look at it with trusting eyes, would have revealed her values and her potentialities for development. According to G., her falseness toward others lay in making them believe that she was identical to the golden layer, while she knew she was not, but she did not realize that it was in considering herself identical to the black layer that the falsification of herself began. And yet the complacency, which bordered on boastfulness, with which she spoke of her so-called "nastiness" was probably only the superficial aspect of the deception carried out, while the most profound aspect lay in adopting false modalities of confidence and inauthentic behaviors to hide her difficulty in being present to herself. With the analyst, however, G. showed that she was conscious of these problems, as confirmed by some of the things she said:

> I always have the feeling that I am not in the place in which I find myself, that I am doing and saying things that are not really me. At times, it is as if I were talking in a dream.

3.2.3.2.7 THE ATTACK ON HOPE

I reflected on a story told by Bion in *Italian Seminars*, which I have already mentioned and which I would like to cite here because I found it particularly significant and enlightening, especially in this therapeutic process. A small group of people managed to survive a shipwreck by clinging to a raft:

> They experienced no fear whatsoever – but became terrified when they thought a ship was coming near. The possibility of rescue, and the even greater possibility that their presence would not be noticed on the sur-face of the ocean, led them to be terrified. Previously the terror had been sunk, so to speak, in the overwhelming depths of depression and despair. So the analyst, in the midst of the noises of distress, the failure of analy-sis … still needs to be able to hear the sound of this terror which indicates the position of a person beginning to hope that he might be rescued.
>
> (W. R. Bion 1977, 1983, p. 21)

The emergence of a feeling of hope within the analytic field immediately unleashed in G. a tempest of destructive forces that sought to negate any good possibility, perhaps precisely because, contemporaneously, she was seized by the fear of experiencing another, even more humiliating disappointment. Moreover, as Bion maintains, only the expression of self can be threatened, only what is vital and has value can be attacked by envious forces. In my opin-ion, while envy can come from others, it can also issue from the Ego, and be directed against the Self if the Ego does not tolerate the unpredictable, and never fully controllable, creative possibilities of the Self. I believe that hope, as referred to above, is not only a feeling, but actually a function essential to analytic work. Hope implies patience, because it orients us toward the future; tolerance of uncertainty, because it contemplates both success and failure (whereas if it were founded merely on certainty it would become fanaticism and violence); and trust, because it implies the recognition of positive potentialities in self and others. In this sense, I see hope as the opposite to passive waiting, since it is a maieutic activity, the bringing to light of things that are still not perceptible to the senses. Panikkar has an even more radical conception of hope as a faculty that concerns, not the future, but the present, because it means "knowing how to see the invisible." After G. had been in analysis for some years, I once said to her that, when we began, she was waiting for a miracle to be worked from the outside, but was unable to hope, and she responded:

> In Spanish there is just one verb: *esperar* which means both to wait and to hope, but there are two nouns. When you go to see a doctor, for example, you say *sala de espera* (waiting room) and not *sala de esperanza* (literally, hope room).

This told me that she had consulted an analyst in the same way that she would have a doctor or surgeon, who are asked to intervene and bring healing without the patient having to participate.

3.2.3.2.8 SPAIN AND SPANISH

I asked myself what our use of Spanish to communicate, and G.'s reiterated plans to settle in Spain as soon as possible, might signify. She would say, in fact, that the day she was capable of moving back to her homeland, she would have beaten her loneliness and overcome her problems. But she was terrified of re-experiencing the disappointment she suffered in her early teens when, upon her return to Madrid, she had had to deal with a reality that obliged her to give up her dreams. From this standpoint, Spain always loomed as the specter that would interrupt the analytic work, since it represented both the ideal place, which was as difficult to abandon in the imagination as it was to make real, and the place that had to rectify the past by giving back to her everything that had once been taken away. I thought that Spain might have embodied the concreteness that prevented her from entering the symbolic order. Did Madrid attract and fascinate her because it was the archetypal image of the mother whose omnipotence would offset the shortcomings of G.'s real mother? Would it have englobed in a primal symbiotic unity the daughter who sought to separate herself from it? However, I thought that both Spain and the Spanish language had an ambivalent side: on the one hand, they were roots that enlivened the present through a sense of the past; on the other, a formula that dragged her back and confined her to repetition.

I wondered which homeland G. was seeking: Would she return to Spain after conquering her inner terrain, and plant the seeds of her future there? Or would she let herself be swallowed up by the past that was embedded in her crystalized memories, and therefore by the place that had not allowed her to be born?

3.2.3.3 The first dreams while in analysis

The first dream that G. recounted to me during the exploratory period represented exclusion, a recurring theme in all her earlier dreams: *"I join two girl friends at a café, but I arrive late. I ask for a strawberry ice cream, but the waiter tells me that there are no ice creams left."* The second dream had sinister and threatening overtones, which I found most distressing:

> I am in prison and I have been sentenced to death. From the window I see the king of Spain pass by, followed by a procession of people, and I think that, perhaps, he could grant me a pardon. I want to shout out but I can't, because I don't know if such an important personage would occupy himself with me, or if my voice would be loud enough to be heard. My mother is by my side, and she says to me: "Don't worry, it'll be quick and painless, you'll see."

At that moment I felt that, as an analyst, I could occupy one of two positions: that of a highly influential, yet inaccessible paternal figure who could not establish an essential relationship with her, or – which was more likely, since I was a woman – that of a maternal figure who, though compassionate and supportive, was fragile and resigned to assuming the role of guardian angel of death. At a countertransference level, therefore, I felt that I was caught in a series of antitheses that seemed to block the path to a possible transformation. I would have had to embody either the image of an omnipotent savior who, being semi-divine, could not be concerned with earthly sorrows, or that of a humble and good Samaritan who comforts and alleviates suffering, but succumbs to resignation, and gives up the fight. Similarly, I would have had to be either totally active or totally passive, totally present or totally absent. In fact, as I have already pointed out, my patient could not conceive of working on herself with another person; likewise, she was unable to maintain a connection between the moment of meeting and that of separation, indeed at the end of each session she seemed to vanish into thin air, making me wonder if I would ever see her again. It appeared to me that the situation of opposing and irreconcilable roles into which I was being forced as an analyst, reflected G.'s dissociated inner state. My mind struggled to mend the broken links in the chain of her psychic experience, but I did not know if my inner vision would one day acquire a coherence and continuity that she, too, would recognize and find meaningful.

3.2.3.4 My concerns

Not long after the dream about the death sentence, I had serious doubts as to whether it was opportune to start the actual analysis, and suggested to G.

that we extend the exploratory period for another three months. She agreed to this, but not without a certain anxiety; in fact, a few days later I received a phone call from her psychiatrist, who urged me to take a decision, because the uncertainty would be harmful to the patient. I explained the reasons for my wishing to prolong the exploratory period to the psychiatrist, as I had already done to G., and we continued with the investigative work.

I believe my doubts reflected not only the aforementioned countertransference difficulties, but also the far more deep-seated doubt the patient had about herself, which always pushed her to the verge of destabilization. Would she have been able to bear the further psychic suffering linked to the analytic process? I also had to determine how serious the risk of suicide was in this case, and whether I would be able to contain the anxiety engendered by it. The patient not only attacked her own hope – that glimmer of hope that could be glimpsed in the depths of her negation – but also attacked mine, that is my faith in the world and in the possibility to transform reality, which as a human being I had been able to preserve through the trials of life, but whose definitive triumph is never a sure thing. I had to decide whether she would be able to make it, but also whether I would, too. I reflected that, even if the analysis went well, beginning this journey with a patient who was nearly fifty would mean working through and bearing with her the grief caused by all the things she had lost, as well as the remorse for the damage which, due to incapacity or error, she had inflicted on her living parts. I sensed it would be a heavy burden! At best, melancholy would be our traveling companion for at least a few years! So, for me, this analysis was a challenge to the meaning of existence and of illness, which was all the more greater because I intuited my patient's real human qualities: intelligence, generosity, emotional depth and courage, all of which lay buried beneath her desperation.

Reconsidering, many years later, my inner turmoil at that time, I think my hesitation was due not only to the doubt and fear that I was unable to resolve, but also to a therapeutic intuition. Indeed, my proposing to continue investigating G.'s existential situation together, without giving her any certainties but also without abandoning her, constituted an antidote to her attack on relation when she sensed that someone respected, accepted or believed in her. Severing the interhuman tie was her means of actively anticipating the abandonment that she feared and saw as inevitable. So the fact that I, the analyst, bore the burden of a doubt, protected her against the irrepressible impulse to put an end to any uncertainty in life by taking refuge in a negative certainty.

3.2.3.5 The elements that led me to take the risk. My "yes" to analysis

Even though the patient declared that she saw no possibility of changing her destiny, that she had no choice but to settle for a limited life or to commit suicide, and that she did not think it was right to work on deep psychic areas at her age, I felt that she still had a strong desire to establish real human contact, and that it was only the fear of disappointment that led her to suffocate all the seeds of future life within her. As the therapist, I felt terribly alone because G. refused to collaborate, but I was strengthened by the thought that, perhaps, she had once felt like me. I also intuited that G. had not really killed her hope, and that she was asking me to look after it until she could recognize and actively express it herself. The elements that enabled me to trust in a transformative process can be summed up as follows: doubt, contradiction, difference, and challenge.

3.2.3.5.1 DOUBT

I think doubt is a critical capacity of great importance, since it shows that one is able to tolerate the uncertainty implicit in the quest for truth. Where there is doubt, there is also a subjectivity that establishes authentic relationships with others and the world. Clearly, I am not referring to the patient's using suspicion to continually taint the image of herself and of others because, in both cases, doubt was nothing but a negative certainty. Instead, I am referring to the doubt that she had expressed during our first meeting, and had also allowed me to glimpse on the rare occasions when she was able to drop her cynical mask. It was then that she showed herself to be disoriented, distressed, and fragile, yet sincere in seeking help. By saying that she was unable to choose her analyst, for example, she revealed that she was conscious of having to take a crucial step that no one else could take for her, and which encouraged her to run the risk. Therefore, it was not true that G. had finished with her existence; indeed, she had showed me her healthy part which, though still immature in some respects, was able to believe in human solidarity and the possibility of receiving the appropriate nourishment for her growth. The temptation to see her failure as inevitable, in order to eliminate the anxiety of possibility, was blocked by a profound, and still partly unconscious, intuition that she, too, was responsible for creating her life.

3.2.3.5.2 CONTRADICTION

When G. mercilessly self-denigrated or contemptuously devalued her analysis (for example, she would compare the analyst to a prostitute whom one had to pay to be listened to), she would often suddenly point out, as if fearing I would take her too literally: "... *yet there is a contradiction in me. I don't believe I can change my life, but I'm here.*" G.'s thinking was often reductive. Her reasoning seemed to curb every vital thrust and to negate the depth of reality. She had probably adopted the mental attitude of her cousin R.G., whom she once compared to a Martian: "*R. G.'s logic is compelling, he's always brilliant and wins everyone's admiration, but it is as if he possessed a lethal weapon that can dematerialize. When I'm near him I feel reduced to nothing.*" I felt, therefore, that it was very important for G. to recognize that she was the bearer of a contradiction, since she was able to perceive an inner state that obliged her to abandon superficial attitudes and to deal with the problems of existence also by embracing irrational, or emotional, dimensions. I thought that inter-preting the experience of contradiction would enable her to accept what she still could not explain to herself, which could constitute the blueprint for her future psychic richness.

3.2.3.5.3 DIFFERENCE

As I have already mentioned, G. told me in various ways that she saw reality as a series of mechanisms that were completely predictable, because, in her experience, they had always repeated themselves identically and could in no way be modified through personal initiative. She seemed unable to conceive that we constantly apply our theories to the world to give them a meaning, that there is a mind that interprets reality, and that, in its turn, this interpreta-tion can transform reality itself. Likewise, she seemed to be asking for a total relationship with the analyst, in which the difference between self and other, consciousness and unconscious, life and reflections on life, was annulled. The analysis was to make the world of illusions concrete and to allow her to remain in a false order, where she would no longer feel alone because she had obtained the complicity of the analyst, but in such a relationship, any changes would have taken place in an omnipotent and magic way. This "folie à deux" could have been counterweighted by the delusional system's being constantly threatened by the irruption of the experience of her early traumas, namely the catastrophe of abandonment, the disappearance of self or other, isolation, and death fantasies.

With the metaphor of the glove and the hand, G. introduced an image embodying the concept of difference into the analytic field. Although she said that glove and hand were so stuck together they became indistinguisha-ble from one another, the existence of the glove itself alluded to the hand that had to use it. The glove would be a useless object without the hand, and therefore refers to something different from itself, to a living and extremely efficient part of the body. The hand, I reflected, is used to caress, to attack, to work, to explore, and to make art. So the glove could also have symbolized the barrier that separated the patient from reality, preventing her from mak-ing direct contact with things, and from feeling and shaping them. The glove protects the hand but, at the same time, anesthetizes and isolates it. G. told me that she was in a state of total confusion, in which she was captivated by everything that came near:

> I feel like an octopus that tries to grab hundreds of objects at the same time, but at least the octopus has a center that coordinates its tentacles, while I have no center ... it is as if it's not me who grabs the things, but the things that grab me...

But in so doing she revealed her intuition that there were differences between things, as instrumental objects that are used but do not possess initiative, and people, as subjects with their own intentionality, and that she herself had the mental premises to clarify them, and thus obtain her personal creative space. I thought that it might be possible to slowly increase the distance – then still virtual because it was only recognized rationally – between the glove and the hand during the analytic work, to the extent that perhaps one day G. would be able to drop the glove and to touch herself and the things of a world that was now recognizable, but no longer alien and hostile.

3.2.3.5.4 CHALLENGE

G. constantly alluded to her deceit, as if she were trying to warn me that I should not trust her, and the subtext were:

> I'm asking you to do an analysis, but don't believe me, I have no intention of paying the price of change. I've warned you: the golden layer is only the façade behind which I hide the black layer, nastiness is my only truth.

She would often tell me she was like the Russian prince in a fairytale who wore a mask of goodness to be loved by his subjects but who, on his death-bed, realized that he no longer knew who he really was, because the mask could not be detached from his face. (It is curious that the meaning of the mask is overturned in this metaphor, since the impossibility of negating evil, implies the impossibility of negating good.) Her telling me this tale could also have meant: *"Don't fool yourself, it's no go with me. The enigma of my identity, if indeed it ever existed, is now indecipherable."* Yet, as I have already said, I sensed that G.'s real deceit took place at a far deeper level than her masks of complacency and rebellion. Perhaps it was the possibility, and not the impossibility, of her doing analysis that she was concealing, because I sensed in her the existence of a nucleus of genuine and vital potentiali-ties that had remained hidden even from herself. It was the positive aspects of her nature, the presence of good and true elements that scared G. so much and mobilized all her powers of negation, because it is precisely the good and true elements that require us to make a free choice. It was not her shadow, but her light that had been removed. Thus the shadow had ceased to occupy its rightful relative space, which is indispensible to the exercise of its function of relation, and it had become an "Absolute Shadow": *"If I placed my hopes in analysis and it didn't work,"* she once told me, *"then I really would be finished, because I came here as a last resort."* Did I therefore have to find the strength to cultivate trust and hope for her, despite her, and in opposition to her, or at least to her defenses? I honestly believe I had no other choice: if I, too, had been taken in by her superficial deceit, and had not revealed the deeper one, the possibility of G.'s turning her life around would have been denied her. During the analysis I often thought about the theme of *La vida es sueño* (*Life Is a Dream*) by Calderón de la Barca. In the play, the father believes the oracle's prophesy that his unborn son will have violent nature, and prepares a destiny of imprisonment for him, to save both his son and himself. He locks him in a tower, where he is forced to spend his life without any knowledge of the outside world, and the son actually becomes violent to rebel against the injustice he has suffered. Similarly, we may ask ourselves: Is it the parents who determine the illness, perversion and unhappiness of the child, because they want to see it unhappy and ill? Or is it the child who becomes unhappy and ill because this is how it felt it was seen, or wanted to be seen, by its parents? The pathogenic element probably lies within the parental relationship, but perhaps it is the child's task to rectify the errors of the parents – as in the Spanish poet's play, where the son changes his destiny by giving the lie to the prediction through his personal initiative (which proved impossible for Oedipus). Likewise, G. could have shattered the prophesy embodied in the destiny reserved for her by her parents (or, more specifically, the destiny that was delineated within the unconscious understanding with her parents, or at least in that understanding as she saw it) which, in her imagination, foresaw her being condemned to die, as illustrated so clearly in the dream she recounted to me. Only by working on herself would she be able to recover the benevolent gaze of positive parental figures within – that same gaze, albeit with the limits inherent to the fallibility and imperfection of human nature, she had once received from her historical father and mother. Besides, doesn't the prince in *La vida es sueño* redeem his father's injustice by saving himself from prison, wickedness, and vindictiveness?

I sensed that G. was engaged in a struggle to the death with life, with herself and with the analyst, and that she was challenging me to a duel of intelligence and psychic strength – what she was really hiding from me was the fact that she could make it, not that she couldn't. This was the real trap that I had to avoid falling into, because I would have been caught in a constellation of impossibility (which actually happened in various transitional stages of the analysis). It was at this point that I thought it was important that G. had chosen to put herself on the line with a woman. Only by plumbing the depths of her feminine nature would she have been able to recover the qualities of feeling, tenderness, compassion and commitment to life, which were all the more frightening to G. because they were irredeemably close to her fragile parts. It was necessary to wait patiently until her sensitivity and her capacity to experience pain while becoming conscious of many distressing experiences – which were not an expression of weakness, as she thought, but of strength – were complemented by the courage and fighting spirit that were part of her temperament. On the basis of all these considerations, I decided to pick up the "gauntlet" that G. had thrown down and, just before the summer holidays, I assured her that I was willing to accept her as a patient, but gave her the responsibility of taking the final decision. She immediately said "yes" and, after having clarified the various points of the therapeutic contract, we made a date to begin in the autumn.

3.2.4 A summary of the first two years of therapy: the analyst's desperation

What I remember more than anything else about this first phase of the actual analysis are my feelings of desolation brought on by G.'s internal landscape, and the terrible doubts I had about the accuracy of my evaluations, which had led me to hope for a favorable outcome of the therapy. I wondered if, by chance, I had been driven narcissistically to believe in an impossible psychic transformation, perhaps because I had identified with certain aspects of my patient's suffering. In fact, G. continued to interrupt the sessions by talking at length about her desire to die and the possible ways of realizing that desire. She frequently mentioned Exit, a British organization that ensures its members access to euthanasia, also in cases of unbearable psychic suffering.

It was probably the sensation that G. really did run the risk of taking her life, which created an anxiety in me that prevented me from thinking and led me to abandon my analytic role, as if I had wanted to grab her when she was about to leap into the void. On the other hand, it appeared evident to me, and irritated me somewhat, that G. tended to equate analytic therapy with the service provided by an organization that would have granted her a painless death. The first signs of a change in the patient's mental attitude only began to appear toward the end of the second year of therapy. These signs were mostly unpredictable and, accompanied by a sense of apprehension in G., seemed to emerge from a field that was still far removed from Ego-consciousness. For example, she said to me:

> "I'm scared, I don't even want to believe it, but this is already the second or third time I find myself thinking that here it's not the same old story of seeking comfort like I did with my grandmother and with Sofia [the Swiss therapist]. Knock on wood [a superstitious phrase that from then on she would say before telling me that she felt different from usual or experienced wellbeing, joy, trust and hope], it really seems as if I'm discovering something new in me, and hoping there's a connection between what happens in analysis and in my life."

Laconic and infrequent, these expressions were immediately contradicted, like slender rays of light obscured by the darkness of an ever-fiercer doubt, as soon as they appeared. With hindsight, I don't think things could have gone differently in that first period of work. In actual fact, I had not misread the situation, but I had not realized that the patient had a tremendous fear of one day having to acknowledge that her desperation had been understood, or that she fought tooth and nail to preserve the destructive defenses to which she had consigned her strength and her substance. When undergoing therapy, many people often feel that if their suffering (mistaken for a form of weakness and inadequacy) is seen and empathically experienced by another person, it can no longer be annihilated or denied, and thus becomes "real." Here, I shall recount the most important episodes that took place in this period.

3.2.4.1 A mise-en-scène of the initial dream: the analyst as a mother who wants her dead

After returning from a trip to Sicily at the time of the Chernobyl disaster, G. told me that she had realized just how unbearable her solitude was, and had decided to put an end to her life without dignity. The danger of radioactivity, which had made many people fear for their own safety, that of their dear ones, and of future generations, had not alarmed her at all. What did it matter to her if humanity was swept away by a cosmic catastrophe, when she had known nothing but endless suffering? She added that while on vacation she had been assailed by the fantasy of throwing herself into the crater of Etna or remaining submerged in the sea, because she wanted to disappear completely when she died, along with her body, as the image of her rediscovered corpse was so repugnant to her. It seemed to me that G. wanted to wipe out all trace of her passage on earth, and, rather than putting an end to life, she wanted to return to where life had never existed.

At this point I told her that, perhaps as a means of defense but perhaps also to stem her despair, she had probably forgotten that a part of her had turned to analysis not to annihilate herself but to learn to live. This made her unleash her aggression on me, but I thought that anger was a more vital feeling than the pantoclastic destructiveness that swallowed everything. Indeed, it was often by working on anger and hatred that we were able to mitigate her depression.

As P. Gobodo-Madikizela writes in her book on apartheid, *A Human Being Died That Night* (2003), anger and hatred can perform the initial function of enabling victims of violence to emerge from the state of complete impotence, humiliation and passivity that has dehumanized them. G. asked me indignantly why I was so moralistic as to want to give more meaning to life than to death, and demanded what right I had to oblige someone to live, when they had a natural tendency toward death! I replied that, aside from any consideration about the meaning of life and death, at that moment I was simply remaining faithful to her complete person, and thus to that part of her which perhaps was not in agreement with the intentions she had expressed. She left with a grim expression on her face, almost without looking at me, and I was extremely apprehensive until the next session, also because there was the weekend in between, which was always hard for her to get through. Fortunately, she arrived punctually on Monday, then told me that she had remained for hours with the barbiturates beside her thinking that, if she wanted to kill herself, she could not ask anyone for help, and had to do it alone. After her despair had hit rock bottom, however, she had gradually been able to admit to herself that she had been unfair in asking me to side with her destructiveness, and her spirits had lifted. I breathed a sigh of relief.

3.2.4.2 The vase

Once I asked G. what it was that prevented her from perceiving the parts of herself that were good and worth believing in, and she replied: *"I'm scared that if I acknowledge my having something positive, a terrible beast will imme-diately awaken in me and destroy everything."* During another session the subject of abortion re-emerged, accompanied by a feeling of distress on her part, but with new overtones of remorse and regret. So I ventured, perhaps prematurely, an interpretation of the event that was not wholly negative, sug-gesting that perhaps she had acted protectively toward herself and the baby. Of course, this brought out the beast in her. She immediately broke off and there was a sudden emotional shift. She stared at a vase on my desk and said she wanted to throw it on the floor. Then she spent the last ten minutes of the session telling me that she wanted to smash the vase and asking me defiantly: *"What would happen to me if I did?"* Her body was incredibly tense, her hands were near the vase, ready to grab it, and she was only diverted from her intent by the need to make a few comments, such as: *"The only times I've smashed an object out of anger I was certain that nothing would have happened to me. I've never had the courage to actually take my revenge, for example by killing and then killing myself."* I maintained strict silence because I realized that there was no room for interpretation. I could only accept what she was feeling without seeking to defend either myself or her, but also without abandoning her. We were on the brink of an acting out, still only expressed verbally, and I knew there was a tremendous amount at stake. G. was threatening the ana-lytic container and she could have repeated, through a metaphorical act, the abortion, this time of her new, still nascent, way of being. Luckily, the session ended without her breaking the vase. From then on, the object was filled with symbolic meaning for us, to the extent that when she almost knocked it over by accident, she grabbed it in time to prevent it from falling.

3.2.4.3 The silence of the sirens

Before the summer of the second year of analysis G. lent me a book titled *The Silence of the Sirens* by a Spanish friend of hers, which she had already spoken to me about. It is the story of a woman who withdraws to a village in the mountains to live an illusory love affair undisturbed. She writes long love letters to a young man who accepts and reads them, but never replies, main-taining that it is a love story that concerns the woman alone, in which he, as an element of reality, has no part. The writer and main character in the book, a young teacher, realizes that this woman who is her friend and has confided in her, is living in a limbo and in another world, and wants to cure her illness. So she suggests to the young recipient of the letters that he refuse them, in order to oblige her to give up her illusion and re-enter reality; however, the woman is unable to bear the severance of her one lifeline, and dies by aban-doning herself to the deep snow. The story ends with a reference to Kafka, which I shall paraphrase here: Ulysses, who had chained himself to the ship, did not know that if the sirens had possessed consciousness, they would have been destroyed immediately. Evidently the book had a profound effect on me, because I sensed that the patient was saying to me: "Watch out, becoming conscious of my inner reality means dying for me." In fact, this warning put an end to any interpretive possibilities, because it threatened catastrophe.

The problem, which I had still not brought into focus at the time, was, perhaps, how to evolve a modality of consciousness in which it was possible to experience a different form of illusion, which was not a counterweight but a symbolic background to reality. As Jung so aptly puts it, and as mentioned above, it is not enough to develop a representation that encompasses the known and unknown to accede to the symbolic order, it also requires an orientation of consciousness adept at "… throwing a veil over the crude reality" (1912/1956, 2014, p. 226). The task of the therapy was therefore to encourage a symbolic conception of things, a "symbolic consciousness," capable of capturing something that goes beyond the concrete fact, and thus of integrating rational consciousness. Today, I think that at this stage of the analysis G. might not have been able to handle such a critical development, which, in fact, occurred much later.

At the time, the sick part of G. that sought to put me under the spell of the unconscious identity between analyst and patient, had momentarily checked her healthy part that wished to differentiate itself and win its independence. I sensed that the patient was about to launch a violent attack on the masculine world and conscious growth as a whole. Then I tried to explain to her that telling a story about death did not signify dying and, moreover, if the sirens had learnt to sing in a different way, Ulysses would no longer have needed rope to bind himself nor wax to stop the ears of his comrades. But since she had brought me a content that was not hers, i.e., the book by her friend and not her own account of the book, she was able to rejoin: *"The book is by my friend, I am capable neither of recounting nor of dying,"* and stymie my intervention designed to effect a transition from the concrete to the symbolic.

It is one thing to illustrate reality with fantasy and then illuminate it through poetry, and quite another to invent an illusory world as a substitute for reality which isolates us from the latter. But perhaps Giovanna saw my considerations as an attack on the only defense modes that she had set up to survive, and therefore vehemently rejected them. The analyst would have had to have foregone Ulysses' rope, and been transported into her crazy alternative world.

3.2.5 The following years

This later period of analysis was characterized by the fact that the positive times were increasingly longer, consistent and articulate, even though, as the patient herself said, they were "bracketed," that is there was no continuity between them and they did not succeed in linking analysis to life. Expressions like the following were significant. *"If I'm better it is by chance or due to favorable circumstances, and, just as they came, they will go."* G.'s wellbeing seemed fugitive, because it was not consciously accepted. What the patient found difficult to accept was that she herself was the person mainly responsible for her gradual improvement and that it was possible, with the analyst's help, to learn how to implement the process. It seemed that G. categorically excluded the idea of her subjectivity as the protagonist of new creations in the present. The idea of a magic cure still exerted its fascination that could not be abandoned, but this was, of course, accompanied by the sense of impending catastrophe. What had not changed with respect to the first phase of analysis was the cyclical progression of the phenomena, i.e., the alternation of positive and negative periods. Indeed, the more qualitatively intense and closer to the Ego the positive phase, the more devastating the negative phase that would follow. But over time we were able to mitigate the destructive drive by anticipating it verbally and interpreting it time and again. To use the metaphor of a primordial landscape, it was as if, at the beginning, there were only tiny islands in a vast ocean, but little by little the land emerged until it formed a continuous network. There was still the alternation of land and water, but the balance was tipping more and more toward the land. Metaphors aside, it seemed to me that early on a framework had been created that was gradually welding the deepest parts of G.'s psyche (a phenomenon which, from a Jungian standpoint, we may suppose as taking place at the level of the Self), but that it was not until much later that the conscious structure of the Ego was able to build bridges to the inner depths. Besides, as I have already mentioned, Jung does not consider the unconscious a by-product of consciousness, but rather its matrix. Indeed, it is in its dark depths that the light of an originary consciousness appears, an "unconscious consciousness" that is also the Self's consciousness of itself, and which shines before the Ego – whose perceptual sensory activity is directed toward the inner and outer world – can visualize it. But for this process to be completed I think it is indispensable that the analyst attend to all the relational pivotal points between his own Ego/Self axis and the Ego/Self axis of the patient. Only through a continuous "intra-" and "inter-" psychic dialogue can individuals be structured to achieve wholeness. Hence I have selected the significant material of this period according to the importance of its meaning rather than a chronological criterion.

3.2.5.1 Interpretation of the Shadow: a homeopathic dose of poison

Since I had seen how much anger my constructive proposals aroused in G., I thought it appropriate to devote a large part of my interventions to the interpretation of her Shadow, especially make her aware of her responsibilities in the use she made of it. I did not consider it opportune to move in this direction during the exploratory period, fearing that it might be premature before the therapeutic alliance had been firmly established. Predictably, this subsequent choice to proceed with the analysis of the Shadow also triggered very aggressive reactions, but every so often, where the ground was more prepared, it was possible to observe feelings of remorse and real pain. For example, G. once told me in dismay: *"But if it wasn't reality that inflicted this whole tragedy on me, then... I lose all points of reference. Must I accept having squandered, with my own hands, so many things that were possible?"*

3.2.5.1.1 DESTRUCTIVENESS AND POWER

The fundamental aspects of G.'s Shadow seemed to consist in destructive mechanisms that served to damage her relationships, and in the impulse to isolate herself in order to gain power and dominion over others. Foreseeably, a large part of her Shadow was projected onto male figures who, on the one hand, represented a fiercely admired and envied narcissistic ideal of hers, and, on the other, the embodiment of all that she hated and furiously attacked. At times she seemed seized by a frenzied desire to paint the whole world and herself black, repeating ad infinitum: *"No one loves me, no one has ever loved me, and rightly so, because in me there is nothing to love."* When I asked her what she thought to arouse in her interlocutor with such machine gun-like statements, she replied: *"Desperation and impotence, I suppose." "When did you yourself feel desperate and impotent?"* I asked, and she said: *"With my mother, there was nothing I could do to alleviate her suffering."* So G. inflicted on everyone the wound that a mother unable to respond with gratitude and joy to a daughter's attempt to help her, would inevitably have given her. She also seemed to gain satisfaction from flaunting her "black layer," which she passed off for "her truth." For instance, she would tell me that she always identified with the wicked characters in fairytales because she thought the good ones were stupid:

> I think I talk to others so that they will confirm my nastiness, a bit like the evil queen in Snow White who questions the mirror to hear it say that she is bad.[3] Unfortunately, I'm unable to be thoroughly bad, just like Doña Urraca [a Spanish comic character] who is never able to do the evil she plans and, sooner or later, simply appears ridiculous.

(This observation, in particular, led me to understand that we would be able to use humor to depotentiate the Shadow.) One day she said to me, point-blank:

> I have no problem in recognizing myself as evil, but I am unable to feel remorse about this. Do you know that I tried to kill a little boy? He was the son of a happy, creative couple and I was envious, so I gave him an LSD pill. The little boy was very ill but no one suspected me. I couldn't stand that child because he was the expression of a productiveness of which I was incapable: I had just ended my marriage and aborted my son.

"You used LSD not cyanide," I said. And she replied: *"Yes, but if I had had cyanide I would have used it."* After a session in which G. had felt particularly understood and relieved by my interpretations, she brought me the following dream: *"I am in a courtyard surrounded by gray walls with no openings. The ground is covered with excrement and I think, to my horror, that it is probably mine."* Translated into words, the dream was saying: "I prefer to remain in

my abominable isolation instead of recognizing that I could receive help in a real human relationship." The image of the Madonna dressed in black, who needed no one, came back to me.

On the basis of all this information I thought about how I could attack and, at the same time, illuminate the Shadow. I intervened more or less along the following lines:

> The real deception is your arrogant desire for power expressed through the triumph of solitude. Recognizing a need for relationships means accepting the limitation of the human condition, but you want to assume the position of a deity. You believe you will be victorious over others because you accuse them of not coming to your assistance, while at the same time ensuring their defeat by rendering futile their every offer of help. This is also a choice that you refuse to abandon, even though you say you don't know how to choose. Why pursue a strategy of deception? You can play at being gods in make-believe.

I realized that my interventions were harsh and I was sorry to hurt her, but I thought a small dose of poison that was tolerable and given at the right moment could serve as an antidote to the massive doses that were contaminating her life, and, in fact, it did. Enlightening in this respect was her account of the conflictual situation that had arisen with her office boss, whom she felt treated her unfairly. One day he had said to her:

> Why are you always concerned with the advantages I might give others? I'm free to do what I think and to give to whomsoever I wish. The truth is, you feel discriminated against because you're envious and bitter. You can't be counted on.

G. explained that although the rebuke was unpleasant, it didn't plunge her into depression like manifestations of trust and encouragement would have done. I told her:

> That was perhaps because your boss' criticism concerned a limited aspect of your character, whereas when you are appreciated an internal system is set in motion that cuts you down to zero. It is as if an inner voice were whispering to you: "You're nothing, a wretched empty being, anything good you or others think about you is not true." External criticism cannot be that brutal and absolute. So maybe we could use a little criticism to weaken such a cruel system?

Now, it seems to me that the denigrating psychic organization that was so active in her can be likened to the figure of the protector/persecutor of whom Kalsched speaks (1996). G. fully accepted my intervention because she herself had guided me with a "Freudian slip," saying "doctor" instead of "boss" when describing her conflictual situation.

3.2.5.1.2 EXISTING THROUGH THE SHADOW

I did not only use reductive interventions in seeking to interpret G.'s Shadow because, like all Shadows, it had deeply ambivalent aspects. Besides negative elements and others irreconcilable with the orientation assumed by consciousness, which had to be deciphered, and a complex construction to be dismantled, there were also potentially healthy contents to be freed. All this became clear to me mainly through a story recounted by the patient. During the period of analysis, G. had agreed to spend some time in Spain to edit a contemporary history magazine, an assignment that offered her the chance to devote herself to the activity she most wished to pursue: writing. But suddenly she was afraid of failing and of having to tell everyone that she had returned to Spain as a loser instead of a winner. *"I felt like a squid,"* she told me, *"that squirts its ink around it to hide from view."* In this metaphorical image, I found it significant that ink, the substance used to express oneself in writing, was utilized to hide. Language, the precious human system of signs that leads to the light of expression, became a means of hiding in shadow. On the other hand, I reflected, the squid thought it could become invisible by enveloping itself in a black cloud, but in so doing it actually marked its presence. It may have been that G. switched light and shadow, but in that case the shadow would still have had a trace of its opposite. Was it therefore necessary to find the manifestation of self behind the hiding place and the vitality behind the sense of death? Once G. had told me: *"Negation is more a part of me than affirmation. A 'yes' always implies the uncertainty of the results and the danger of failure, but by saying 'no' I'm much stronger because I'm sure of winning."* *"Perhaps you are afraid that if you relinquish your 'no,' you'll have nothing left? Do you think you can only exist through your destructive fury?"* I observed, and she replied: *"Exactly, I'm scared of looking at myself, scared of experiencing the horror of the void."* This brought to mind a consideration of Freud in *The Ego and the Id*: "… we are driven to conclude that the death instincts are by their nature mute and that the clamour of life proceeds for the most part from Eros" (1922, 1962, p. 36). In G., in fact, anger, hatred, and vindictiveness seemed like a cry of protest, and thus could have hidden her passion for life. *"Perhaps you can't forego destruction because an extremely vital energy has remained trapped in it?"* I commented. *"Do you think that if you lose what you call your 'badness,' your 'black layer,' a truly essential part of you will disappear?"* G. smiled at me and murmured: *"I think we've come very close to an important nucleus of truth."* For my patient, the Shadow had become the only means of access to existence, because she had not been able to experience any others.

3.2.5.2 Positive phases

I think it is important here to describe some of the situations in which new and optimistic attitudes toward life and herself prevailed in G. Once she told me that she had experienced great happiness while watching the film *The Sky Above Berlin* by Wim Wenders, because she had felt as if she had met the director, and thus emerged from her solitude. The film expressed an insight with which she could identify, and she thus realized that inter-human communication was possible: parallel ideas could spring up simultaneously in the minds of several people and one's feelings could be confirmed by the understanding of others. The angels in the story renounced their immortality to become flesh and blood, accepting the limitation of human existence, suffering, time with its inevitable deadlines, and love, as long as they could take part in the story of the world.

On another occasion, after a break in the analysis due to an operation I had to have on my leg, she exclaimed as she watched me move around: *"How well you're walking; it's a real transformation!"* This made me think that a space able to accommodate "her" own transformation had now opened up in her.

During a later session, while she was telling me about a trip to India, she said that she had been able to go with the flow of reality without undergoing the "glass" experience, as she put it. By this she meant that she had no longer had the usual feeling of seeing everything through a veil, as if she were a mere spectator. She had been able to experience the "sensuality" of imagination, an activity that, as she herself said, differed from daydreaming because it did not separate you from the world: *"It was as if the things 'out there' belonged to the same order as my inner reality that made itself visible."*

At various times, she told me that she had enjoyed the company of dear friends. She had felt herself brimming over with intimate, warm feelings that, though simple, were truly hers. As she looked back on her life, pleasant memories also emerged. For example, she recalled her mother as not only weighed down by affliction, but also as a woman who, when G. returned from her aunt and uncle's village, came into her room every morning, singing and throwing open the windows to wake her up, happy to have the daughter she had wanted, and loved so much, with her again.

Lastly, she told me that on one occasion she had again been seized by her pessimistic "machinations": *"I am not loved, my office boss persecutes me, I'm only capable of watching TV, and so on,"* but then she said that, at the same time, she was surprised to hear another inner voice replying to her, as if a debate were being conducted within:

> [The words] were like sparks that flew out of my reasoning and responded: "But you can also decide who you want to love; the disaccord with your boss is something circumscribed and cannot threaten your whole life; there are other ways of watching TV besides gorging yourself on images!"

This brought to mind Jung's essay on the unconscious as a multiple consciousness, in which he holds that consciousness can manifest as countless little luminosities, or sparks, even in the depths of the unconscious, before actually constituting the consciousness that the Ego has of itself.

3.2.5.3 The dream about hooligans, or the mitigation of the Super-Ego

While on vacation in Spain, G. was seized by a nostalgia for analysis and made an appointment with a Jungian analyst who had given a lecture. This provoked feelings of betrayal in her: *"I felt responsible for interrupting the analysis,"* she confessed, *"it was as if I had wanted to prove to myself that you were not indispensable to me and I could always replace you with another analyst."* Shortly after this episode, she had the following dream which, according to her, took place in a different register from the usual ones:

> I'm in an unfamiliar apartment. I climb the stairs to my bedroom because I'm really tired. As soon as I get into bed, I remember that my dog is shut in the basement and I think he will die if I don't go and feed him right away. However, I don't have the strength to get up and I fall asleep with a vague feeling of guilt. Suddenly I hear a knock on the door, I think I'm dreaming, but then the door opens wide and I realize it's for real [of course, this was happening in her dream]. Some young men come in, who have been to get my dog, fed him, and brought him to me. He's a beautiful cinnamon colored dog who's so happy to see me again. I'm also very touched that he was saved. In the meantime I begin to suspect that the youths may be hooligans because they plant themselves in my room with an aggressive attitude. They sit on my table with their arms folded and a cigarette in their mouth, and look at me reprovingly, as if to say: "If it wasn't for us your dog would be dead."

I thought that the hooligans embodied, on the one hand, Giovanna's self-criticism for having neglected her affective world, and, on the other, the healthy energies of her deep psyche, because they restored to her a vitality and goodness that was denied, or at least ignored, by her conscious Ego. In fact, the dog is well and, instead of retaliating, shows that it is happy to see her and forgives her. G.'s Super-Ego has been mitigated because, although judging the Ego strictly, it does not make it pay with self-destruction, but pushes it toward a reparatory attitude. This time the patient did not see herself as having some kind of natural defect or indulging in unacceptable behavior, but simply reproached herself for a lapse that she could have avoided without any great effort. The appearance of a tolerable guilt feeling, configured as the awareness of a mistake, seemed to be the most meaningful sign that G. was now ready to adopt a responsible and free approach to life.

3.2.6 Two dreams that marked a turning point

Toward the end of 1990 there were two dreams that revealed a radical change in the patient's inner orientation. In the first dream G. went to visit Maria Zambrano, and she and a male friend were walking around her house, following a quadrilateral path. At a certain point she stopped in dismay, and said to her companion: *"She doesn't know we're coming, perhaps it would be better to stay where we are and wait till she dies."* Maria Zambrano was a prominent figure in Spanish culture and a good friend to G., and, in my opinion, represented the propulsive center of the patient's transformative process. In fact, although the Ego was still desperately employing its defenses to sabotage the encounter with this center and to oppose change, there was already a deep inner movement, a circling around the crux of the problem. I did not think it accidental that G. had used as a defense precisely the symbols of circular movement and the square, which are at the root of life and orientation in the space-time order. After this dream, the patient did actually pay several visits to Maria Zambrano, then old and ill, thus giving her friend the opportunity to chide her kindly: "Why didn't you come to see me anymore? I waited for you so long." G. was able to mend the relationship she had broken off some time earlier by disappearing and not getting in touch, like she did with all the people who meant something to her in her life. A few months after this dream, Maria Zambrano died, and I felt relieved that G. had gone to see her in time to return her friendship, fulfilling a debt of love and relieving herself of the additional burden of grief that, otherwise, would have been difficult to work through.

I think that in this dream the patient was also making a request to her analyst: "Stay close to me for a while, accompany me like a good friend, and don't talk about the end of analysis, because I'm still unable to bear separation." The subject of our possibly concluding the analysis had already come up between us, in fact, and G.'s meeting with the aged Maria Zambrano also meant that she was willing to experience firsthand the pain of a more or less imminent loss.

The patient remembered the second dream at a session in which she expressed a doubt as to whether she should stay in Italy or move back to Spain. I stressed that the one important thing was that she made the choice herself, and both of us undoubtedly felt that going back to Spain at that time would be a return to her roots, but within the context of a new self-awareness. We also mentioned the light that could be generated by her genuinely seeking the meaning of her existence. She suddenly made a connection:

Speaking of light, I remember a dream I had a few nights ago. The evening before I had read about the tribal feuds in South Africa in the *Venerdì di Repubblica* magazine. There was the photo of a negro's charred body, and I thought to myself that life was full of the most unspeakable atrocities. How could a black mother bring a black baby into the world amidst such tragedy? Perhaps I did well to refuse to have a child and to place it in such a tragic world. In the dream I went into a cave and found a new born baby who was all black and dressed in rags. It looked dirty and I thought: "This is the child I did not have." I picked it up and set off for home. Then the little boy was white, he was about six or seven, and was walking by my side. As soon as we got home I said to him: "You see?

What sense was there in bringing you home with me? All I can offer you is this small living room and this TV." The boy looked at me in silence and smiled at me with a certain mocking air.

It emerged from the dream associations that six or seven years earlier G. had arrived in Rome and begun analysis. *"It was the most desperate moment in my life,"* she told me. *"I went into analysis to pass the time, until I could find the strength to kill myself. For me everything was lost. I remember a Rome that was always dark, always rain-soaked."* "It was the darkness of your imprisoned consciousness," I thought, "the wetness of so many tears that had never been shed." In this dream, like the one about Maria Zambrano, G.'s Ego was still resisting the unrelenting movement that was pushing her toward the encounter with herself. But her resistance seemed to be gradually weakening, to the extent that she was able to foresee it ending, as was evident from her use of the conditional in speaking to the boy: *"What would have been the point of bringing you with me?"* Meanwhile, the image of the boy was there, together with her, and could hardly be denied, since it embodied a profound and authentic part of her being that she could no longer cancel.

As G. continued to reflect on the image of the boy, she remembered that when she was about six or seven she received her first communion and everyone fussed over her, including her mother, who was crying, as usual. However, it was the first time in her life that she thought she had experienced, quite clearly, the sensation of being false, which caused her considerable anxiety. She was dressed in white but she felt black inside; she had confessed but it seemed to her that she had not told the truth. This experience was perhaps mainly triggered by something that had happened earlier in the day: her grandmother had sent her to the nuns to be admired in her beautiful dress, and had secured her rosary beads around her wrist so that she wouldn't lose them. The nuns praised G. for the clever little idea, and she accepted the compliments without admitting that it was not hers. She told me:

> I was left with the impression that not only was I deceiving people, but also that I would only be able to receive appreciation for things that weren't mine. The same thing happened to me as an adult when people congratulated me on an article I had signed for a friend who was not able to put his name to something publicly because of his political position, and had asked me to do him the favor. I could not contradict the official explanation, but I felt as if I was hounded by a curse that repeated itself.

In the light of these revelations, I thought that the boy in the dream not only represented G.'s inner world transformed by the analytic interaction, but could also offer us practical indications to overcome her painful experience of inauthenticity and the conviction that she could only live and be accepted by offering a deceptive image of herself.

I am transcribing below some excerpts from the sessions devoted to dream interpretation. My thoughts, when not explained verbally, appear in brackets.

A: What do you think is behind the boy's smile? What could he be saying?
G: I think he would tell me:

> I don't believe you. You say that you have nothing to offer me except this small living room and this television just to avoid your responsibilities, but I know it's not true. Besides, you don't consider the fact that, in any event, I'm much better off here than in the cave!

A: Could the image of the boy could be a synthesis of the image of the dog and that of the hooligans from your other dream?
G: I was thinking exactly the same thing, but I don't quite know why.
A: On the one hand the boy, like the dog, is a bearer of affection that is given without asking anything in return, and without even asking himself if it is deserved; on the other, like the hooligans, he embodies a consciousness that observes and also judges you.
G: Yes, but the boy does not judge me disparagingly and ironically like the hooligans. True, there is a certain reproach and mockery in his gaze, as if he were saying: "I have seen you now, and you can no longer deceive me." At the same time, his smile is not sarcastic but sweet, bright and serene. He has a calm, confident look, which is almost disturbing. I think: "And what am I going to do about this boy now?"
A: (So, neither affection without vision, nor the critical and reductive vision of the intellect separated from love, could help my patient. The boy loves her at first sight, thus placing her in relation to her positive and negative aspects, i.e. her entire personality, worthy of being accepted in its indivisible oneness. I remember a dream that G. had many years previously, in which she was holding a strange newborn: a miniature adult who spoke. Perhaps it represented a form of thought that derided her new possibilities of life. The boy in the current dream does not speak, he does not allow himself to be trapped in dialectic, probably because he is the bearer of a very profound message that alludes to the integrity of the person that he wishes to make whole again.)

By exposing your deception, does the boy make you real?
  G. In what sense?

A: A lie can persist only as long someone believes it; once it has been exposed it turns to dust. If anything, the liar remains, and therefore the question of why you felt obliged to lie, but this is already a search for truth. Behind the deception there is not the emptiness you feared, but a real person, although she has made mistakes. Then again, only real people can make them.
G: Sometimes it's easier to attribute to ourselves all the worst things that are not ours, rather than admit the errors, albeit contained, which are truly ours.

A: (Finally, G. can take responsibility without it crushing her, she can see her Shadow without being invaded by it.)

Now you can accept yourself lovingly, even while alive?

G: What do you mean by that?
A: Only the dead are perfect.

G. smiles knowingly and nods. After reflecting for a moment, she continues:

G: The boy seems to me the exact opposite of the characters on TV that I see, while I cannot be seen.
A: (Right, the boy looks at her, joins her, without being put off by appearances; he sees her, but remains present. He does not disappear and does not abandon her). Does the boy's gaze illumine you and make it possible for you to look at yourself, too? Like the "sparks that flew out" of your reasoning, does the boy resemble that "other voice" that destroyed the pessimistic argumentation of reason by emphasizing your positive aspects instead?
G: But the boy is also little, dirty and covered with rags.
A: Yes, but he reveals your values to you; in fact, he discovers that you deceive because you want others to believe that you have nothing, rather than something, to give. Your generosity is the treasure you have been hiding, not your emptiness.

G. cries, overcome by emotion, and recites a Spanish poem that has come back to her. The poem mentions empty hands that have given everything but can still give themselves:

> *Te doi mis manos.*
> *Vacias de tanto que dar.*
> *Vacias de tanto que dar.*
> *Sin tener,*
> *Sin tener,*
> *Pero son las manos mias .*

> G: I give you my hands
> Empty because they have given so much
> Without possessing anything
> But they are my hands

Finally her hands were bare, they had cast off the gloves, and could now touch reality. The schema of the false Self, or perhaps we should say the false Ego, had been abandoned. It was no longer necessary to G., because she could bear to appear vulnerable, to trust in the empathy of others, to allow herself to be seen as she really was without losing faith in being loved. If she reproached herself for something, it was because she knew that she could forgive herself; but she was also aware of her capacity to love.

In the end, the curse of an impossible meeting had been broken. In the analytic space, G. underwent the experience of being able to recognize herself and, at the same time, of being recognized. There was no longer an isolated subjectivity on the one hand, and a world that excluded and condemned her on the other. Her Ego was able to humanize reality by transforming it with the gaze of consciousness, and reality was able to come to G. as a welcoming space that made her real.

It was then that G. told me she intended to take a year's leave from work in order to organize her future return to Spain. This time it was not an escape but a project pursued in harmony with the overall meaning of her life. At the same time, we decided to conclude our analytic path by meeting a few more times before her definitive departure for Spain. G. was sure the year would mark a turning point: *"Next year will be very important because 1991 is a* capicua [palindromic] *number, i.e., a number that is the same when read backwards."*

I was struck by the exceptional coincidence, since this combination occurs only once every hundred years, and also by the fact that, as I have often seen, the themes discussed at the beginning of the analysis reappeared toward the end, almost as if the beginning and end of a process each contained each other. This therapy also confirmed that psychic transformation truly demands the synchronic involvement of both components of the analytic couple. In the image evoked by G., the black of the squid was a shadow that hid and at the same time revealed, and thus represented both the patient's use of the Shadow to disappear and the state of confusion between analyst and patient that the former must recognize and abandon, if he hopes that the patient will be able to do the same.

The squid ink may have been the very ingredient that permitted me to recount the journey of this analysis, and G. to express her new parts of herself and come into the light. It took almost seven years of work to rebuild the broken structure of G.'s real Self and to enable her to reconnect her life experiences. The most profound parts of G. were oriented in a new direction, and no longer turned toward death, but life. G.'s future commitment would consist in attaching these parts ever-more firmly and coherently to the structure of the Ego. But soon she would have to do battle in the front line, and consciously assume the task of taking care of herself.

I caught myself thinking: "And now, what are we going to do about this little boy?"

3.3 Luca's case: indirect treatment. Sadness as liberation from a fatal antimony

Here I shall recount some salient episodes in the story of a boy of thirteen, whom I shall call Luca. I do not know him personally, but his mother, who was in therapy with me for several years, spoke to me of him in detail. Indeed, for a long time Luca was practically the only subject of conversation between myself and the patient, because his problems were so deeply enmeshed with her own that she saw therapy solely as a means of alleviating her son's suffering. During her childhood and adolescence, the mother had always felt discriminated against with respect to her brother, whom their parents allowed considerable freedom of movement and choice, whereas she, as a female, had to do exactly as they wished. She remembered, for example, that her brother could go out with his friends and acquaintances without telling their parents who they were, and could come home late at night; while the people she saw were vetted and she had to be back by a certain hour. During the years of her marriage she passively complied with her husband's every wish, just as she had submissively obeyed her father's orders, thus adopting a behavioral scheme that made her slave to the male world.

She confessed to me that she was disappointed when she gave birth to a boy. She would have liked a girl, perhaps to free her own femininity from the limits that had been imposed on her, and to redeem herself from the humiliations she had suffered. She told me that she was afraid Luca knew how she felt, because when he was little he had said to her: *"Mommy, you didn't want me, you wanted a baby girl, didn't you?"* When her son entered adolescence he was very difficult to manage, also because her husband's work took him away from home for long periods, and the boy would only obey his father. Luca was prey to sudden destructive attacks and acts of violent rebellion against his mother and his daily obligations. For example, he refused to study and sometimes even to go to school; he spent hours at his play station, and if she tried to turn it off or take it away, he would lose his temper, throwing everything he could lay his hands on onto the floor or dirtying the house. Sometimes, he stood in front of an open window and threatened to jump, worrying his mother sick, or hurled things off the balcony. When she came home one day, she found all the books from the bookcase on the floor and the shelves covered with toilet paper! She told me how she had tried to reason with her son: *"Why do you behave like this with me, and obey your Dad?"* to which Luca had replied that he was scared of how his father would react if he did not do as he asked, but he was not frightened of her because she was "weaker." In response to the questions she fired at him when she went into a panic, he once said: *"You see, Mom, there's a bad part and a good part in me."* Taking this as an opportunity, she proposed a way out: *"OK, let's give this bad part a name, that way we can talk about it and try to get rid of it or, better still, make it go away!"* to which her son replied: *"Mom, you didn't understand, I'm a combination of both, it's just that my good part wants to die, and my bad part feels strong."* I think this clearly reveals how, in this case and also in other situations, destructiveness can be a desperate cry for help to emerge from existential despair that one neither wants to, nor can, accept. The gift of understanding from another was also categorically refused by Luca, because it was associated with fragility: better to be bad and strong, than weak and comforted. From this I deduced that Luca's destructiveness was a kind of energy he drew on for support, to avoid succumbing to despair and anxiety. I worked intensely with his mother at the transference and countertransference level, in order to construct with her a model of authoritativeness that did not imply imposition, command, orders to be given and punitive reactions. One had to understand her boy's desperation and show him a new kind of "strength," which neither opposed vulnerability nor eradicated feeling; a strength capable of empathy and compassion, which we could call "capacity of soul." Ultimately, it was a question of reconstructing the truly feminine strength that she had not been able to draw on, which would have enabled her young son to have discovered it through her, not as something that was not his, but rather as a means of complementing his male gender. In fact, we may say with Jung that "male" and "female" are poles of the psyche and, as such, pertain both to man and to woman. Perhaps this was the path that would have led us to integrate the "good/bad" poles and to transform destructiveness into something constructive?

I would like to conclude this brief account with a poem by Luca that his mother told me about, since it shows he was developing a new inner constellation that possibly would have allowed him to emerge from the perverse impasse in which he was trapped. On the one hand, there was deep depression, in which obedience was identified with passivity, and led him to quash his desire to live; on the other, anger, acts of aggression and the feeling of conquering everything and everybody, precisely by opposing all indications from his mother and her attempt to guide him. I think it was actually Luca's mother who was able to offer him the image of an existence with room for hope, because through her own therapy she had constructed a new possibility of mirroring her son's inner space.

The poem is significant because it also reveals a tragic, yet extremely mature, form of spirituality in a boy in his early teens. Here it is:

Il fuoco del destino infernale

E' piacevole provare il caldo infernale della tristezza.
E' un fuoco da cui, almeno una volta nella vita, bisogna farsi bruciare.
Cielo grigio,
neon blu,
foglie marroni.
Sono bei momenti, noi non soffriamo, noi godiamo.
Fatevi bruciare dall'inferno per capire se è quello il vostro destino.

The Fire of Infernal Destiny

It is good to feel the hellish heat of sadness.
A fire you should be burned by, at least once in your life.
Grey sky,
Blue neon,
Brown leaves.
These are beautiful moments, we do not suffer, we enjoy.
Be burned by hell to see if that is your destiny.

These lines seem to represent the process of overcoming a state of utter desperation and loss of the future; a state that induced a death wish in Luca when he was in what he described as a "state of goodness," which was none other than a feeling of extreme fragility, instability and nullification. But also of overcoming anger and destructiveness, which made him feel strong and that he had conquered others and his depression, and which he called "his badness." In fact, the poem does not speak of depression but sadness, which reactivates feeling, whereas depression seeks to annihilate it.

As Eugenio Borgna writes (Borgna 1994), a distinction should be made between depression as a state of mind and depression as a thematic category in psychiatry that embraces reactive depression, provoked by a traumatic situation, and endogenic or psychotic depression, which is apparently without cause. Deep and overwhelming, the latter is accompanied by the radical compromising of vital functions (*corporeal* functions as a whole) and an irresistible fascination with the death wish (p. 36). On the other hand, depression as a state of mind, as *Stimmung*, may be called the "emotion of sadness." This sadness can also derive from profound contact with our being and with the world, and from our capacity to feel and to empathize with every living being, precisely because all of reality is subject to becoming, to the passing of the seasons, to comparison with the splendor and joy it conveys but also with its finitude, with suffering, and death. As Borgna states: "… sadness is painful but it is *also* a means of understanding the suffering that exists in the world: visible and invisible, latent and evident …" (ivi, p. 31). He continues:

> When I detach myself from the frenetic, uninterrupted flow of things (events), and return in the manner of Augustine to my inner self, I cannot but sense, in *certain* situations, the precariousness and finitude of reality; the ephemeral fragrance of certain things sought and desired, which have become evanescent and elusive.
>
> (ivi, pp. 32–33)

Memorable are Freud's considerations on sadness as mood and on its almost impalpable fragility, as well as his thoughts on its previously unconsidered possibility of instilling courage. He expresses these in a text in which he describes a walk he took with a young, already well-known, poet friend through a flourishing summer landscape. The poet admired the beauty of nature around them, but did not enjoy it. He was bothered by the thought that it was destined to die when winter came, in the same way that all human beauty perishes. Freud comments:

> Everything he would otherwise have loved and admired seemed to him devalued by the transience for which it was fated. … We know that from such sinking into the decay of all that is beautiful and perfect, two different mental impulses can emanate. One leads to the painful world-weariness of the young poet, the other to rebellion against the fact being asserted.

No, it is impossible that all these glories of nature and of art, of our sensory world and of the world outside, should really melt into nothing. It would be too senseless, and too foolish to believe in it. They must be able to continue in some way, removed from all destructive influences.

(Freud, 1916)

Sadness also seems to be the feeling that enabled Luca to emerge from a fatal antinomy: on the one hand, an urge to destroy his life when he felt too fragile to tackle tasks that he could only have partially fulfilled and thus would have been subject to judgment, since everything we are able to realize is always imperfect and ephemeral; on the other, an equally irrepressible impulse to be "strong" through anger and destructiveness, which produced a more certain and definitive result than the necessarily nuanced work of creating. Sadness, linked to the feeling of transience, was a source of poetry for Luca, because things that have a value, as Freud states, cannot "melt into nothing"; they are not marked simply by chronological time, but belong to the dimension of quality and intensity that cannot be measured in hours, minutes and seconds. In fact, it was precisely through sadness that Luca experienced the feeling of *Dasein*, and being in the "here" and "now," which is painfully fleeting but at the same time goes beyond the flow of becoming and opens up to the infinite. Returning to the thought of Raimon Panikkar, eternity is neither a reality that begins after death nor a time that lasts forever, but the non-measurable and therefore not strictly "temporal" root of time. This is well-expressed by the word "tempiternity," the true foundation of our existential experience. From this point of view, an intensely experienced present can correspond to a feeling of eternity experienced in the temporal dimension of life. Spirituality cannot be separated from history, of course, but it helps us to distinguish between "things" as they happen and the "sense" of things, which always has a spiritual valency.

In *The Confusions of the Young Törless* the author Robert Musil profoundly intuits the devastating effect that stifling sadness caused by the absence of dear ones can have on an adolescent's soul. When the Törlesses leave their son alone at boarding school, he is tormented by an acute longing: "He saw everything as if through a veil, and even during the day often found it hard to choke back a persistent sob ..." The boy only drew comfort from thinking that in the evening he would write his daily letter to his parents, because then

it was as if he had, hidden on an invisible chain, a golden key with which, when no one was looking, he would open the gate to wonderful gardens. ... When his "homesickness" grew less acute and gradually faded away, this aspect of it became fairly clear. Its disappearance did not bring a long-awaited feeling of contentment, but left a void inside young Törless. And it was this emptiness inside himself that made him realize that it had not been simple longing that he had lost, but something positive, a psychological force, something that, under pretext of pain, had blossomed inside him.

(Musil 1906, 2014, pp. 6, 7)

To conclude, I think that Luca's sad mood offered him the chance to have a real creative experience which, by indicating a new horizon, freed him from the pre-established modes of behavior in which he was trapped, and consequently from the sense of being persecuted by an implacable destiny. Luca's verse does not, in fact, appear to refer to a destiny imposed on us by alien powers and to which we are forced to submit, but to destiny as "destination," i.e., the goal and fulfillment of our life. Furthermore, as he expressed so well in speaking of goodness and badness, and especially their synthesis as the essence of his being, the goodness of feeling – even when it is feeling steeped in sadness because it signifies being aware of all the sufferings of the world – can be combined with strength (which is no longer badness). This enables us to understand emotions and share them with our fellow individuals, and to feel involved in and able to change human destiny.

As Giacomo Leopardi reflects in his *Zibaldone*: "If there is any true poet today, if ever he feels true poetic inspiration, and he composes poetry in solitude, or writes on any subject, the source of that inspiration, whatever it may be, will certainly be melancholic..." (Leopardi, cit. Borgna, p. 35).

3.4 The wolf man. The impossible choice between symbiosis and isolation

At the beginning of a course of therapy with me, a male patient had a dream in which he was with some men impeccably dressed in a suit and tie, but when he looked at them more closely, he noticed they were wolves. As he was scrambling up a small hill to escape them, he realized that the men/wolves were in pursuit and that he only had three objects which, in his opinion, were absolutely useless for fighting them off: a cup, a pen and a torch. At that moment, he woke up in a state of anguish. This person's relational style was marked by extremely defensive, and at times aggressive, characteristics, because during the primary experience with his mother he had felt that he risked losing his identity, and his male identity in particular. Hence the Other, and especially the "female Other," the woman, were suddenly experienced as enemies and darkened by suspicion, since they would have sought to engulf him in their world of demands or imposed on him an alien will that would have forced him to exist solely in relation to their expectations. This man oscillated between two situations that caused him equal anxiety: one in which he restricted interhuman relationship and always kept a place where he could isolate himself and seek refuge, which made him feel that his inner contents were dispersed, and that *"his identity had drained away, like water without a container."* And the other, in which he maintained a symbiotic relationship but sacrificed his individual differentiation, which made him furious and forced him to attack the relationship itself because it was an unsuitable container for his identity. This destructive swinging back and forth naturally had its effect on the therapeutic situation:

I have the feeling that you will betray me as well. I have always relied on someone whom I then felt was empty, absent, or against whom I had to defend myself. ... I am afraid of pouring myself out, of being liquid. In this deconstruction of my identity you should be my container to collect the liquid and then give it back to me, but I have never trusted anyone completely, and I do not want to need you, analysis, or this merciless exposure of myself. Then again, who knows ... perhaps where I see emptiness there is a fullness that is not threatening and the malice of absence is more presumed than real.

For my part, I had never forgotten that first dream of his, or my previously unvoiced consideration that, contrary to what he thought, the cup, pen and torch that he was holding were actually the only effective tools for engaging with the wolf-men. In fact, it was not a question of defeating them, but of changing them into complete human beings.

The patient had told me that he was experiencing a time of considerable hardship because he had committed some administrative errors – due to distraction, laziness, unconscious rejection, but mainly a form of systematic rebellion that always ended up harming him – and now he had to pay out a considerable amount of money. From this he had deduced that his inner orientation was evidently at odds with his goals; indeed, instead of moving toward stability he had been thoroughly destabilized, not only financially but also psychologically. I told him that it was probably not his identity that was dissolving, but a form of identification to which he could no longer relate, and that to find himself he should perhaps broaden his sense of relation. For him, the Other was still a mortal enemy, an alien, the outsider who must be defeated in order to avoid defeat; in other words, he was the "wolf-man." And the patient had never been able to constitute himself as an interlocutor with whom it would be possible to establish the inexhaustible dialogue that weaves the story of our existence. His relations were conducted solely on the basis of the diversity between I and You, who were engaged in unrelenting combat and had never constituted themselves on the identity of *We*, on the Other's profound appurtenance to our own world. As Panikkar writes, being happy means finding the source of our joy precisely in the *You* who is not the "Other" revealed by the intellect, but the You of love (2004, 2005, p. 111). The cup in the patient's dream, which he himself had offered as a gift to the analyst, could have represented the container for a relation based on We, while the pen and torch could have alluded to the words exchanged between ourselves and the Other in dialogue, illuminating the encounter. Here I was not thinking about words governed by reason that defines, explains, and excludes, and not even of words as an interpretative moment in the analytic process. Instead, I saw them as a creative expression of our whole reality, I was thinking of the word "revelation," in the sense that Panikkar uses it, or the word "symbol," which enables us to go beyond the narrow confines of our Ego; indeed, the *Others* whom we carry inside will also speak in us, and the You, whom we address, will offer a significant destination for our words. Without interlocutors we could not converse, or even exist, because relation *is* our reality.

According to Panikkar, the phrase famously attributed to Aristotle, "man is a rational animal," would be better translated as "man is the animal through which logos – language – passes" (1981a, p. 57).[4] Ultimately, we may suppose that our identity is constituted precisely in the borderland where the intra-subjective dialogue between the diverse elements of the personality and the inter-subjective dialogue between I and the Other than I take place. Thus, identity will never be a monolithic whole into which the diverse parts in dialogue are assimilated and their distinction lost, but will consist in an interweaving of relations. Apropos of this, Emmanuel Levinas writes poetically:

> The relation between men is certainly the non-synthesizable par excellence. We may also wonder if the idea of God, especially such as Descartes thinks it, can be made part of a totality of being, or if it is not, much rather, transcendent to being. The term 'transcendence' signifies precisely the fact that one cannot think God and being together. Similarly, the interpersonal relationship ... is not a matter of thinking the I and the other together, but to be facing in inter-personal relation. The true union or true togetherness is not a togetherness of synthesis, but a togetherness of face to face.
>
> (1982, pp. 71–72)

And Martin Buber points out that the true dialogue with another human being begins when the other becomes a "You" and ceases to be simply an "It," or rather a mere individual, an "object of my knowledge." Only then does the dialogue become inter-personal and intersubjective:

> If I face a human being as my *Thou*, and say the primary word *I-Thou* to him, he is not a thing among things, and does not consist of things. Thus human being is not He or She, bounded from every other He and She, a specific point in space and time within the net of the world; nor is he a nature able to be experienced and described, a loose bundle of named qualities. But with no neighbour, and whole in himself, he is *Thou* and fills the heavens. This does not mean that nothing exists except himself. But all else lives in his light. [...] All real living is meeting.
>
> (Buber, 1937, pp. 8, 11)

When I conveyed the above thoughts to my patient, he was very touched and his anxiety melted away.

3.5 Giorgio's case: the difficult conquest of freedom[5]

This young man, whom I shall call Giorgio, came to me for therapy because he was suffering from strong panic attacks. He was seized with anguish when he found himself in cramped, crowded and unfamiliar places, but also in wide open spaces. He was terrified if he had to travel along a busy flyover or if he had to take a plane. The panic attacks had begun when he had decided to leave a religious organization set up by a priest who had always been a presence in his life and that of his parents, offering advice, guidance and care, since he also saw himself as a psychotherapist. With the passing of time, Giorgio felt that the organization had become increasingly fundamentalist and dogmatic, and he had found the courage to leave and to follow his own independent path. He had first experienced panic attacks just before his school leaving exam, and they had disappeared when he entrusted himself to the priest and followed his guidance. The path of life already laid out by the priest calmed the anxiety experienced by Giorgio when faced with choice and freedom, which obviously imply the possibility of error and failure. One of the first dreams he described to me had occurred several years earlier, precisely when he joined the religious organization. This is the dream:

> There is an enormous pyramid with some slaves whose hands are chained together and who are dragging stones. I am one of the slaves, but by repeatedly wrenching my wrists apart I am able to break free from the chains. At that moment, I see myself with a different face that I do not recognize. Then everything around me goes black. The red desert stretching out before me also becomes black. I am seized by a terrible fear, and I bind my hands together again. Giorgio commented: "Today I am stronger. I broke the chains and everything turned black, but will I come out of this alive? The one thing I know is that I must not seek another yoke."

In the early stages of analysis, Giorgio recounted the following dream, which still reveals anxiety in the face of freedom:

> I am in my house in Rome, where I live, and I am alone with my maid. We have been told that there is a wolf in the building and we barricade ourselves in the apartment. There is an atmosphere of terror because we know that the wolf is fierce. At a certain point I decide to tackle it, I take a pair of kitchen scissors, and go toward it. I notice that the wolf actually has a docile look and doesn't seem to want to attack me, but I am scared and I slit its stomach with the scissors. Blood comes out of its belly, along with a seafood salad with shrimp and carrots.

The morning after he had this dream Giorgio saw an image of a wolf – identical to the one in his dream – accompanied by the caption: "Say no to culling wolves," on Facebook. I was astounded by this extraordinary instance of synchronicity. Giorgio cited the well-known story of the wolf of Gubbio:

Only St Francis could approach the wolf and talk to it, because he wasn't afraid of the animal. That is why it ceased to be a wild beast that killed livestock and children, and became the protector of the city.

Giorgio added that that perhaps the wolf represented the attitude that had led him toward freedom, and in the dream he killed it because there was a part of himself that was terrified by freedom and did not want it.

It reminds me of the Israelites who complained to Moses when he freed them from enslavement to the Egyptians: "Why didn't God let us die in comfort in Egypt, where we had lamb stew and all the bread we could eat? You've brought us out into this wilderness to starve us to death..." So I kill the wolf and find myself with the food I eat at home, which my maid often prepares!

I commented that the food coming out of the wolf's belly might also represent the particular generosity that comes with opening up to freedom, and that it was affective nourishment, which reconnects us to our story, that had emerged, rather than loneliness, fear, the loss of all existential points of reference, or a challenge to society, the guiding figure and the past. With hindsight, I saw the shrimp and carrots as symbols of a primitive psychic fabric: carrots are roots embedded deep in the earth and, as Jung observes in the *Basel Conferences*, shrimp are archaic creatures, devoid of a cerebral-spinal nervous system and possessing solely a vegetative nervous system, making them the authentic expression of instinctiveness that draws on phylogenetic experience. Hence, true freedom is not something that takes us into a rarefied dimension where consciousness is separate from the body, but an experience that reconnects us with our roots, instincts, and family story, as well as with human and pre-human history. This leads me to conclude that freedom cannot be won solely through the egoic dimension, because we would be too isolated, and it would end up being confused with will. This would result in the aspiration to an heroic role, far from, and above others, without our being able to recognize the fabric of our common humanity. We can only be free by realizing the Self, because it enables us to reacquire a sense of the past and of solidarity with all of humanity that is around us, that has preceded, or will follow us. Only then can we stay at home and eat our regular fare without feeling imprisoned; only then can we follow a guide without becoming slave to him, because we are able to see that this guide is not speaking in his name, but is the humble exponent of a trans-personal dimension.

I would like to conclude this brief clinical excursus with a mini-fable told to me by Giorgio, which he made up about the figure of the wolf when he was still in his early teens. It shows just how much his youthful consciousness was still linked to the original wisdom of the unconscious, precisely because it was capable of expressing itself in symbolic form, and was already preparing him to experience freedom in a productive way. In fact, the story reveals a double awareness. On the one side that freedom implies the ability to distance oneself from those guides who, by presenting themselves as leaders, presume to determine our existential path in the best possible way, but demand blind faith, loyalty and absolute obedience in return. And on the other, that freedom does not signify being the sole arbiters of our destiny and proceeding in a state of coldness and isolation, but being able to draw on the wisdom that comes from the depths of the soul, through the great archetypal images. These last are a source of inspiration for those who guide us and for ourselves, as long as we do not, of course, fall prey to the temptation or illusion that we can identify with them. This is the fable:

> One day a wolf, who lived with a pack and was dominated by the leader, saw the sun and decided to go and seek it. Alone, he climbed the steepest and most impenetrable mountains. When he reached the peaks he met the moon, who said to him: "Look, I have received the rays of the sun and that is why I can reflect them and illuminate things. You can do the same as me." When the wolf died, the sun, in the form of a little boy, changed him into a constellation, and cast him into the sky.

Notes

1 I also discuss this case in the volume, edited by myself, entitled *Introduzione alla Psicologia Analitica. Le conferenze di Basilea (1934) di C. G. Jung.* Transcribed by Roland Cahen. Moretti e Vitali. Bergamo 2015 (private edition); in my book *Silenzio a Praga.* Moretti e Vitali. Bergamo 2017, and in my correspondence with Murray Stein, *Temporality, Shame, and The Problem of Evil in Jungian Psychology: An Exchange of Ideas*, Routledge, London and New York 2021, also published in Italian under the title, *Temporalità, vergogna e il problema del male*, Moretti e Vitali, Bergamo 2019.

2 Term coined by Murray Stein to define the experience of time that cannot be measured, in *Temporality and Shame*, Ladson Hinton and Hessel Willemsen 2017 and in *Temporality, Shame, and the Problem of Evil in Jungian Psychology*, Murray Stein, Elena Caramazza, Routledge, London and New York 2021.

3 Although in the fairytale the evil queen apparently questions the mirror to hear it confirm that she is "the fairest of them all," in actual fact she could never have supposed that it would have told her she was more beautiful than Snow White. G., on the other hand, has understood the queen's real intention and reveals that her innermost desire was not to be the most beautiful, but to obtain power through nastiness and evil.

4 Some of these thoughts were expressed in my article: 'Il mio incontro con Raimundo Panikkar: la religiosità come dimensione costitutiva dell'essere umano,' in the magazine published by Aracne, 2014, and *Rivista di Psicologia analitica: Spiritualità e psicologia del profondo: Andare a fondo è il contrario di affondare*, new series, no. 38, vol. 90/2014.

5 I have already recounted this case history in my book, *Silenzio a Praga*. Moretti e Vitali, Bergamo 2017, pp. 176–179.

Chapter 4

Destiny and intergenerational shadow

I would now like to focus on a particular type of Shadow which I call "intergenerational," since it is passed on from one generation to another, thus preventing the constitution of a unique authentic Self with its specific characteristics. This Shadow insinuates itself, like a foreign body, in a person's psychic fabric and is made up of mental contents, fantasies, desires, and anxieties that are projected by the progenitors on the descendant, who cannot but project them, in his turn, on the Other or on his own child.

On the other hand, since the Shadow is generally a relational place and not an independent entity, it is always the product of complicity: a Shadow can only come into being through the collaboration of two or more psychic instances and at least two people. A fortiori, the intergenerational shadow is like a condensation of phantasms that draw on intersecting projections, but, paradoxically, it obstructs the process of knowing the place in which it originated and thus blocks the relation between the Self and its internal agencies and between the Self and the Other, paralyzing the intra-psychic and interpersonal dialogue. This shadow falsifies all relationships and interrupts, through its deception, the energetic current that nourishes them. We may therefore expect childhood to be the phase most conducive to the formation of this Shadow or, at least, of the foundations on which the adult's corresponding future Shadow will be constructed. In fact, the most significant interactions for the individual are unquestionably those established with the parents in the first years of life, i.e., in the period in which the environment, as Winnicott (1965) reminds us, must be considered an integral part of the child's psychic structure. Thus, the conscious or unconscious fantasies that the parents, and especially the mother, entertain about the child before or after its birth, will crucially influence its destiny. If these fantasies are constructed on the lines of a potential or actual response to the child's messages and needs, they can act as the soundbox that will shape the nucleus of his authentic Self. On the other hand, if they are the expression of the parents' narcissistic needs, they can only transmit contents that are foreign to its nature, thus alienating the child from itself. In such cases, we can consider the effects of projection from the point of view of the recipient, that is, the child. In fact, whether the images fantasized by the parents are of a grandiose

DOI: 10.4324/9781003261872-5

nature, for example, that of the hero son, great artist, or savior of the family, or whether they are negative, such as that of the sick or deformed son, or future killer of the parents – themes that also appear in various myths – they are always the expression of a Shadow, since they can steal the identity of the child and, even if they allow it to exist, prevent it from feeling real and authentic. Through this mechanism, the individual can remain incorporated in the magic circle of familial constellation, and thus unable to follow the path that would enable him to realize his uniqueness. Bernhard would speak of a "pseudo-Shadow," because the person who is unable to evaluate himself from an individual standpoint, cannot acquire the ability to discriminate between his values and his disvalues and, consequently, will switch his personal Shadow and his aspects of light: "If the yardstick is the parental instance, the individual, insofar as he deviates from the parents' evaluation, is the 'Shadow.' Through the internal instance of the Super-Ego, therefore, the individual would shape his individuality from the Shadow, a 'family Shadow'" (1969, 1985, p. 34). It is precisely the degree to which this Shadow prevents a person from dissolving his identification with the archetypal image of the parents and from drawing on the resources of his own Self, that, in my opinion, makes its characteristics similar to those of the Absolute Shadow described earlier, which I suggested was responsible for the manifestation of a negative destiny. Another thought expressed by Bernhard follows a similar line: "To the extent that man goes with his uniqueness, he has succeeded. Life can be difficult, but there are never catastrophes, it always proceeds productively, it has a direction, an internal consequence, a meaning. Otherwise it becomes unhappy, absurd, full of catastrophes. In the first case, destiny takes man happily along with it, in the other it is seen as 'bad'" (ibid., pp. 32–33). I believe, however, that in such situations it would be more exact to speak of a double projection of the Shadow, enacted respectively by the parents on the child and the child on the parents. The grandiose or negative way in which parents see their child is probably a derivative of the ancient archetypal image of their own parents, who, in their turn, were heirs to the archetypal image of the Penates. An image that, after having brought a child into the world, they projected on it, with the hidden intention of recovering the ideal of narcissistic perfection that had inevitably come to nothing, but whose loss they had never elaborated. Paradoxically, even the most extreme form of destructiveness is a part of perfection, since it is an expression of absolute power. Thus, the child who cannot help but construct its psyche with internal parts of the primary reference figures will find itself unconsciously inhabited by the mental contents of its parents and grandparents (and, going back in the chain of generations, of its ancestors), whereas the child itself will inevitably project onto its real parents the archetypal parental image that is the product of an ancestral experience of the human species. The dual aspect of the image of the parents, which is fascinating and destructive at the same time, is related, as I have already said, to the omnipotent character of the archetype in general, because omnipotence comprises everything, even the illusion that any possibility can be realized without having to go through effort, uncertainty and fear, or to accept limitation. Thus, the archetypal parental image with which one identifies "... is capable of diametrically opposite effects and acts on consciousness rather as Yahweh acted toward Job – ambivalently" (Jung 1909/1949, 2014, p. 321). Moreover, for Jung, the extraordinary and magic energy with which the parental imago influences the life of the child is not attributable to an ordinary person, to a real parent in fact, but to an archetypal model. The danger, which may be seen as the Shadow flooding the whole personality, lies in the Ego's unconscious identification with the archetype: "... not only does it exert a dominating influence on the child by suggestion, it also causes the same unconsciousness in the child, so that it succumbs to the influence from outside and at the same time cannot oppose it from within" (ivi, p. 316). According to Jung, its hypnotic fascination lies at the root of the powers of destiny when, uncontrolled neither by consciousness nor by will, they exert their influence on a human being's life.

> If we normal people examine our lives, we too perceive how a mighty hand guides us without fail to our destiny, and not always is this hand a kindly one. Throughout we believe ourselves to be the masters of our deeds. But reviewing our lives, and chiefly taking our misfortunes and their consequences into consideration, we often cannot account for our doing this act and omitting that, *making it appear as if our steps had been guided by a power foreign to us.* Therefore Shakespeare says:
>
> *Fate, show thy force: ourselves we do not owe;*
> *What is decreed must be, and be this so!*
>   (*Twelfth Night*, Act 1, Scene 5)
>   (ivi, 314, including note[1])

In short, this Shadow that extends along the chain of generations and expresses the impulse to merge with the idea and sense of the absolute, is generated by the Shadow and generates more Shadow. Inherited from one's parents, it is first redirected at the parents themselves and then projected onto the children, but we cannot know whence it originated since it is not only the expression of a consequence and of a response, albeit inadequate, but also of an initiative. Like a specter, it circulates within the first relationships of life and will continue to contaminate adult relationships until we understand that our primary narcissistic wound cannot be remedied, being neither fault nor illness, but the very condition of our psychic birth.

To conclude, we may also see this Shadow as the product of a narcissistic relationship between parent and child. As Racamier perceptively observes, if a mother, who is always on the verge of depression, is hostile to her own desires and reacts with horror to the child's libidinal desires, she will need "... her child [to] complete her or, more exactly, that it remain an integral part of herself, like a vital organ," and she will presume "to keep the child inside herself once and for all, as if this narcissistically seduced offspring had never been born. The child cannot bring about the second birth, which is a psychic birth; it cannot grow, think, desire or dream. For the mother it will remain her embodied dream: a living fetish. But can someone who is a dream have dreams?" (1980, 1983, pp. 83–84).

Miller is also of the opinion that if a mother narcissistically invests her child, she may love it with all her heart, but not for itself. When the child has become the object-Self of the mother, it will make every effort to live up to the expectations she has of it, but consequently find itself obliged to disavow the validity of its perceptions and its affective motions. The indispensable condition for preserving maternal love is that the child never abandon its false Self (1979, 1994).

On the other hand, Racamier also writes, "narcissistic seductions exert a fascination on the child that is by no means minor, since it enables him to form with the mother an omnipotent Whole, to never lose her. … Moreover, the law of relation in narcissistic seduction remains unchanged: it is an invertible relation, in which the human beings involved are interchangeable, since each takes the place of the other. Narcissistic seduction abolishes otherness" (ivi. p. 84).

4.1 The Louis Althusser case

I would like to recall here the story of Louis Althusser, as recounted in his autobiography,[2] since it is emblematic of how a shadow formation that develops in early childhood within a disturbed relationship with the mother can later reemerge in a couple relationship, to the extent that the Shadow of one partner seems to evoke, actualize and, above all, activate the Shadow of the other. In this way, a loving interaction between man and woman, capable of promoting growth and integration of the personality, is replaced by a destructive interaction between Shadows which, stronger than the will of the individual, would, in Althusser's case, seem to have been the architect of a tragic destiny. In his autobiography, Althusser honestly and rigorously reconstructs the weave of internal and external events that led him to play out the drama of his life to its horrific, irreversible climax: the killing of his beloved partner, Héléne. History tells us that Althusser was not tried as a criminal but committed to a psychiatric clinic for many years, since he was judged to be mentally irresponsible. As Althusser writes, the commonly held view is that "mental illness" is a destiny because the mad person is seen as permanently ill and consequently should be committed for life: "*Lebenstodt*, as the German press so aptly puts it" (1992, 1993, p. 22). In effect, Althusser felt he was one of the living dead because the non-prosecution procedure prevented him from explaining himself publicly, from reconstructing the sense of his actions, and from exonerating himself: "beneath the tombstone of the non-lieu, silence and public death […] I had to survive and learn to live" (ivi. pp. xi and 28). All this led him to explain himself publicly through his memoir: "First and foremost, I am doing it for my friends and for myself too, if that is possible, to remove the weight of the tombstone which lies over me" (ivi. p. 27). He goes on to explain that the public "will know nothing [...] of his desperate efforts to try to understand and explain the reasons, both distant and immediate, for the tragedy into which he has literally been plunged in his madness and delirium" (ivi. p. 25).

The memory of the days preceding the crime remained forever impenetrable to Althusser. He was only able to reconstruct the hellish atmosphere that had descended upon himself and Hélène as they became increasingly isolated, finally shutting themselves up in their apartment without seeing or talking to anyone, swept away by a kind of double delirium. The last clear image he is able to evoke, to his horror, is that of Hélène stretched out on the bed, already dead because her eyes are motionless and the tip of her tongue is lying between her teeth. He is kneeling beside her and his muscles and forearms ache after massaging her neck for a long time. He realizes he has strangled her: "I rushed, screaming, from our flat towards the sick-bay. ... My fate was sealed" (ivi. p. 254). In fact, the coroner's report stated that Hélène died of strangulation, but no sign of self-defense on her part had been found. Althusser repeatedly asked himself and his psychoanalyst how he could have been able to kill Hélène, and once suggested that it could have been "a suicide by proxy." By this he probably meant either that he had killed Hélène, because she had repeatedly said that she wanted to commit suicide and, not having the courage, had asked him to kill her with his own hands; or that by killing Hélène he had killed himself, since his relationship with her was so fusional. There had already been, in fact, a particularly conflictual and dangerous episode in their relationship. Althusser had enticed a young woman into a rough, stormy sea and engaged in erotic play with her before the eyes of a terrified Hélène. As in other similar situations, his intention was both to provoke Hélène and to obtain her approval, just as he had wanted that of his mother when he embarked on a love affair as a young man; however, she had always withheld it. With difficulty he managed to return to the shore, where he met with Hélène's indignant, indeed furious, reaction, since she had feared, on the one hand, that he would perish in the stormy sea and she would lose him forever, and, on the other, that she would die inside from the insult to their relationship.

After the tragedy, Althusser reflected: "The fact is: for the first time my own death and hers were fused. They were *one and the same death* – the cause might be different but the end product would be the same" (ivi. p. 179). One of the most emotionally vibrant memories evoked by Althusser is of Hélène's face, which was always receptive to the emotions of others and to the surprises of life, but also capable of hardening into "a mask of intense pain, as her suffering welled up from the depths of her being." It was as if the hollows in her cheeks were "marked and lined [...] by her long and terrible 'negative struggle,' as well as the personal and class battles in which she had engaged in the labour movement and the Resistance" (ivi. pp. 156–157). In fact, Hélène came from a Jewish family from a region on the Russian/Polish border, which had fled from the pogroms and found refuge in France, where she had been born. In the past she had been a militant in the Communist party and an active supporter of the worker's cause; she had also lost several much loved friends, who had been shot by the Nazis during the period of the Resistance in which she herself had participated. The agonizing separation from so many people dear to her had etched on her face "the marks of death and despair" (ivi. p. 158). Althusser movingly remembers her hands: "They had been fashioned by work and bore the marks of hard physical labour, yet her touch had a wonderful tenderness which betrayed her heartbreak and helplessness. They were the hands of a poor, wretched old woman who had nothing and no one to turn to, yet who found it in her heart to go on giving. I was filled with such sorrow at the suffering engraved on them. I have often wept into these hands, and they have often made me weep, though I never told her why. I feared it would cause her pain. [...] Hélène, my Hélène ..." (ivi. p. 159).

As he sought to reconstruct Hélène's problems, Althusser became convinced that there was terrible hatred between his wife and her mother. In fact, as she herself told him, her birth flew in the face of her mother's wanting a boy and upset all her plans. She never breastfed her daughter, never took her in her arms, and never made any gesture of tenderness toward her. She hated Hélène because she herself had rejected her, and she saw her as a little rebellious animal, black and wild, impossible to tame and always prey to fury and violence, which, Althusser observed, must have been her only means of defense. Thus, Hélène identified with a negative image of the mother and, above all, with the negative image she supposed the mother had of her. She had an irrepressible fear of being a horrendous woman, a hag who spread evil around her, incapable of controlling her terrible outbursts that a force, more powerful than her, unleashed without respite. Althusser points out that "... her original phantasy was not arbitrary, but linked to real 'signs' through which her mother's unconscious and 'willed' desires (her implacable desires) revealed themselves" (ivi. p. 117). It was as if Hélène had no choice but to embody and act out the image of the ugly, naughty child that the mother imposed on her so that she might hate her without a hint of remorse. But this meant that the daughter was caught in an unresolvable paradox: either she had to be how the mother wanted her, in order not to lose her (which happens to every child); at the same time, however, she had to be repudiated by the mother because, if she put on that face, she was unworthy of love. Moreover, the "original phantasy" must to some extent also have been Althusser's, since he himself recognizes that he was compelled to provoke Hélène with humiliating behaviors. These included his making up to other women in front of her – implicitly seeking her approval – which was designed to provoke an irate reaction on her part, because she would feel as if she had been transformed into a harpy and was forever condemned to be a "bad mother." It was almost as if Althusser felt obliged to impersonate Hélène's mother, who in this case was assimilated to his own mother, while Hélène became his child self, annihilated by a maternal gaze which (as actually happened in his childhood and I shall go on to explain) was directed at another love precisely through him.

Althusser's biographical precedents were just as traumatic as Hélène's, in fact. When he was born his mother decided to call him "Louis" after his paternal uncle, whom she had loved passionately and who had died when his plane crashed during World War I. She always considered her marriage to Louis' brother, Charles, who had survived the war and was Althusser's father, as a fallback, a betrayal of herself and her great love. Althusser would never feel loved by his mother for himself but as a substitute for another – dead – man. The very name Louis, similar to *lui* ("he," in French), led him to feel like the shadow of another man he could never be. He comments on the pronoun: "...*lui*, which deprived me of any personality of my own, summoning as it did an anonymous other. It referred to my uncle, the man who stood behind me: *Lui* was Louis. It was him my mother loved, not me" (ivi. p. 39). Remembering his mother in the early years of his childhood, he writes: "When she looked at me, it was not me she saw but another person, the other Louis, who was not me but whose name I had been given and who had died in the skies over Verdun, those pure skies which belonged to her past but which were ever present. [...] It was as if she looked through me. I disappeared under her gaze, which reached out beyond me, beyond death to recapture the face of another Louis who was not and never would be me [...]. In her 'love' for me, something chilled and marked me from earliest childhood and determined my fate for a very long time. It was not a phantasy but the very reality of my life. That is how phantasy becomes real for each individual" (ivi. pp. 53–54).[3]

Althusser, no less than Hélène, had found himself prisoner of a fatal conjuncture: to be like his mother he was obliged to betray the person he loved, and, to respond to his mother's wishes, he had to betray himself and his most authentic aspirations: he had to become "another," but, above all, he had to die like his uncle had died. Althusser describes more of his experiences: "... my mother whom I loved with all my heart loved someone else through and beyond me, using my physical presence to remind her of a person who was absent, or rather seeing his presence through my absence [...] How therefore could I make my mother love me, since it wasn't actually me she loved? I was doomed to be merely a pale reflection, that of a dead man, perhaps even a dead person myself? Clearly, the only means I had of escaping this 'contradiction' or ambivalence was [...] to win my mother's affection in order that I might become [...] the man behind me, in some infinite and imaginary sky which was forever marked by his death [...and] to *seduce* my mother ... *fulfilling her desire*" (ivi, pp. 53–56). Thus, to be loved by his mother (which for a child is equivalent to being), Althusser sought to offer her everything that she would have expected from the other Louis: wisdom, purity, virtue, pure intellect, a disembodied state, academic success, a literary career and, to complete everything, a position at the École Normale Supérieure (ENS), where he became a well-known philosopher. When Althusser asked himself if he really would have been able to seduce his mother, his answer was literally yes and no: yes, because in seeing the son as the means of realizing her desire she was happy and extremely proud of him; no, because in seducing her he would inevitably feel that he was not himself and he only existed through "artifice" and "deception." The price of such an act, therefore, was the loss of his authentic existence and the betrayal of his personal vocation and own desire: "I existed only through my mother's desires, never my own, which remained inaccessible" (ivi, p. 58). Furthermore, once Althusser had followed the path of seduction, he could no longer acquire the capacity to give and receive real love. Through simulation and falsification, which were acted out unconsciously but soon led to consciously deceptive acts (which would result in the anxiety of not existing changing into a *sense of guilt* for not existing), he won the admiration and approval of others, precisely because he embodied both the ideas they had of themselves, and the unconscious images of their fantasies and hopes. But this kind of admiration, which is actually a form of idolatry, is merely a pitiful substitute for love, which offers only narcissistic compensation for narcissistic seduction and forces the partners involved in the game to engage in a ruthless struggle for personal dominion one over the other. The freedom to freely reveal oneself to the gaze of the other, male or female, will be forever banned. In fact, Althusser felt powerless to love: "It is as if I had been deprived of what might have constituted my physical and psychic integrity." In actual fact, he had not yet realized that by assuming attitudes that were first childish then later rendered more sophisticated by all the intellectual faculties of an adult, he himself had relinquished love in order to fully exploit the power of sick psychic mechanisms. After beginning his affair with Hélène and consummating his first sexual act with her (at the age of thirty!), Althusser repeatedly suffered episodes of deep depression followed by hypomanic states that obliged him to be hospitalized and to undergo electric shock treatment. We may suppose that this first experience of love disturbed him, because he had violated the taboo of "purity" that represented the implicit pact with his mother. This is how he remembers it: "… we made love on the bed. It was new, thrilling, exhilarating and violent. When she left, I was plunged into a profound state of anguish from which I could not escape" (ivi. p. 124). However, Althusser himself recognizes that in his depressive and hypomanic phases it was as if deep down he sought to draw on a form of omnipotence, because in both situations he was able to manipulate others, using them according to his needs. Indeed, as his psychoanalyst later explained to him, in hospital one returns to being a small child, lulled by the certainty that one will never be abandoned again. The whole world, namely the doctors, the nurses, the people who love us and visit us, is at our beck and call. "With nothing to fear from the outside world, you are all-powerful like a child with various loving mothers" (ivi. 143). Althusser comments: "My fear of being totally impotent and my desire to be all-powerful, my megalomania, were two aspects of the same phenomenon: the desire to possess *what*

I lacked which would make me a man, at once whole and free ... I was haunted alternately by the same dual phantasy (hence its ambivalence) in the unreal nature of my all-powerfulness when I was depressed and in the megalomaniac all-powerfulness of the manic state" (ivi. p. 144).[4]

Another aspect of Althusser's ambivalent omnipotence complex, as clearly exemplified by his relationship with Hélène, was manifest in his need to create a "reserve of women" to deal with his fear of loss or abandonment, a need that was also expressed through his habit of accumulating material goods and money. As indicated earlier, "It was a way of living constantly in the same present, never having the courage or rather the simple freedom to face the future (without a prior guarantee of reserves) other than as an accumulation of the past" (ivi. p. 106). Althusser also recalls a perceptive comment by a dear woman friend: "What I don't like about you is that you are determined to destroy yourself" (ivi. p. 97).

To conclude, we may posit that Althusser's Shadow, corresponding to an omnipotence/impotence complex and thus to an "absolute" Shadow in the light of my previous considerations, took the place of his personality in organizing his destiny. Constructed like a mosaic, also by incorporating psychic fragments of people who were important points of reference (first his parents and later Hélène), this Shadow would have sprung from connivance and reflected a familial, genealogical and relational unconscious. This last element of its genesis was probably responsible for its power to cause a tragedy which, strangely enough, neither its protagonists nor all the human help available and offered at the time, were able to avoid.

It would be useful to ask ourselves what was overlooked, or not understood in time to change the course of events. In this particular case, unfortunately, it was necessary for the pathogenic complex (perhaps precisely because it had a transpersonal root) to be acted out and for Althusser to suffer for many years before he could finally say, at the end of his life: "I have also, I think, learnt what it is to love: being capable, not of 'exaggerated' initiatives, of always going one better, but of being thoughtful in relation to others, respecting their desires, their rhythms, never demanding things but learning to receive and accept every gift as a surprise: and being capable, in a wholly unassuming way, of giving and surprising the other person, without the least coercion. To sum up, it is a question simply of freedom. Why did Cézanne paint the Montagne Sainte-Victoire at every available moment? Because the light of each moment is a gift. So, despite its dramas, life can still be beautiful. I am sixty-seven, and though it will soon all be over, I feel younger now than I have ever done, never having had any youth since no one loved me for myself. Yes, the future lasts a long time" (ivi. p. 279).

4.2 Shadow and pre-oedipal problems

In the light of my above reflections on the genealogical Shadow, I would now like to re-examine the Oedipus myth from the parents' as well as the child's point of view, and through an interpretive key that primarily considers pre-oedipal problems. In fact, we cannot fully understand Oedipus' destiny without taking into account the complexes of both Laius and Jocasta, because the oedipal impulses of children are also aroused by the "counter-oedipal" impulses of the parents, which are specular to those of the children. Thus, if the oedipal complex is not the work of the child alone, the presence of real or symbolic parents is necessary for it to be dissolved. An oedipal structure of mind, which implies going beyond endogamy, separation between generations, and the psychic co-presence of the two principles, paternal and maternal, is achieved through the cooperation of all three components of the triad.[5]

In particular, it is not enough for the father and mother to have harmonized within the male/female and paternal/maternal polarities and be the bearers of the two functions.[6] Each of them must be able to represent the other real parent in their mind, i.e. the mother to carry inside the image of the father and vice versa, so that they can both offer these images to the child. Only in this way can the child open up in itself a place to receive a third image, before actually discovering it as an object in reality. In sum, creating an oedipal structure in the mind implies that father and mother have both a reciprocal relationship and a relation with their partner as an internal object; a relation that obviously includes the child. In both parents the paternal and maternal function will not be exaggerated, but will be mitigated in turn and integrated.

Returning to the Oedipus myth we could say, first and foremost, that the fateful oracle which leads Laius to sacrifice his son, represents the voice of God wrongly interpreted by a human being. In psychological terms, this would mean that the most profound agencies of the psyche, pertaining to the Self, were misunderstood by the rational consciousness of the Ego. The real meaning of the oracle's pronouncement, "This son will kill his father and marry his mother," can only be interpreted in a symbolic sense, i.e., "This boy, like all sons, will carry out a new work that will outlast his parents, and will draw on the universal experiences of the human race." This means that "from the mother he will inherit the resources of her body's profound wisdom concerning the mysteries of the transmission of life, and from the father he will acquire the capacity to realize a project that is completed in the dimension of time and therefore limited but, precisely because of this, open to the other and to the elsewhere." In fact, for a child to fulfill his or her true purpose in life, the parents must accept that they are mortal individuals, while at the same time knowing that the child will develop agencies deriving from the depths of human nature where no temporal boundaries can be drawn. In particular, for a child to realize itself, the mother must embrace it but not bind it to her, and the father must indicate to it the meaning of life without imposing specific obligations; provide rules without considering them absolute; and present the principle of the limit not as prohibition but as a value that permits contact with otherness. In this sense, as I have already inferred, the limit can be defined as a "boundary" that separates and, therefore, relativizes each human being, while also allowing them to connect with the reality that transcends them: a boundary which, as indicated by the Latin term *cum-finis*, is the sharing of one's own finitude with the other than self. The paradoxical nature of the limit, which truly unites paternal and maternal, history and myth, time of life and the transtemporal dimension, is what enables us to experience the mystery of the origins and the aims of destiny, this last understood as our "destination" and fulfillment. In transmitting a sense of the "finite," and thus the contingent and transient, the limit also opens the door to the infinite. This sheds new meaning on the comment made by Marco, whose story I recounted earlier: *"How worthless was the perfection I strove for, and how rich and, in a certain sense, 'infinite' is this limit I shunned!"*

In the light of these considerations, we could ask ourselves what might have been the characteristics of the possible complexes of Laius and Jocasta, which would have determined the unfolding of the drama. It is reasonable to suppose that for Oedipus' parents the oracle's pronouncement that their own son would kill his father and marry his mother, expressed a joint unconscious fear that existed – as often occurs – in parallel to an unconfessable desire. For example, they may have seen the act of procreation as personal power, rather than a willingness to receive the action of a force that passes through an individual, in order to implement an unfathomable plan that extends beyond the project of a single life. In this case, the son could have been conceived by the king and queen with the hidden intention of denying their own limit and mortality, almost as if they wished to eliminate the generation gap by deluding themselves that they could superimpose their own life on his life, and consequently imagine that through him they could actually project themselves onto the entire future. This kind of omnipotence fantasy would have prevented the son from being seen in his diversity and otherness, and he would have found himself caught in the web of his parents' unconscious desire of living and asserting only themselves, through him. In this event, the only path open to the son would be to expose and consciously thwart his parents' plan, in order to implement the original project of his life. But this without disowning his real parents who are not identical to the omnipotent images (or, it might be said, to the archetypal images transmitted from one generation to another, and therefore common to the two generations) by which they are either inhabited or they have projected onto themselves, but who, instead, are imperfect and limited beings. Should he fail in this task, he is bound either to remain a prisoner of the intentions of the past or to rebel, falling prey to a violent reaction. In the first case, he would be condemned to repeat obsolete forms that bring nothing new to the world; in the second, the link with his origin would be severed and he would inherit the inflationary omnipotence fantasy, this time in the form of self-generation, which would deny him the productive meeting with the other than self. Going back to the myth, if Oedipus' father had imagined his son as both an extension and a copy of himself, it is likely that, on the one hand, he would have expelled his terrible feeling of guilt by projecting it on his son, and thus imagining him as his future assassin; and on the other, he would have feared that his son might actually have committed parricide in a desperate attempt to preserve the uniqueness of his life, to avoid becoming one of the "living dead." The transferred guilt and the fear would have been expressed in the words of the oracle: "This son will kill his father," while the presentiment of the dream of omnipotence coming to nothing would have been configured as a vengeful act by the son. There is, however, something even more disturbing about Laius' wrongdoing: to protect himself from his guilt feelings, and also the truth, he commits the crime of pedophilia and then abandons his newborn son. From this standpoint, it is likely that the king interpreted the Delphi oracle as an announcement of the revenge of the gods, who one day would arm and set his son – a boy as innocent as the king's victim – against him. So, should we consider the killing of Laius as a consequence of his guilt or the denial of his guilt? In my opinion, it is precisely his guilt, unacknowledged and unexpiated through psychic suffering, which caused the drama and was unconsciously unloaded onto the son, triggering in him the irrepressible urge to act out, quite unknowingly, his father's murder. As Jung says, no one is redeemed for a sin he has not committed. The exposure of the son to a near-impossible state of survival would have permitted Laius to avoid actually murdering him and to protect himself from the capacity for violence that he attributed to him. We are at a pre-oedipal level because the conflict between father and son is not linked to an erotic rivalry to obtain the love of the same woman, but to the desire/fear of a reciprocal assimilation, to fascination, and to the danger of their both remaining in a state of unconscious identity, inflated, moreover, by the imminent danger of homosexual incest.

For the mother Jocasta, on the other hand, the dream of omnipotence could have taken the form of being able to eternally reconceive and give birth to her son without depending upon a partner (the sons of her son are, in fact, also hers). And thus never to separate herself from her son; indeed, to be one with him since he is, at the same time, the fetus in the womb, the little boy dependent on her care, and the beloved husband or lover. In this way, mother and son would have formed a self-sufficient unit in which all generational power would have remained imprisoned, and otherness abolished. Here, too, we find ourselves at a pre-oedipal level, because, once again, the events are not conducted by Eros, but rather the need for fusion that makes two people interchangeable and in which the omnipotence fantasy also subjugates sexuality. So where the mother is concerned, the oracle's response could be both the expression of her desire and her feeling of guilt (also projected on the son) concerning her husband, since the aspiration to form a perfect unit with the son, an hermaphroditic totality in a certain sense, implies the rejection of her partiality as a female being and the elimination of the other than self, of the man, who can no longer be recognized or loved. In fact, in the actual drama Jocasta acquiesces to Laius' command to sacrifice their son, thus failing in her task of accepting, protecting and empathizing with the helpless little boy. The mother's wrong is extended by her attempting to keep from Oedipus the truth of his origin, in order to bind him to her in a state of tragic unconsciousness.

The authors of *Figli e Genitori*, which I referred to earlier, ask themselves in what way the hidden aspect of myths, i.e., what is "not said" in them, has distorted our knowledge of the essence of man. A consequence of what is "not said" in the Oedipus myth, which concerns precisely the parents' wrong-doing, would be the Freudian theory of the Oedipus complex pertaining solely to the son, whose resolution was entrusted entirely to Freud's endopsychic work. For example, the operation that he would have performed on the text of *Oedipus Rex* by Sophocles would have been to substitute the familial relationships and their role in Oedipus' life with his unconscious fantasies. Later, the hypothesis of unconscious fantasies supplanted the theory of seduction and of real trauma, leaving its mark on psychoanalytical science for a long period (C. Albini Bravo, P. C. Devescovi, 2004, p. 28).

In order to shake off a destiny marked out by intergenerational forces, Oedipus would have had to acknowledge his parents' complexes that had parasitized his psyche, as well as to what degree these complexes had possessed him and become his own, through an irresistible movement of unconscious identification with their power. As Marco, the patient of whom I spoke earlier, said: *"Once it was my mother who prevented me from being and feeling differently from the way in which she conceived it, that is in a perfect way, thus preventing me from arriving at my truth… now, it is a terrible anxiety… which has no face, no name …."*

Oedipus knew nothing of his own story, but when a wayfarer hinted that his Corinthian parents, Polybus and Merope, might not be his biological parents, he ignored the doubt that most certainly must have arisen in his mind. When he heard the Delphic prophecy, he thought he could avoid its coming true by leaving Corinth, but in so doing he prevented himself from discovering his true origin. Likewise, he was sure that he had defeated the sphinx by revealing its enigma and reducing it to a children's riddle, but was unaware that enigmas are such precisely because they are veiled, i.e., they cannot be deciphered as they stand, but only by intuiting the invisible and unfathomable truth to which the veil alludes by hiding it (as mentioned earlier, the Latin root of reveal is *re-* "back," "again" + *velare* "to cover"). The real enigma was the sphinx herself. A figure that, as Jung writes, represents the desire of the son to become one with the primeval mother by immersing himself in the undifferentiated unconscious identity of the origins, as if wishing to reacquire "something of that mysterious and irresistible power which comes from the feeling of being part of the whole" (Jung 1912/1952, 2014, p. 178). While this could have been the creative aspect of a symbolic regression that leads to rebirth after reaching the depths of the psyche whence springs a form of consciousness that precedes Ego-consciousness, Oedipus' movement seems to stop at the desire for regressive incest that implies the refusal of separation from the mother, of differentiation, and of the conquest of an autonomous individuality. Hence the sphinx encountered by Oedipus also represents the murderous, devouring mother who tends to reabsorb the son to whom she does not want to give birth, so as never to be separated from him and to form with him an absolute totality. To escape his incestuous destiny Oedipus would have had to decipher his unconscious impulse to rejoin with his real mother and to transform it into a desire for, and movement of union with, a symbolic equivalent of the mother. This would have enabled him to penetrate the mystery of his origin, to avoid taking literally the stories told him, and to go beyond the curse of the oracles and the violence of paternal punishment. At the same time, he could only have avoided identifying unconsciously with his father and symmetrically replicating his wrong, by "pardoning" him. To pardon does not mean to forget, and implies much more than refraining from revenge. From the Latin *per dono*, to pardon means to offer anew to real people, also as we see them in our minds, the entire nebula of possibilities they have not yet taken up and acted on. Possibilities that could have been realized and are part of a human being's totality, that constitute our base, depth and richness, and are no less real than concrete facts.

Seen in this key, Oedipus' drama is specular to that of Laius and Jocasta. He, too, is tempted to seduce his parents narcissistically, a trap he seeks desperately, and unsuccessfully, to avoid. He thinks that he can fathom the mystery of life through reason and that he has defeated destiny by solving the sphinx's riddle. In reality, he does not know how to penetrate his Shadow, namely the desire for omnipotence that drives him and colludes with the analogous desire of his parents. Consequently, he is not able to trace his origin: instead of recognizing himself in his father and, at the same time, differentiating himself from him, he wishes to be identical to Laius, indeed to be the king himself, since he will usurp his crown. Instead of becoming a man, conscious of belonging to a different gender from his mother, and meeting a woman he can love, he continues to be united, to identify with his mother through the inevitable ambiguity of his sexual definition, because by generating children that are also his brothers and sisters, it is as if he were generating himself in the absence of a father, i.e. in a unified whole with his mother.

I think that Oedipus confuses origin with beginning. Almost as if wanting to stop time, he aspires to rediscovering the magic moment in which the psyche had still not received the narcissistic wound inflicted by the fracturing of the totality without spatial limits or the temporal division that enveloped it, and by its entrance into becoming. And so he seeks the actual moment in which this extraordinary situation was experienced, by swimming upstream against the current of life. It is precisely the past that cannot die which leads him to parricide and incest. Origin, instead, can only be traced at a symbolic level, since it does not pertain to *Chronos* but to *Kairos*, the time of meaning; to consciousness that experiences the moment knowing it will pass but, precisely because of this, that it is also in relation with its eternal foundation. The origin contains the blueprint of an entire life, to which it is always possible to return as the nucleus of one's own individuation project, since it embraces both development and meaning. It is no accident that, try as he may, Oedipus is unable to discover who his real parents are. He loses his origin, that is he abandons his real self when, through his complicity, the phantasm of eternity and omnipotence (of being similar to God) takes over his destiny and occupies the space reserved for the living and for those who accept death together with life.

Notes

1 The quote within the quote, which appears in the note by Jung, is from A. Schopenhauer, 'Transscendente Spekulation über die anscheinende Absichtlichkeit im Schicksale des Einzelnen,' in R. von Koeber (ed.) *Parerga und Paralipomena*, vol. 1, Berlin 1891. Eng. trans., David Irvine, "On Apparent Design in the Fate of the Individual," *Parerga and Paralipomena*, Watts, London 1913, p. 26). The italics in the quote, aside from those of the verse, are mine.

2 *L'avenir dure longtemps suivi de Les Faits. Autobiografies.* (*The Future Lasts Forever*, Eng. trans. Richard Veasey, The New Press, New York 1993) Edizioni Stock/IMEC. Paris, 1992; 2007.

3 In this regard, it is interesting that Karl Abraham finds there is often a correspondence between a patient's ideative contents and the meaning of his/her name. Clearly, a name can have a meaning because it represents something that is known, e.g., a situation or a function, or it evokes the characteristics of a person who has already borne it, such as a member of the family (as in Althusser's case), a forebear, or an historic personage (Abraham 1911).

4 While in a manic state, for example, Althusser proudly informed Hélène of his ability to engage in shoplifting without being caught or actually to steal an atomic submarine, sending her into a terrible panic.

5 This theme is explored in depth in the book by Camilla Albini Bravo and Pier Claudio Devescovi: *Figli e genitori. Note a margine di un mito amputato*, Moretti e Vitali, Bergamo 2014.

6 The authors of the abovementioned book specify that solely the accommodation of the two functions within by the parent can also lead to mothers who act the father, excluding their male partner, or to fathers who mainly play the part of the mother.

Part II

Chapter 5

Fate

The term "Fate" would appear to have a broader and more ancient meaning than "Destiny," since it refers not only to the forces that influence the path of human life, but also to those that organize the whole structure of the universe in time and space. Thus, the world, gods and men find themselves incorporated in an order that both considers and dominates them at the same time. The sense of Fate pervades the whole of Greek culture. Though particularly keen in Homer, it originated in earlier times, around the 5th century BCE, in civilizations that preceded writing and outlined the colossal features of a real and proper archaic astronomy in which "many motifs and thought levels were intertwined in a whole that possessed a compactness and formed a unitary vision of the cosmos" (De Santillana 1968, 1985, 2004, p. 12).

5.1 Revelation and symbolic consciousness

The Indo-European etymological root of Fate is *bha*, in Sanskrit *bhati*, from which depart two branches of meaning: one concerning the word and speaking; the other embracing the idea of light. In Greek, for example, the nouns related to this idiomatic nucleus are φημι', I say, I affirm; φάτις, word, divine voice; φημη, φάμα, oracle, prophecy, revelation; φαινω, φανεω (equivalent to *bhati* in Sanskrit), I make manifest, I show, bring to light, reveal; I shine; φῶς, φωτός, man, hero, husband, bridegroom; φῶς, φάος, light.[1] In Latin: *fari*, to speak; *fatum*, what has been spoken; *fatidicus*, prophetic. In Sanskrit: *bhanati*, to speak and *bhà*, luce.[2]

Fate can therefore be understood as the word of a god who illuminates and reveals – but what is this word? It is certainly not the word of the intellect, which could instead be called a "term" (in the sense of "end," "termination"), because by defining being it de-termines it and, by abandoning the area of the symbolic, places it within the rigid boundaries of its presumed thinkability. Panikkar emphasizes that the last twenty-six centuries of Western thought have been bound by the formulation first coined by Parmenides: thinking and being are the same (but only if thinking is seen solely as a logical procedure). The polarity being/thinking, from which the dichotomy subject/object originates, informs our entire culture, making possible, among other things, the

DOI: 10.4324/9781003261872-7

astounding phenomena of science and technology. But at a very high price: the sacrifice of freedom and of joy. According to Panikkar, if we start from the assumption that thinking tells us what being is, being will forcibly have to obey thinking and will not be able to manifest anything of itself that cannot be comprehended by a mental formula: "We have tamed being, we have dominated it by making it follow thinking" (1986, p. 42). It is also Panikkar's view that Indian philosophy, presumably like that of other cultures, centers on the being/speaking, rather than the being/thinking, polarity. The word has taken the place of thought, but follows a completely opposite path to the latter. Being can speak, "in the sense of expressing itself, of expanding in a way that is absolutely unprogrammed, unthinkable and, therefore, not even logical: it can burst with a meaning that nobody knows" (ivi, p. 43); it is the scope of the word "as revelation, as manifestation of what being is" (ibid.). I think that the revolutionary aspect of Panikkar's message lies in his intuition that it is possible to radically change the structure of consciousness that has informed an entire civilization. A consciousness that stops at investigation, that insists on questioning reality within the bounds of its experiments, will only get answers conditioned by the basic data entered by the experimenter himself. He will certainly know more and more about the causes of certain phenomena and the laws that govern them, but he will be none the wiser about their purpose and meaning. Rather than being understood as further characteristics attributed by thought to being, purpose and meaning should be seen as the very energy that moves being, its entelechy (or ὁ ἔχει εν εαυτῳ το τέλος, that which bears its goal within itself), as Bernhard writes (1969, 1985, note. 20); in other words, the ability to make qualitative leaps of change and to generate, rather than submit to, one's own future. Only a consciousness that is open to listening and to receiving unprogrammed messages from the external and internal world will be able to enter the current of becoming in a new way and collaborate with its irreplaceable function on the transformations of the psyche and the cosmos. For Panikkar, "India [with India standing for this new form of consciousness that Jung would have called symbolic because it is capable of 'seeing the invisible,' i.e., that which is not visible to the eye, capturing precisely what goes beyond representation at its face value] lets being speak, spread, empty out, and go on its way in a kind of expansion of the universe" (1981, p. 57).

Rediscovering Fate today could thus foster the transition from a dogmatically- to a symbolically-oriented consciousness. This would signify the birth of a "new vision of the world," and even the birth of a "new world," in the sense of a future unforeseeable to the current tools of intellectual investigation.

5.2 Reality is relation

Fate can thus be understood as reality manifesting itself to a consciousness awakening from its sleep and learning to formulate the images and language of reality, without falsifying them through the Ego's arbitrary interpretations.

Phanes, the luminous motion of the ether, was the first deity to appear in the Greek world, and the divine has always represented for man the mysterious trace of his origin, the source from which everything sprang. Fate is, therefore, both an epiphany and theophany, because it reveals being and its foundation to a consciousness that expresses them in a form that can be grasped in lived experience. Consequently, its disturbing announcement is that things cannot be said "in themselves," but rather through the network of relationships that link them and reconnect them to their beginning. Illuminating in this regard is the myth of Prajāpati, which is recounted by Panikkar and of which I have already spoken. Prajāpati is the god who decides to escape from his solitude by creating the universe with his own substance, since, being absolute, he has no other matter with which to create it. His is an originating rather than Original Sin, because from his immolation a world and order of contingency is born. However, seized by the anguish of dying he invokes his creatures so that they might reconstitute his dismembered body. Thus, the second act of the creation beings, in which the creatures, resisting the temptation to situate themselves in a state of radical independence, rejoin with their origin, their creator, and their finality, reconnecting contingency and the absolute, beginning and becoming, the eternal and time. As Panikkar writes:

> Sin is temporality taken for substance. Existence would indeed be a fault and even sin if it were considered and accepted as simple *sistence* cut off from its source and destiny, as a mere fall – into nothingness. Culpable ignorance (*avidyā*) is to consider yourself something "in itself," to substantialize your self...
>
> (Panikkar 1979, p. 111)

This new sense of Fate could interrupt the construction of a Shadow understood as a tendency to identify with the absolute, since it suggests that relationship, and not the absolute, is the most profound essence of the real, i.e., what creates its unity and its very totality. Perhaps this is why, as Galimberti reminds us,

> Jung does not speak of the Ego and the unconscious in themselves, but of the relationship (*Beziehung swischen*) between the Ego and the unconscious, because only through this "relationship," in this "between" can an Ego that does not think itself absolute come into being.
>
> (1984, p. 171)

Thus, the other than me, which I have always seen as extraneous, and at times as an enemy and tyrant, cannot only become "different," that is the person who delimits my identity through engagement and diversity, but can also give a previously unknown depth to my actual being. Without the You, the Ego is not just isolated but cannot arrive at the Self, or the meaning of its belonging to itself.

Moreover, a meeting with the "other" – that other who "inhabits our inner-most self, as what the Ego is not, being separate from it" (ibid. 1984, p. 171) and which appears to us with the mysterious face of God and Self – will also take place at an intrapsychic level. If we are able to perceive the sense and the poetry of the Jungian metaphor, in fact, and as I have already said, we see that the image of God and the image of the Self are indistinguishable, God's word will also be that of the Self, which reveals itself to the Ego as the trans-formative force of life.

So it is precisely a new approach to Fate that can reunite us with our fellow human beings, all other beings, the cosmos, and the originary principle of the psyche and the world, by linking us to the element that transcends the dichot-omy of being/not being because it is the profound source of all reality. The "alter" of our journey toward the integration of the unconscious will thus be the truly other, the unnamable, the God of the Bible whom we cannot behold without perishing; but, at the same time, it will be the "ipse," our innermost center, the generating nucleus, equally invisible and inexpressible, from which we have differentiated ourselves, but to which we return to receive new lifeblood.[3]

In psychological and meta-psychological terms we could perhaps say that the Ego establishes a relationship with the entire arc spanned by the Self, from the infinite beyond the astral constellations to the infinite within the human soul (from God of the heavens to the inspirational principle of my dreams). This enables us to reconnect with the harmony of archaic astrology, in which there existed a perfect correspondence between the movement of the stars and planets, and the rhythms that marked earthly existence. This is illus-trated by a Chinese proverb: "The accord between the music of ritual flutes and the calendar is so perfect that not even a hair could pass between them" (De Santillana, 1968, 1985, 2004, p. 169).

5.3 Necessity and freedom

For the ancients, the order that underpinned the universe was inviolable not because it was imposed by an arbitrary will, but because it expressed the very quality of its structure. When Zeus wishes to know the fate of Hector in the decisive duel with Achilles, he places a scale on his knees and, upon seeing the balance tip in favor of Hector, accepts, even though he is a god, the response of Fate, along with the pain of seeing his beloved hero die. Likewise, when Diomedes asks Glaucus to tell him his name before killing him, Glaucus understands the vainness of man's presuming to know reality by naming it, and replies: "Brave Diomedes, why ask my lineage? Like the generations of leaves are those of men. The wind blows and one year's leaves are scattered on the ground, but the trees bud and fresh leaves open when spring comes again" (*The Iliad*, Book VI). This concept of a powerful Necessity that binds everything to its constraints was not considered an affront to human free-dom, since its implementation relied on the correct intuition of the forces that transcend the Ego (which here are transegoic but not superegoic) and compliance with their plan that did not betray the vocation of the individual but, on the contrary, faithfully expressed it by bringing it into harmony with the totality of a person in his relationship with others and with the world. Being, in relation to Fate, signified that man had the difficult task of developing the capacity to participate in his own becoming in the cosmos. Not the cosmos understood in the Aristotelian sense, i.e., as bound to the rigid temporal sequence of causes and effects, but rather as the place where each individual being is determined by the whole and, synchronically, determines the whole. As De Santillana writes, it is a "world... that is over-determined – on different levels that conspire between themselves; oversaturated with determinism, where total Necessity reigns, yet at the same time remains freedom" (1968, 1985, 2004, p. 169). In this case, the Ego would be neither totally active nor totally passive, but transformed and transforming, together, through the network of relations that constitute it. The Self could not come into being if the Ego did not speak its own words, but the Ego would not know who it is if it did not recognize itself in the image offered by its unfathomable depths. From this standpoint I believe, as stated earlier, that Narcissus perishes because he cannot distinguish the entity of the Ego from the dimension of the Self, and loses the capacity to establish an intrapsychic relationship. He mistakes the purely concrete, static, and superficial vision of his identity (a mere appearance that manifests in the pond) for the profound and dynamic image of his individuation, which the Self would only reveal to a gaze directed at the invisible. Narcissus does not really love himself, because he wants to rejoin with his simulacrum and loses himself in an image that is neither deep, substantial nor real.

The "profane" gaze that captures "what is in front of us," what is clear and evident, should be combined with a "religious" gaze that searches our interiority and also embraces what is not immediately evident. The realization of one's own destiny, therefore, will require the Ego to participate in, execute and interpret a plan it did not formulate, but which only it can fulfill; thus freedom will also be the supreme expression of faithfulness to oneself. As I suggested earlier, Aristotle's profound observation "man is the animal through which logos – language – passes" is erroneously translated as "man is a rational animal" (Panikkar 1981, p. 57). Our passing through this world does not require our assent, but our actually being able to feel that we ourselves are the passing requires being consciously open to the proceeding of life in its supra-personal dimension. Then, our entering becoming, sojourning and passing through will also mean permitting the Word that has preceded us and which will find its completion "beyond us," to pass through us. In this event, even the unrelenting passage of time, which in the negative destiny complex seems to be the prototype of everything that degrades and destroys, could be transformed through the rhythm entered into by the individual to participate in the global work of the universe.

5.4 Justice and synchronicity

The sense of harmony that pervaded the ancient concept of the cosmos reflected, above all, a dedication of unequalled measure, because in the cosmos justice was also characterized by precision, and, more specifically, the capacity to be in the right place at the right time. As De Santillana writes: "...there was a time when right meant, above all, correctness, and sin was incorrectness" (De Santillana, 1968, 1985, 2004, pp. 169–170). He also describes a myth that was widespread from the Pythagoreans to Polynesia, and then evoked by Dante, in which the souls of the deceased crowd the seashore, waiting for the boat that will transport them from time to eternity. There were only two moments of the year, which coincided with the equinoxes, in which the Sun when it set was open like a door (whence the classical name *Portae Solis*), since it was positioned on the zodiac and the equator simultaneously. The magic boat had to follow the long trail of sunlight reflected in the water and reach the Sun before it sank below the horizon, sail through it to pass from time to eternity, then climb up along the Milky Way toward the souls' last resting place. Those who "missed the boat" had to wait on the shore for six months (ivi, p. 27). Thus, precision provided both a physical and an ethical law to the cosmos. The transition from one world to another contemplated various points rigorously marked in space and time, "nodal links" that connected otherwise-divergent parameters such as time and eternity, finite and infinite, earthly life and spiritual path. In Platonic language, as De Santillana explains, it is a question of points "where the circle of the Same coincides with that of the Other" (ivi. p 27), while in psychological terms, we could say, as mentioned earlier, that the meeting with oneself cannot occur without the meeting with the other than self. It would seem, therefore, that these nexuses of significant coincidences are not governed by the law of cause/effect and of identity/non-contradiction, but rather relate to the Jungian notion of synchronicity. In the first place, in fact, two heterogeneous phenomena share the same meaning and are linked, not because one produces the other and precedes it, but because they find a reciprocal orientation that simultaneously alters both; in the second place, these same phenomena mark different events that are nevertheless part of a single reality. The experience of Fate, as a rigorous measure, is therefore also the experience of καιρός, the incidence of the single moment, the right time, which, according to the Greeks, "decides between being and nonbeing" (ivi, p. 169), and the instant in which situations light years apart come together, producing a creative contact. This experience clearly does not only concern the moment of death, but all the moments of life that constitute a turning point, a truly qualitative leap in the individuation process. In this sense, καιρός, while demanding attentiveness and promptness on our part, is not merciless like the chronological time of history in which each event is irreversible and therefore cannot be corrected or redeemed. Within καιρός, we can always find new meanings for the past and new orientations for the future.

"How many times have I made away with!," exclaims Mephisto, the spirit of negation, in *Faust*. "And ever circulates a newer, fresher blood [...] From Water,

Earth, and Air unfolding, a thousand germs break forth and grow, in dry and wet, warm and chilly" (Chap. 3). There is a parallel between Goethe's image and the dream of a young woman who was in depth analysis with me:

> I am on the edge of a deep well. I slide downward and plunge into the darkness. But as I go deeper, there is a glimmer of light that becomes brighter and brighter, as a voice off proclaims: "It's useless, in the depths of death there is always life, no matter what the human being does."

These intuitions would seem to indicate an inversion of the chronological sequence of events by triggering the dimension of the new precisely from something that ends. Thus, they emphasize the power of Eros, not as the son of Aphrodite but of πόρος (fullness) and πενία (lack), and thus permanently full due to his pertaining to the paternal nature and permanently empty due to his pertaining to the maternal nature. And also to Eros as the pilgrim, who is both rich and beggarly at the same time, and, like the Arabian Phoenix, dies and rises every day from his own ashes. But at what register of meaning can these images be read to avoid lapsing into a kind of madness of desire? Obviously only in the order of a symbolic time that attributes to the relationship between beginning and end a different meaning from the one existing in concrete time. The irrefutable truth that death necessarily concludes (and, from a certain viewpoint, interrupts) life, which we cannot forget on pain of being swept up into the vortex of a manic pathology, can be associated with another truth, perceivable by the soul and not the senses. Namely, that there is also an end that reconnects with the beginning and with the project of our deepest being, and thus becomes meaning and fulfillment.

There are many occasions on which we might seek our origin – even if we have lost it – and begin again, albeit at different levels and stages of life, to trace the secret design it contains. The most ancient civilizations, characterized by a pre-historical consciousness of time, utilized ritual to re-actualize the cosmogonic moment in which a cosmos arose from chaos, and thus to repossess the potentialities of their own destiny (Eliade 1949). Καιρός, the time of meaning, that intensely lived present from which a sense of the eternal bursts forth, could be configured as the symbolic place where our own ritual takes place: the maturation of a consciousness which, while not ignoring history, can open up to trans-historical dimensions. As Panikkar writes poetically:

> Those moments for which we would have given our whole life, those aesthetic experiences that seem atemporal, those spheres of existence that open up "beyond the heights" in deep meditation, and the ecstasy experienced when contemplating the mysteries of life, suffering and death, could all be examples of the irreducibility of human consciousness to historic consciousness.
>
> (Panikkar 1981/1984, p. 19)

There is a particular sense of justice that reflects the law of retaliation, since it interprets misfortunes as the price to pay for individual and collective wrong-doings. By contrast, the law of Fate, understood as the strict adhesion to one's place and task in the cosmos, contemplates a form of suffering inherent to life, which is not guilt-related or pathologically used as a hiding place or a weapon to brandish vengefully against the presumed culprits. When experienced as transit, suffering is accepted but also abandoned, since "justice" would also mean a "capacity to give oneself to joy."

Notes

1 In more detail, φήμη also means: novella, proverb, tradition, memory; φατός, sayable, renowned; φάσις ἄστρων, apparition, rising of a star; φανερός: visible to all, evident, manifest, renowned, illustrious; φαντασία: spectacle, splendor, appa-rition, phantom, vision, imagination, fantasy; φανός: bright, shining, radiant, flaming torch, lantern.
2 In more detail φήμη means also: news, proverb, tradition, memory; φατός: what may be said, famous; φάσισ ἄστρων: apparition, rising of a star; φανερός: visible to everyone, manifest, famous; φαντασία: show, glamour, apparition, ghost, fan-tasy; φανός: full of light, radiant, torch, lantern.
3 I believe that the Christian notion of the Trinity, with its concepts of transcend-ence and immanence, offers us an image of how the divinity itself (metaphor-ically comparable to its corresponding psychic reality, i.e. the Self) split the absolute through a circularity (περιπατέσις) of giving (in the original sense of κένωσις, kénosis, the complete emptying out of self) in which the obsessive-com-pulsive defenses of subjectivity no longer exist. To sum up briefly Panikkar's thought, which I find the most innovative on this subject, the three figures that constitute the Trinity are placed in a condition of radical relativity one to the other: everything that the father has he transmits to the Son who is *his* being, his expression, his word, while all the other beings, *through* the Son and the Holy Spirit, i.e. by following their existential path and maintaining the contact with the depths of their inner being, return to the Father, to the source whence they sprang (1989; p. 73 and ff.)

Chapter 6

Destiny and individuation process

Tyche was one of the pre-Olympian Greek deities, "a goddess whose name means 'what may hap' or 'Chance,' a deity of whom no particular stories are told, but whose power – like that of the three Moirai and the threefold Hekate – proved stronger than the rule of Zeus" (Kerenyi, 1951/1958, p. 41). Since there was no particular story attached to Tyche, we may suppose that she was a beginning unto herself, the initiator, she who ignited the spark of invention. Thus, her decisions were not justified by a cause or born "from" something, but "for" something whose meaning lay in the future.

In the past, the unpredictability of Fate aroused considerable anxiety in human beings, probably because it conjured the image of a tremendous flash of lighting that struck the path of life and sent it completely off-course. For this reason, it was held in check by a series of laws and norms designed to neutralize its power and place it within the bounds of a recognizable horizon. I think that the unpredictable datum "chance" was truly misunderstood and that man, in attempting to rid himself of his fear, also eliminated the innovative element heralded by chance. In our desperately seeking to reduce Fate to a destiny "of which I am master and I shape with my own hands," we have lost the possibility of liberating ourselves, at certain moments, from the burden of the past and of preparing a future that is unforeseen, since it is not the product of an obligatory sequence of events, and, above all, it is "still not known." In seeking to prevent our existential path from being deviated by another hand, we have actually betrayed it and rendered it sterile. This is why we need a new sense of destiny in which we see ourselves neither as acting alone nor as crushed by overwhelming powers, and which, far from alienating us from ourselves, would give us back our creativity. As Galimberti writes, there is in every language:

> a certain number of words that imply destiny, such as fortune, fatality, chance, predestination, vocation, individuation. [...] They all suggest an image of the world that is not the image that man has rationally constructed. Destiny eludes the logic of reason that the notion of causality substantiates, while causality eludes the sense of mystery jealously guarded by destiny. The idea of destiny expresses the cosmic nostalgia

DOI: 10.4324/9781003261872-8

of a soul that has lost its homeland and wanders through foreign lands, where it may find means of subsistence and reasons for living, but not meaning. [...] There are moments in which every form of causality in the outside world is overturned and an overriding need for a meaning asserts itself, which no causal system is able to satisfy.

(1984, pp. 114–115)

A patient once recounted a dream in which a man was standing in a circle of light with darkness all around. In describing the dream he imagined possible ways in which the oneiric image might evolve:

The man, who has the air of an orchestral conductor or a ringmaster, could remain alone in his space, illuminated like a stylite atop a pillar, or he could have the powers of a wizard and create his orchestra or circus by some magic trick. He could also suddenly see the lights come on, and then the orchestra or the circus, previously in the darkness, would appear.

The first solution would appear to represent an autistic choice: the man isolates himself, encapsulating himself in a form of radical self-sufficiency and severing all his ties with reality. The second solution, instead, denotes a narcissistic choice: the Ego attributes to reality the value that corresponds to its need to be grandiose, and others are only seen if they coincide perfectly with the characters created by its design and they recognize it in the role it has attributed to itself (*"The truth is the formulation of which we can convince others,"* a patient mentioned earlier once told me.) The third solution expresses a creative choice: reality is not an invention of my mind, nor is it subject to my commands. It can manifest freely, as it wishes, and I will define myself within the relationship that I establish with it. The conductor and the ringmaster are such, in fact, because they have an orchestra or a circus to direct, which exists independently of them. *"This last event is a revelation,"* the aforesaid patient exclaimed with a certain excitement.

In this regard, it may be said that what we call "revelation" necessarily involves both an objective and a subjective dimension. In fact, on the one hand, we find ourselves faced with the world that "offers itself" to a transformative process that introduces new perspectives; on the other, this new opening would only trigger a turning point and avoid remaining sterile if it were captured by an observing gaze capable of recognizing it and reflecting it in the deepest psyche.

The aforementioned patient's account of the possible developments of his dream shows that the sense of destiny will vary according to the different positions assumed by the Ego, which may remain bound to the construction of a form of Shadow or transform itself into the light of existence. If the Ego is invaded by persecutory ideas and sees itself threatened by an ever-imminent catastrophe, it will defend itself by withdrawing in its proud isolation or by seeking to dominate reality with the same absolute power that it imagines itself to be governed. If, instead, the Ego has faith in the innovative faculty of the world and in its own capacities, it will be willing to perceive the "revelation" of reality and to interact with it in a creative relationship. Then the Ego will rightly feel that it is the creator of its work, since it is supported by its own inspiration as well as its desire to express it, and by an authoritativeness that it has not usurped arbitrarily but which has been conferred upon it by reality itself – the reality of the orchestra and the circus that needs a director whom, to some degree, they choose and elect. In this case, it may be said that the image of one's own destiny is translated into a sense of adhesion to the individuation process, i.e., the establishment of productive relationships between Ego and Self, Ego and Shadow, I and You, soul and world. Bollas conceives destiny as an impulse of the Self, since it expresses the real Self's tendency to elaborate the personality's potential:

> There is [...] an urge to establish one's self. This destiny drive is that force imminent to the subject's idiom in its drive to achieve its potential for person elaboration. Through mental and actual objects this idiom seeks to articulate itself through the "enchainments" of experience.
>
> (Bollas 1989, 2019, p. 26)

But doesn't the Jungian concept of the individuation process also contemplate the path followed by the Self's impulse toward its self-realization? In my opinion, the powerful love of Fate offered to us by the spirit of the ancient world provides an opportunity to revisit Jung's intuition, and thus to associate our individual destiny with the becoming of human collectivity and the cosmos itself.

The idea of Fate as the word of the god who illuminates and reveals seems to link it, first and foremost, to a key moment in the individuation process: the broadening of consciousness. However, this should not be understood solely as Ego-consciousness, nor would it concern a knowledge of reality in which thought (reduced to its rational dimension) would appropriate, though the application of its categories, the laws governing phenomena and would dominate the latter. Instead, it should be seen as a consciousness that emerges from the deepest layers of the psyche, an "unconscious consciousness," as Jung calls it, or the consciousness of the Self in which, as mentioned earlier, multiple luminosities are kindled. In harmony with their free rhythm, the evoked images would reveal themselves to the Ego, shifting its point of view and widening its horizon Thus conceived, the unconscious would be not only an object to study but also a subject that expresses itself, asking to be looked at and listened to. In the depths of the collective unconscious, in fact, as Jung states, "I am the object of every subject, in complete reversal of my ordinary consciousness, where I am always the subject that has an object" (1934/1954, 2014, p. 22). This place of every subject, this "we," which is concretized in the community in which we live when we take part in satisfying its needs, cannot but have an equivalent in the Self. Hence, the dialogue between Ego and Self becomes intersubjective, possessing all the dignity and disquieting unpredictability that such a dialogue implies. If this is so, do the others, the world, and the Self exist because I see them, or do I exist because the others, the world, and the Self see me? Does Ego-consciousness bring the object to light or does the light of the object communicate itself to Ego-consciousness? It probably works both ways, because if I am able to recognize myself and I am recognized at the same time, I not only feel that I exist, but also that I am true and real. From this standpoint, Fate could be the process through which a person expresses himself to himself and others, and receives an enhanced image of himself from the Self and others. It is precisely in this sense that Fate is superimposed to the Jungian concept of the individuation process. Indeed, for Jung individualizing is much more than becoming conscious of what we are. And how could consciousness, constituted within precise limits, embrace the infinity of unconsciousness without distorting and betraying it? Hence, the achievement of individuation not only involves a quantitative broadening of consciousness, but also a qualitative change: the transition from a dogmatic consciousness, which tends to absolutize itself and to interpret reality solely through the parameters of reason (also in order better to master it and bend it to its purposes), to a symbolic consciousness, which is open to the further meaning contained in the unconscious, to that inexpressible and unknowable mystery that always lies at the bottom of every revelation. As Galimberti writes:

> … in the Ego-Self dialectic, Jung perhaps gives one of the most apt descriptions of symbolic consciousness, which is none other than human consciousness saved from the confinement within the rational dimension to which Western culture has consigned it.
>
> (Galimberti 1984, p. 185)

As Mino Vianello reminds us, there is also the fact that ever since the days of permanent settlements society has been dominated by a male chauvinist culture. This lies at the root of Western rationality, which can also be described as "instrumental," since it pursues solely goals of spatial conquest and dominion over various forms of life and culture. Therefore, it is necessary to introduce another face of the Absolute Shadow, namely the Male Chauvinist Shadow – cause of war, femicide, gender discrimination – and to understand this we must take a look at history and the Neolithic.

Permanent settlements were a novelty in the history of the human species. They sprang up following a discovery made, thanks to women, around seven thousand years ago: agriculture, which paradoxically marked the end of gender equality. In all areas crossed by great rivers, in Mesopotamia and the Fertile Crescent in China, there developed settlements linked to agricultural production (Vianello, 2022, pp. 19–28), where males dominated females by monopolizing public life. This was a reaction to their frustration – relatively mild during the age of Man-the-Gatherer (90 percent of the history of the human species) – provoked by their incapacity to produce the most beautiful thing in the world: another human being, thought to be generated by a mysterious power that was activated from time to time in the depths of a woman's body (Vianello and Caramazza, 1992, 1998), and which the male did not possess. This frustration could not even be mitigated by an awareness that the conceived baby was the result of fecundation, i.e. the union of a generative male and female element, since at that time no one knew that the sexual act between man and woman was linked to the beginning of a new human life. Paradoxically, however, the envy and deep-seated anger triggered by female procreative power lived on in the male psyche, becoming far more deep-rooted than Freudian penis envy in the woman, even when the relation between coitus and pregnancy gradually came to be recognized.

In the period preceding the Neolithic, all religions were pervaded by a female ethos. With the arrival of permanent settlements, however, the myths of the Great Mother were ousted by the myths and worship of angry and violent gods (Bolen, 1984, 1989), and all religions became fiercely male chauvinist. This gave rise in the individual and collective unconscious to another kind of Shadow, the "Male Chauvinist Shadow," from which women themselves are not exempt. The "Male Chauvinist Shadow" contains the anger, the reaction to humiliation, and the vindictiveness of the male, who felt inferior to the female due to his lack of generative power and thus presumed to dominate woman and subjugate her completely by degrading her.

In Jungian terms, we could say that, since then, the archetypal image of the woman in the male psyche, i.e., the Anima, has lost its characteristic sensibility, capacity for compassion, tenderness, and profound intuition of the most authentic value of every part of creation, from the animal to the human being, from flower to celestial vault. Thus the Anima, which speaks to man's consciousness, could no longer express itself or inspire him, being reduced to an internal presence judged to be inferior and weak, which was incapable of asserting itself, degraded and voluntarily removed, becoming an inferiority complex to eliminate by projecting it onto woman herself.

For her part, the woman sought to react by allowing herself to be guided by the same power complex that man used to oppress her. Hence she was no longer able to make use of the male archetypal image in herself, the Jungian Animus, as a totality of factors that would have given her determination, strength, and even a precise understanding of the reality of the world, through the exercise of judicious thought. Instead, the Animus was transformed into a kind of "animosity" through the will to dominate others in its turn, especially the male, and even its own femininity that was seen as fragile. Thus, for some women the Animus became a form of "Male Chauvinist Shadow" by which they were possessed, unconsciously losing themselves in it, or with which they consciously identified, to the extent of considering their feminine characteristics inferior and refusing to accept them as part of themselves. And so *male chauvinist culture*, like all dominating cultures, also *became that of women themselves*, for whom worship of the strong, "virile" male became a myth. All this was able to happen because the male chauvinist culture had acquired the upper hand in the socialization process.

In the light of these considerations, the "Male Chauvinist Shadow" could be seen as a type of "Absolute Shadow" because it abolishes the dialectic between the different instances of the psyche and between self and other than self. In this case, personality enrichment through the dialogue between man and woman in the interpersonal reality and between the male and female principle in the intra-psychic sphere would be overwhelmed and abolished by an "absolute power complex." In the interaction between man and woman communication, reciprocal complementation, and the sense of having a common destiny would cease, and solely the will to abuse and to dominate the other would prevail.

To return to the Jungian concept of the individuation process, we could say that it encompasses the stages of psychic development that embraces individual differentiation and, precisely through the confrontation with mythological images, the integration of the archaic function of the psyche in the global context of the personality. This process unfolds through the constructive dialogue between Ego and Self, and since the Self includes the world, cannot disregard interpersonal dialogue, involvement in the concrete needs of the community, and relationship with the whole of reality.

Enlightened by this new conception of Fate that embraces an ancient wisdom reinterpreted in the light of the concept of individuation, we can perhaps conceive of our destiny in new ways. Instead of viewing it as a sense of the inevitable, as what has been determined from above to enchain our evolution, or as confidence in being able to manage existence voluntaristically – all of which are equally inadequate – we could see it as becoming our specific and unique life project, as the development of our innate potential, and as the drive that will allow us to trustingly consign the nucleus of our innermost essence to the future.

Chapter 7

Conclusion

I would sum up the fundamental concepts of this book by saying that I have sought a greater understanding of the Shadow – one of the most difficult themes in Jung's oeuvre – through an interpretive grid based on both my studies of analytical psychology and my clinical experience. I have discussed a specific configuration of Shadow, which I have called the "Absolute Shadow," drawing inspiration in particular from an image described by Jung in *Memories, Dreams, Reflections*, since it seems to prefigure his concept of "Shadow" that was later developed in multifaceted ways. The image occurs in the passage in which Jung evokes, in metaphorical form, a crucial existential experience he had at the age of twelve:

> I was taking the long road to school from Klein-Hüningen, where we lived, to Basel, when suddenly for a single moment I have the overwhelming impression of having just emerged from a dense cloud. I knew all at once: now I am myself! It was as if a wall of mist were at my back, and behind that wall there was not yet an "I." But at this moment I came upon myself. Previously I had existed, too, but everything had merely happened to me. Now I happened to myself. Now I knew: I am myself now, now I exist. Previously I had been willed to do this and that; now I willed. This experience seemed to me tremendously important and new: there was "authority" in me.
>
> (1961, 1989, pp. 50–51)

This telling imagination of Jung's seems to represent his emerging from the state of fusion between the Ego and the unconscious that he had experienced during his "infantile neurosis," which had begun when he was nearly twelve. It all started when a schoolmate pushed him and he fell down, striking his head on the curbstone, and almost losing consciousness. However, he recalls deliberately playing on his condition, just after he suddenly had the thought: "Now you won't have to go to school any more." From then on, he suffered a nervous crisis every time he had to go back to school or his parents told him to do his homework, which resulted in his being absent for over six months:

DOI: 10.4324/9781003261872-9

Above all, I was able to plunge into the world of the mysterious. To that realm belonged trees, a pool, the swamp, stones and animals, and my father's library. But I was growing more and more away from the world, and had all the while faint pangs of conscience. I frittered away my time with loafing, collecting, reading, and playing. But I did not feel any happier for it; I had the obscure feeling that I was fleeing from myself.

(ivi, p. 46)

He further explains:

What had led me astray during the crisis was my passion for being alone, my delight in solitude. Nature seemed to me full of wonders, and I wanted to steep myself in them. Every stone, every plant, every single thing seemed alive and indescribably marvelous. I immersed myself in nature, crawled, as it were, into the very essence of nature and away from the whole human world.

(ivi, p. 50)

Thus, we can say that the Shadow is only embodied later, when the Ego begins to constitute itself. By separating from the unconscious, the Ego distinguishes itself from its own Shadow and sees it at the same time: it is the cloud behind Jung.

Jung's emerging from his infantile neurosis therefore meant his refusing to drown in a sea of feeling, where it was as if he had identified with the totality of the universe and was no longer obliged to come to terms either with his limits and his duties, or willed initiatives that can result in success or failure; in other words, with the dimension of the Ego. And it was this refusal that enabled him to have the vital experience represented by the image of the dense cloud.

When a conscious Ego is established it is as if one was able to perceive an area of shadow or mist in which, though still not clearly defined, objects can be seen and, to some extent, circumscribed. The cloud could represent the unconscious and, in this case, the Shadow would be superimposable to the unconscious itself. This would mean that one has arrived at the vision of a relative Shadow that no longer takes over one's whole being and is, instead, a source of creativity, because it contains the unknown future. To conclude, the Shadow can only begin to represent a part of the totality of being, with which the Ego can then enter into relationship, after the psyche has been divided into consciousness and unconscious, indicated by the cloud and the observing Ego. This gives rise to both an "intra-" and "extra-" psychic relational dimension, that is a meeting and exchange between consciousness and unconscious, Ego and Self, soul and world.

Conversely, what I have called "Absolute Shadow" could be represented by a state of total immersion in the cloud or in the realm of nature, which would prevent one from seeing both the cloud and the world as it really is. From this standpoint the Absolute Shadow, which may be defined as a state of total indistinction between Ego and non-Ego, as well as between Ego and unconscious, could not be configured immediately and only reconstructed *a posteriori*, after the birth of consciousness. In fact, Jung is only able to talk about the cloud in which he was immersed after he emerges from it and sees it. We should therefore speak of it as a virtual image, inasmuch as it has no contours and is not definable, or perhaps as an attempt to depict a motion of being. A motion that, fantastically speaking, could lead either to annihilation or to the conquest of a phantasmal form of totality and perfect happiness because, at that level, nothingness and the all would both have the value of an absolute with which one identifies or of which one is part. There is, as I mentioned earlier, an analogy between the danger of going back to merge with the Absolute Shadow and remaining engulfed in it, and the psychic movement that Jung called "regressive incest." For Freud, the desire for incest is sparked in the phase of the Oedipus complex that is established when the child is already in a triangular situation and, therefore, experiences a conflict of ambivalence toward the parent of the same sex and an erotic attraction to the parent of the opposite sex; whereas in the situation of regressive incest we find ourselves in a pre-oedipal and, perhaps, pre-sexual phase. Here the risk to mental health is certainly much higher, since it is almost a matter of going back through the barrier of psychic birth, i.e., the moment in which the child is able to bear, albeit for brief moments, the perception that its body is separate from that of the mother and that there is a difference between me and not me, between me, as the beginning of subjectivity, and objective reality. In such cases, we seem justified in speaking of an Absolute Shadow, since the already constituted Ego is in danger of floundering in the primordial unconscious, in that undifferentiated Self which, as the maternal womb, had once contained and nourished it, but which must be distanced at the right moment, in order to activate a development toward the realization of a complete and integrated personality. In fact, the Self as the goal of the individuation process is quite different from the originary Self, because it is constructed through the ongoing dialogue and interaction with the Ego dimension.

As stated above, I would distinguish the concept of "Absolute Shadow" from that of "Archetypal Image of the Shadow," because in the case of the latter we would be dealing with the prototype of all that is negative a/o unknown, and thus with an already established dialectic between consciousness and unconscious, value and disvalue. Contrastingly, in the Absolute Shadow the Ego loses itself in the non-Ego and the sense of its value is lost in a feeling of disvalue. In Kleinian language, we could say that in the phase during which the object splits into good and bad, the Ego does not evolve toward the depressive position but tends to shift toward a pre-ambivalent and pre-conflictual position in which the opposites are neither split nor integrated, but indistinct and, in a certain sense, interchangeable. Here, too, good and bad would be held together but not diversified, because it would be impossible to perceive the object and the Self as an entity composed of many parts articulated in a larger whole; moreover, diverse and contrary aspects of the internal and external reality would possibly move toward a superimposition rather than a complex composition, which is more articulated than mere synthesis. It would seem more appropriate, therefore, to liken what I have called Absolute Shadow to the archetypal image of the parents (still not distinguished as father and mother but encapsulated in a single form steeped in omnipotence), which re-emerges in every violent desire for fusional relation. In fact, this archetypal image always has aspects whose ideal grandiosity is fascinating and seductive, or whose persecutory power alternately (and sometimes contemporaneously because we are dealing with a paradox) subjugates and destroys. At this level, as René Girard states, there would occur a paradoxical convergence of opposites and one would no longer be able to say that an object is good a/o bad, loved a/o hated, but that it is good "inasmuch as" it is bad, and loved " inasmuch as" it is hated. Then the opposites may be forced into a single existential space and suddenly convert into each other or give rise to switched meanings. For example, death could be sensed as a life rendered immortal; the sacrifice of an actual relationship as the means of saving an ideal union that is suffused with a romantic aura, indissoluble and blissfully happy; and the achievement of total independence, free from needs (what amounts to isolation), as the possibility of being the sole person to enjoy all the riches of the Earth. Emblematic in this regard is the definition of birth given by a patient of whom I spoke earlier: "*Birth is the abortion of a desire that cannot be realized.*" This suggests the existence of a particular form of desire that does not concern the aspiration to reach a goal or a yearning to be one with the loved object, but is rather desire "without object." A form of desire, I would say, whose specific aim is unlimited expansion, which can also act as a resistance to enter life and becoming, since both of these dimensions are always inscribed within a limit.

At the same time, and as I have already explained, my attention was attracted by a whole series of clinical situations in which patients seemed seized by a sense of their own destiny as "the inevitability of a catastrophe." As De Santillana writes: "Fate can be summed up as follows: every great enterprise ultimately seems bound to fail" (1968, 1985, 2004, pp. 16–17). "Pre-" and "super-" ordained factors, extraneous to one's own individual characteristics, combine to weave a web in which the person is inevitably caught. While the desire and need to change one's life and give it a meaning are implicit in the request for depth analysis, overpowering forces that drag the person toward incomprehensible goals are also imagined and felt. This brings to mind the words of Prometheus in Aeschylus' play, "I stopped men thinking of their future deaths," and his response to the chorus when they asked what cure he had discovered for the disease: "Inside their hearts I put blind hope." The image of failure and dying can exert a hypnotic fascination that paralyzes the flow of life and turns life itself into a kind of anticipated death. The resistance to life, therefore, would appear to be related to the refusal of its limit, symbolically and concretely represented by the prospect of death. In this event, blind hope would be the start of imaginative activity that creates a space for the works of existence and belief in their meaning, even though they are inscribed in a relative order: the blindness of hope could be precisely the capacity to remain in the "here and now" without being overwhelmed by the anxiety of death that always underlies a desire for immortality. Prometheus is able to gift men a divine spark precisely because in accepting the temporal boundaries of their life, they forego being gods. However, I think that the "blind" quality of hope has another even more profound and mysterious meaning. It would not only prevent us from being paralyzed by the vision of what awaits us at the end of our life but, above all, would make us open to contemplating an infinite space-time, which can only be seen in the "here and now." This space-time goes beyond the concreteness of the perceived image and arrives at the inexhaustible root of the Self, of the archetypal sphere where the experience of the whole of humanity is condensed, and of the nucleus that is not only marked by time but also veils the eternal, giving to the temporal dimension an "imperishable" quality. We live in "tempiternity," as Panikkar would say, because the intensely experienced moment cannot be measured like the chronological dimension of time. It can expand infinitely, and is the bearer of the meaning of life. Thus, the acceptance of limitation and mortality combined with an awareness that an imperishable dimension could enter our life, would give a non-transient meaning to what we meet, create, and feel: we are not gods and we will forever renounce being such, but we are in intimate and essential relation with a dimension that may be called "divine."

These thoughts show, once again, the importance of Jung's intuition of how fundamental the relationship between the entity of the Ego, which defines us as individuals, and the reality of the Self, which makes us part of the universe, is in the realization of our whole personality. It took Jung a long time and lengthy reflection to unite these two dimensions, which in him were embodied in what he called "personality No. 1" and "personality No. 2." Apropos of this he recounts poetically in *Memories, Dreams, Reflections*:

> ...there was always, deep in the background, the feeling that something other than myself was involved. It was as though a breath of the great world of stars and endless space had touched me, or as if a spirit had invisibly entered the room – the spirit of one who had long been dead and yet was perpetually present in timelessness until far into the future. Denouements of this sort were wreathed with the halo of a numen.
>
> (1961, 1989, p. 87)

And when Jung contemplated Gothic cathedrals he truly had the impression that the world of things, nature and human beings was nourished by an eternal rhizome:

> ... there the infinity of the cosmos, the chaos of meaning and meaninglessness, of impersonal purpose and mechanical law, were wrapped

in stone. This contained and at the same time was the bottomless mystery of being, the embodiment of spirit. What I dimly felt to be my kinship with stone was the divine nature in both, in the dead and the living matter.

(ivi. p. 89)

When destiny is seen as tragic, it is as if a shadow had fallen across and covered it. The sense of negativity projected onto destiny as a force that overwhelms, prevents or coerces, appears to embody the idea of a power that is feared but also invoked, and perhaps also used, by the Ego to cope with its experiences of fragility. Whether it opposes destiny by displaying its ruin as an expression of revenge, or identifies with it as a persecutor, the Ego seems to make use of an absolute power that enables it to experience a form of triumph. It does not much matter whether this power is destructive or constructive, because in the absolute one extreme can always suddenly become its opposite. In particular, as I said earlier, the idea of death or failure of one's existential project may contain an impulse to drown in cosmic dimensions that would fancifully restore to the Ego the totality lost when it entered becoming. Thus death would be confused, on the one hand with "non-birth," and on the other with immortality, i.e., a situation immune to the space-time limit of life. In this context, the suicide project could represent the recovery of a power that was eclipsed at birth, and would contain both the Ego's sense of failure and the denial of this failure due to its merging with the whole. This aspiration to being "immeasurable," this merging with a totality that contains indifferently positive and negative, is the situation in which the Absolute Shadow operates.

It also seemed to me that revisiting the conception of Fate in the ancient world could offer us the chance to change the sense of our individual destiny. In understanding Fate as the word of a god who illuminates and reveals, the human being would no longer feel obliged to fit into a scheme preconstituted by powers above, but would discover his own unique place as part of the cosmos, pervaded by "divine" resonances, and the meaning of his own existential path.

I would like to conclude by briefly discussing two dreams that a patient of mine had on the same theme, but one year apart. In the first dream this young woman was looking at herself in the mirror and noticed that she was losing a suntan that was "fake" or had been obtained too quickly: her face was becoming lighter in the center, whereas she still had a dark area on her forehead. Then, in the same dream, she was watching a little boy, who was unable to benefit from the love offered him by his foster parents because he could not forgive his natural parents for having abandoned him, and remained a prisoner of his bitterness and his need for revenge. In the second dream, a small boy who had lived in an institution for abandoned minors or orphans in the early months of his life and had been subject to maturational delay, responded positively to the care of foster parents and was able to repair the damage he had suffered. Here we could say that we are dealing with an intergenerational shadow, since the shadow of the parents who are guilty of abandoning their son extends precisely to the abandoned boy who, filled with anger, can neither forgive nor benefit from reparative actions by working through the affront experienced and healing the pain. The shadow is well represented by the image of the "fake" tan, since it is a shadow transferred from one generation to the other and therefore does not originate with the child. Even so, its effects are extended to her life, as is clear from the dark circular area on her face. It would seem, therefore, that through the process of elaborating an "inherited" Shadow, precisely by dissolving what we might call a family complex, this patient found a way to allow love to circulate within her relationships, as is well evident in the second dream of the adopted child who receives the gift of love from his new foster parents.

This is, however, a process that concerns every human being, because we could say that, in a certain sense, we are all adopted children. To meet our "real parents," in fact, we are sooner or later obliged to see their limits, recognizing the good things they have given us – obviously in ways congenial to their nature – and the eventual and inevitable difficulties that have prevented them from responding adequately to our needs – also because, in childhood fantasy, needs are often steeped in a thirst for total and immediate satisfaction. So we shall have to accept that we will find our parents different from the ideal image with which we had identified them, which is the result of our desire, our expectations and that fervent childish longing (which perhaps cannot be suppressed by human life) for a love that fills our sense of emptiness. If we do not work through our mourning of the "archetypal parents," then the disappointment and anger we experience due to feeling abandoned and betrayed will inevitably be transformed into the Shadow of a persecutory feeling. The capacity to tolerate the primary narcissistic wound gives us access, over time, to the more mature awareness that it cannot be healed, because it is not disease, and neither can it arouse negative reactions, because it is not wrongdoing. On the contrary, it is the very condition of an authentic existence, and perhaps our most valuable therapeutic tool.

Afterword

Destiny and Fate in couple therapy

The Indo-European etymological root of the word destiny – Caramazza writes (p. 4) – is composed of the prefix *de*, which means a movement from above to below, and *stha* (standing), which forms the prefix of the Latin *statuere*, to set up, to establish.[1]

Hence, destiny would appear to intervene from above and define a trajectory that causes the individual's existence to revolve around points of attraction that deflect its orbit. Diseases that cross several generations, unmindful repetitions of what has already occurred, and constant unconscious modalities that govern relationships are activated, imposing a conservative procedure on a transformative possibility.

Destiny in the form of an "imposed plan," as Caramazza specifies (p. 4), can assume the character of evil intentionality and, in this event, its unfolding raises questions concerning the problem of *guilt*. Guilt is generally projected onto parents, a partner or the analyst, "because we projected onto them the archetypal image of an ideal and omnipotent parent." At times, though, guilt is assumed by the Ego, thus giving rise to a depressive connotation.

"Responsibility and guilt are radically different," Caramazza reminds us. "A sense of responsibility [...] suggests the adoption of a *compassionate* attitude toward what has happened to us, and encourages reparation. [...] Whereas a sense of guilt [...] demands punishment and expiation" (Caramazza, p. 6). The author also emphasizes that it is important to acquire a sense of responsibility through the recognition of error.

Responsibility cannot be assumed, or, one might say, our own Shadows cannot be integrated, if "a Shadow formed by persecutory fantasies, i.e., projected blame, since our parents, God, nature, or our hereditary genetic constitution are considered responsible for our being fated to submit to an unfavorable destiny" (Caramazza p. 29) plays an active part in the structuring of a *negative destiny complex*.

In couple therapy we also encounter the influence of personal and familial Shadows that the partners unconsciously superimpose and bind to, and interweave with, the relationship, to the point that emotionally charged

DOI: 10.4324/9781003261872-10

contents are configured as destiny trajectories. When the *negative destiny complex*, of which Elena Caramazza speaks, oppresses one or both partners, it can act in the unconscious area shared by the couple, combining a sense of destiny as inevitable with the fantasy of being able to avoid it in and through the relationship.

In this case, the unconscious area shared by the couple constitutes the *unconscious dovetailing* first described by Dicks (1967, 2016), a field of *collusion* that immobilizes, when it is dominated by archaic defensive mechanisms. If this happens, the couple tends to maintain sufficient stability, but neglects to elaborate the Shadow aspects of each partner. In analytical psychology, this area is defined as the *Shadow of the couple* (Homerin, 2000), to whose construction aspects of the personal and familial Shadow of each partner, with the respective archetypal nuclei, dynamically contribute.

Many authors have dealt with the transmission of the negative between generations. Jung, in his early studies, emphasizes the pathogenic role of family secrets and of particular family complex constellations (Jung 1909, 1973). Kaës points out that the "family secret" is the most common form of shared unconscious family alliance: "What is transmitted is therefore what one does not contain, what one does not retain, what one does not remember" (Kaës, 2009, p. 190).

In this regard, the concept of *White Shadow* has been formulated in analytical psychology (Gallard-Drahon, 1987). It consists in the dynamic area encountered in cases in which the presence of secrets, silences, or of something unnamable in parents and preceding generations has created a "white," a kind of hole in the psychism. This type of negative inheritance is no less burdensome for those who bear it, nor less difficult to deal with than the "black" Shadow created in the personal story of each individual by rules, values and ideals of the familial and social group to which s/he belongs.

The problems linked to the white Shadow require an individual analysis, and a particular kind of work that focuses on the unconscious of the parents and grandparents, on what Dumas (1985) calls the *genealogical unconscious*, which one can imagine as an intermediate function between the personal and the collective unconscious described by Jung. We, too, believe that the concept of Shadow can be extended from the sphere of the personal unconscious to that of transmission between generations (De Benedittis, Fersurella and Presciuttini, 2016; De Benedittis, Fersurella and Presciuttini, 2019).

Also in Jung we find a clinical reflection on destiny, especially in Jung 1947/1954, 2014 and in Jung 1952. Vitolo (2004/22) stresses that, for Jung, destiny is present both in the idea of intergenerational transmission and in that of symbolization. The symbolic perspective is an invitation to seek meaning by looking beyond.

When the search for meaning appears to be blocked by an inevitable and negative destiny factor, another possibility may arise to give a meaning to one's destiny through the interaction between analyst and patient. In this field, *past* events can gradually be assimilated, the individual's encounter with the real can be elaborated in the *present*, and the potentialities of one's development in the *future* can be reflected upon (Trapanese 2004/22). In order to give "meaning," we always need the mind of another who, through relation, can enable a different thinkability of both the past and present (Boccara, 2004/22), thus releasing us from the prison of repetitiveness.

When a couple seeks to modify negative destiny trajectories defined by illnesses and unconscious modalities that cross several generations, the "mind of another" seems to make reference to the third area of unconscious communication that is created between the partners and the analyst, that is to the "multifaceted subtle body" (De Benedittis et al. 2019) that comes into being between the participants in the session.

This is what happened with Paolo and Gianna, who started therapy after a year-long crisis marked primarily by his beginning dialysis, and her serious work problems.

The couple had met at group therapy, and he had immediately fallen in love with her. Gianna, who had just come out of a stormy divorce and already had a boy of ten, did not want to begin a new relationship, but Paolo had shown himself to be so capable of listening to and reassuring her, that she had soon agreed to live with him.

In fact, the couple relationship was based on a strong need for mutual support. They were both extremely insecure and lacking in self-esteem, and felt lucky to have found a partner to whom they could cling, through collusive projective identification. The collusion was interrupted at times by the presence of Gianna's son, who made Paolo overbearingly jealous.

Gianna and Paolo were both forty-five; she was an office worker and he a technician, and over the years they had become increasingly averse to external relationships. The couple experienced their first crisis after the birth of their daughter, who was breastfed for over two years.

With her baby daughter, Gianna had sought to fulfill the need for symbiosis that her mother had not been able to satisfy in her. Gianna's parents were peasants from the south of Italy, rough, violent individuals. They had rejected her because she was the third daughter, and had thrown her out of the house when she was in her early teens because she "went out too much," unaware that she was pregnant with her first child. Her pregnancy had sped up her marriage to the father, one of her teachers at high school, who had a disability and was also violent. Gianna had felt manipulated by her husband and, when he forced her to have an abortion after she became pregnant a second time, she had decided to divorce him. For her, love had always been bound up with violence and that was what she had continued to seek until, thanks to group therapy, she had allowed herself to be seduced by Paolo.

Paolo had also had a difficult childhood: for a long period he had been virtually abandoned in hospital due to a chronic bone infection. At that time his mother, who already suffered from a serious hereditary kidney disease, was experiencing a difficult pregnancy. When his own baby girl was born, Paolo, as had already happened when his baby sister arrived, had felt that the attention of the woman he loved was no longer given *first* to him! Out of anger, he had started to withdraw into himself and had stopped talking to his wife.

So Gianna had once again found herself experiencing love shot through with violence, but psychological this time: with his silence Paolo seemed to be telling her that she did not exist for him!

The two partners felt hounded by an *evil destiny* which, in forcing them to repeat the past, had plunged them anew into the dramatic suffering of their childhood.

The lack of a maternal female model had left an immense void in Gianna. This wound, which had traumatically reopened when she had become a mother in her turn, made her incapable of allowing her children to separate from her. And Paolo had actually renounced his paternal prerogatives, to seek to establish an illusory symbiotic tie with a maternal figure.

The fact that her son had moved to another city and their daughter was older, had recently enabled the couple to access a new transitional space in which they could seek to experience and work through their continuous oscillations between fusion and separation. However, this difficult and dynamic equilibrium had collapsed a year before they started couple therapy, when both partners had gone into severe crisis, from which there seemed to be no way out.

Like his mother who had died prematurely when she was about his age, Paolo had gone into kidney failure due to the same hereditary disease from which she had suffered, and had had to undergo peritoneal dialysis. While on the waiting list for a transplant, he had to hook up to his home dialysis machine at night and could no longer sleep with his wife. The *negative destiny complex* made Paolo think only of his illness, and he had become both self-centered and egoistic. In this difficult year, Gianna had also had to deal with a bullying *Black Shadow*: a stubborn new office boss who, just like her mother, with whom he was identified, thwarted all her attempts to emancipate.

The two partners felt they had lost the fertile area of dialogue, where even their partially suspended boundaries enabled them to oscillate between states of non-integration and states of integration of their shared experiences. This was why they had decided to undertake couple therapy.

They both blamed themselves; he for not being able to deal with the frustration of his illness and she for being intolerant of her problems at work. They were both incapable of recognizing their rights, due to their childhood experiences.

The therapist had the feeling that Paolo and Gianna were used to navigating stormy seas in a boat that was in danger of sinking at any moment. For a long period, the therapist had also experienced a similar sense of precarity, and thus was able to truly understand their emotions that veered between fear and hope, between feeling overcome by events that dominated them and wanting to participate freely in the realization of their own destiny.

Thanks to the intense exchange that took place in the third area, and even though the traumatic situation could not be verbalized because it was beyond the psyche's capacity for integration, something in the couple began to change. However, it was only after the first year of therapy that the partners started to feel compassion for the needy child in each of them. They both seemed to be initiating – as Caramazza states – a new kind of reparation toward themselves, gradually abandoning their feelings of guilt.

In the second year of therapy, the two opposites, rights and duties, were interwoven with all the threads of the relationship. In the third area, that multifaceted space of interaction where the therapist also comes into play, the dialogue between consciousness and unconscious favored a situation where Ego and Shadow, rights and duties began to find a way to meet.

Gianna accused her husband of not relating profoundly, of thinking only of himself and his being ill. But then she wondered if perhaps it was she who was not allowing him to see her.

Paolo reprimanded his wife for offending, insulting and hurting him in their arguments. Then wondered if perhaps it was he, with his fear of relating profoundly, who was exaggerating in seeing her outbursts as so negative.

In this phase each of them began to claim their own rights and to look at both their own and the other's Shadow.

Two dreams seemed to show that transformative valencies were moving in the field.

Gianna described a dream: *"I hit the roof. I told Paolo that I was mad at the father of my son."* Paolo was asked to associate first, in order to reveal the relational aspect of the dream, and saw that the badness belonged to Gianna's past. His partner added: *"The profound suffering caused by everything that happened in my life, led me to understand that I had to change myself."*

A few days later, Paolo dreamed: *"My car had been stolen. I discovered I could move more freely on my bike."* His wife associated that her husband usually escaped when he was afraid of being rejected, but now he thought more before acting. Paolo commented that he was trying to face criticism. Gianna confirmed that, thanks to the therapy, her partner was less on the defensive.

At the end of the second year Paolo, who had willingly agreed to use his "bike," was awaiting a "new car" and a transplant that would change his life, and Gianna had managed to move to a different office. He found that now they accepted and listened to each other more and, having clarified many aspects of their relationship, they felt able to take their responsibilities in relating with each other.

During this period, Paolo was called in for his transplant.

A year and a half later, Gianna phoned the therapist to tell her that everything had gone well. In the meantime, she had begun an individual analysis. Paolo also wanted to follow a course of his own and asked if he could do this with the couple therapist. The latter felt that this impossible request was a kind of "thank-you" for the transformative process then underway, which saw both partners increasingly in charge of their own destiny. They seemed to have grasped the importance of the images of their inner theatre with regard to new possibilities for their destiny and for realizing their own fate.

How do *Destiny* and *Fate* differ? And how are the two concepts related? Toward the end of her text so rich in content, Elena Caramazza expresses a reflection on the subject of Fate and distinguishes it from Destiny, offering us another view of therapy.

In Greek Culture, Caramazza writes, the "ancient concept of Fate" differs from destiny in that it derives "from a cosmic order superior to both humans and gods." It is not a persecutory force, but rather "brings the human being into harmony with his existence and his becoming in relation to the cosmos" (Caramazza, p. 8). So Fate does not become blame and, as De Santillana maintains:

> The idea of Fate comes into being when man does not succumb like an animal, but seeks to understand and does not accept the gift of origin, *le grand don de ne rien comprendre a notre sort* (the great gift of understanding nothing of our fate).
>
> (De Santillana 1968, 1985, 2004, cit. by Caramazza, p. 8)

Fate, therefore, can

> offer us the chance to change the sense of our individual destiny. [...] the human being would no longer feel obliged to fit into a scheme preconstituted by powers above, but would discover his own unique place as part of the cosmos, pervaded by 'divine' resonances, and the meaning of his own existential path.
>
> (Caramazza, p. 168)

In examining the distinction between *Fate* and *Destiny* in psychoanalytical literature, we have found that some authors use the terms as synonyms, while others see the relation between fate and destiny as mirroring the one described above. For Bollas, in fact, *destiny* indicates the potential course of a person's life, whose realization also depends on the will of the individual in question. To distinguish fate from destiny, Bollas refers to the passage in the *Aeneid* in which Juno invokes *fate* to intervene on her behalf against Aeneas, only to see her wishes thwarted because Aeneas' destiny does not permit such an intervention. For Bollas, destiny corresponds to the individual's specificity, which he calls "idiom," and to the realization of his creative potential; whereas fate, which "emerges from the word of the gods" (Bollas (1989, p. 25), indicates the sensation of being constrained by a life history, of not being free.

Bollas believes that the person who enters analysis can be seen as an individual struck by fate, who has lost the *raison d'être* of his future development and the energy to oppose the forces of inertia and anxiety. Ultimately, in his view, the psychopathological structures that dominate the personality determine the potency of fate, while freedom coincides with liberating oneself from their power. Many Freudian analysts see analytic work as seeking, when possible, to transform a person's sense of fate into a sense of their personal destiny. In fact, it is destiny that "makes a person feel able to move with life as it progresses, to have a meaning and a direction, and to play an active part in his own human story" (Pandolfi 2004, p. 83). This is because, as de M'Uzan points out, "when destiny and repetition seem in some way tied together, it is, luckily, often only an impression" (de M'Uzan, 1984, p. 30).

Balsamo considers the equation of fate with destiny redundant, since one term precedes the constitution of the individual and the other has more to do with planned construction. This author is in favor of the continuous and dynamic interweaving of a force underlying individual reality, whether it is called fate or destiny, with each person's subjective translation of that force. Every fate and every destiny is experienced within a social, familial and individual story in which phantasms and defenses, which make analytic work possible, come into play. Analysis "dissolves destiny, suggesting another meaning where destiny with a fixed meaning weighed heavily" (Balsamo, 2004, p. 44).

Instead, Caramazza's line of thought suggests that a particular idea of fate can offer release from an oppressive negative destiny linked to the transmission of Shadow through generations or to other historical factors that influence personal life. This idea of fate as the "word of the god who illuminates and reveals" (Caramazza, p. 159), evokes an impersonal factor superior to generations and to history.

Let us consider the experiences that can be powerfully activated in the love relationship. In some cases, the discovery of the sense of Fate, and therefore the symbolic rather than logical orientation of consciousness of which Caramazza speaks, takes on a specific significance in the couple. The meeting with the "soulmate" can then occur as something for which one's personal destiny was perhaps preparing, but into which the element of "fate" introduces something completely new and unpredictable, with which one nevertheless resonates.

The sense of Fate, unlike the negative destiny complex, does not necessarily paralyze development, negating the possibility of hope. It is in fact a sense of Necessity which, as Caramazza reminds us, is not felt as an insult to the freedom (Caramazza, p. 152) of a human being, but as a link to his most intimate and, at the same time, universal essence.

This particular sense of Fate bears a similarity to the experience of synchronicity that sometimes pervades the love relationship, when the meeting with the other reveals a diverse sense of time and creates a new possibility of meeting oneself. This kind of encounter is not linked to a causal series rooted in the past, but represents a new discovery open to the future. In this case, destiny can perhaps seem linked to a Fate that favors and protects individuative development, both personal and of the couple itself.

Destiny and *Fate* would therefore seem to correspond to two possible ways of interpreting one's own life. The first is linked to a *personal* dimension, founded on the conscious and responsible subjectivation of events and one's own choices; the second to a *transpersonal* dimension, based on an objectivation of events, which are reinterpreted in an archetypal, universal and, one could also say, cosmic sense.

In the Jungian conception of treatment, these two visions are interwoven like the threads of a constant narrative re-vision, for the subject in therapy. Thus, the analytic process, both at an individual level and for the couple, becomes a new quest for Meaning that focuses on the Ego and the Self, i.e., the personal and the transpersonal dimension. This was the case with Serena, and her analytic journey.

Individuation and Destiny... between consciousness and knowledge

On the pages of Elena Caramazza's book, the reader finds himself visiting the places inhabited by *absolute feelings* that are often opposite and irrepressible, the product of traumatic experiences yet to be worked through. It may be said that in these places of the psyche, as the author points out, there is insufficient "capacity of soul" (Caramazza, p. 14) i.e., an absence of the profound dimension of the psyche that is able to penetrate the *most obscure events* of life, to restore their transparency, and to bring out a possible pattern of meaning, a new narrative.

Hillman states that "A trauma is not a pathological event but a pathologized image" (1983, p. 47), thus emphasizing that it is not the event in itself but the intolerable and unmodifiable image of the event that is constellated as trauma for the subject. Furthermore, Hillman believes that trauma radically affects an individual's destiny and hence his life: "Our wounds are the fathers and mothers of our destiny" (Hillman, 1979). This is what happened in the life of Serena: the premature death of her mother, when Serena was very young, is the event that marked her destiny. Still today, as an adult, Serena is not able to "think herself" beyond that death, which for her is charged with anguish and with doubts about the actual dynamics of the event.

For Serena everything begins and ends in the "vortex" into which her mother vanished so many years ago, and which still continues to engulf every new experience of Serena's life. Everything seems to be at a standstill for her: she and her father are locked in a prison of grief that has never been elaborated.

The initial dreams she had during therapy, revealed a desperate searching for the mother. In a first oneiric image, Serena entered the room of her already dead mother, and nostalgically looked for her clothes; in another image she pursued her, but was only able to see her from behind. Much later, after some years of therapy, it was precisely a dream that marked a turning point in the treatment: Serena saw a reflection of her own face with her mother's face beside it. While recounting the dream, she herself stressed that this was the first time a clear image of her mother's face had appeared next to her as an adult.

Thus in the dream, the experience of the past and of the present come together in a psychic time that has finally started to flow. The current image of Serena, as an adult woman, is reflected beside the early one of her young mother, and the face of each seems to give greater definition to the other. In the dream, therefore, there is a new mutual recognition between mother and daughter, which is no less *real* than an event that has actually taken place.

For the dreaming subject, the oneiric event can be as "real" as one that has occurred in reality. For Jung, "real" is what is *effective*, and the oneiric experience can become an effective and transformative experience for the dreamer, not in the sense of a tangible but of a *symbolic* experience, elaborated during analysis and born of the dialogue between unconscious and consciousness, between *transpersonal* and *personal* factors. In fact, this dream would launch Serena toward a new *self-consciousness* and a new *sense of her own destiny*.

We would therefore like to further explore one of the profound and radical themes addressed by Elena Caramazza: "Revelation and symbolic consciousness" (Caramazza, p. 149). Accessing *symbolic consciousness* is, in fact, the pivotal act performed by the subject's psyche in elaborating trauma – which was the case in Serena's therapy.

In traumatized personalities there predominate dissociative phenomena that invalidate not only the subject's intrapsychic ties, such as the body–mind and unconscious–consciousness relation, but also interpersonal ties, such as the I–You and I–World relation. The traumatized individual has recourse to a narcissistic, defensive subjectivation of reality, since s/he is trapped in a vicious circle of procrastination and self-referential meanings, which are unmodifiable precisely because there is no open engagement with Otherness. It is always, in fact, the *relation* with the Other which, by provoking my subjectivity, obliges me to *relativize the absoluteness* of my feelings, thoughts and experiences, and to reconsider the *one-sidedness of my consciousness*.

Caramazza stresses that "Reality is relation" (Caramazza, p. 150) understood as both I–You and I–World interpersonal relation and consciousness-unconscious and Ego-Self intrapyschic relation:

> Ultimately, it is not only consciousness that illuminates the unconscious, enabling us to know its contents, but also the unconscious that illuminates consciousness by thrusting upward and rendering intuitable profound psychic realities. These realities either precede the birth of consciousness or lie outside its perceptual area, and enrich it with new and complex representations.
>
> (Caramazza, p. 36)

As clearly shown by Erich Neumann (1952, 2000, p. 28), in fact:

There are various forms of *unconscious knowledge*; regarding these Ego consciousness represents only a specific form of knowledge, which is forced to pay the high price of one-sidedness for its rigor, its precision, and its concrete applicability for the Ego (Neumann, 1952, our italics).

For Jung, the one-sidedness of consciousness can only be transformed when the Ego is able to remain rooted in the Self, the unconscious psychic totality that is present from birth: "The self, like the unconscious, is an *a priori* existent out of which the ego evolves. [...] *It is not I who create myself, rather I happen to myself*" (Jung, 1942/1954, p. 259, our italics).

In the Jungian model, therefore, the functionality of the Ego–Self relationship is the backbone of psychic life. The Self may be understood as the center of the whole psyche, a kind of unconscious and creative dramatist, a *"conglomerate soul"* (Jung, 1950, p. 357) that seeks to realize its own parts, by guiding the Ego in living multiple experiences and relations. The Self, on the other hand, should be understood as the theater director, the one who actually maneuvers the various *souls* of the *Self* in the here and now on the stage of the world. Without the Ego, the Self can have neither form nor reality, but the Ego, without the Self, knows nothing of its own origin or its identity, and has no profound knowledge of the meaning that animates it.

It is along the Ego–Self axis, then, that the counterpoint between consciousness and knowledge takes place, namely the alternating relationship of figure and background that is played out in the labyrinthine depths of the psyche. Neumann writes: "Man's task in the world is to remember with his conscious mind what was knowledge before the advent of consciousness" (Neumann, 1949, p. 54).

Hence, we can access *revelation* and *symbolic consciousness* when we consciously remember the primordial knowledge of the unconscious, when our Ego remembers the Self. It is not a question of delegitimizing consciousness in favor of the unconscious, but of temporarily *suspending* judgment, of momentarily *veiling* sensible immediacy, and of *exiling* oneself from the presumptuousness of certainty. Only then will we emerge from "the congenital darkness of light" (Zambrano, 1979, p. 30) and be able to capture the real essence of things as they slowly reveal themselves to us. Indeed, for Zambrano *remembering* can also restore depth "to beings and things always only half-grasped by the intellect, violently perceived, or let pass without reacting, which have all plummeted into the netherworld where what has only been half-seen lies moaning" (Zambrano 1997, p. 72).

But to what kind of memory did Serena have access in the dream about her mother? Certainly not the historical memory of real events. Serena's adult face had never been reflected with that of her young mother before. The oneiric function created a *paradox for consciousness* by realizing, in the dream image, a temporal event that was impossible, not only due to the mother's premature death, but also to the adult age that unites the two women in a single reflected image.

Here we could say that the dream gives rise to a *symbolic memory* in the Jungian sense, i.e., a memory rooted simultaneously in the conscious and unconscious, in the past and present. In fact, dream images arise in the darkness of sleep and of the unconscious, and are evoked by memory in the light of consciousness, as the dreamer recounts them. So, the more the analytic couple engages in the *reverie of the dream*, in a *remembering that is dreaming*, where there is a flowing dialogue between conscious and unconscious, the more the analysand's consciousness loses its one-sidedness. This gives the couple access to a *new knowledge*, to an unexpected meaning of the real, which is not the factual reality of the event or its apparent meaning, but more precisely its *quintessence*.

This results in *revelation, insight*, or, we could say, the *becoming "O"* of Wilfred Bion. In fact, Bion stresses that interpretation should not lead to greater *intellectual knowledge* in the analytic couple, but rather to its *transformation*, "[...] since it must cause O, as representative of the ultimate reality of the 'thing-in-itself,' 'to incarnate itself' in the person of the analysand" (Grimberg, Sor and Tabak de Bianchedi, 1991, p. 162.

Bion also discusses the function of memory: on the one hand, he encourages the analyst to access his own negative capacity, foregoing memory and desire in the analytic listening; on the other, memory appears fundamental to Bion's conception of oneiric work. On the dream and memory in Bion, Civitarese writes: "The function α transforms β elements, which are protosensory or protoemotional, into α elements or thoughts of the dream that can be stored in memory and used to dream or to think" (Civitarese, 2013. p. 84).

Hence, in the dream, and especially in the "dream redreamed" during the session with the analyst, a *symbolic memory* is established, since in oneiric space and time, conscious and unconscious, Ego and Self interact freely with each other, creating what Jung sees as *symbols*, and Bion as α elements. We may suppose, therefore, that oneiric work engenders for the dreamer a new temporal-spatial experience and a new narration of the trauma, and that his mind extends beyond the boundaries of consciousness, toward an *unconscious knowledge* of the real.

Bion sees this new knowledge as deriving from a *"becoming O,"* from a being in *"at-one-ment"* with the *"thing-in-itself,"* with "the Origin." While for Jung it comes from the *transcendent function* of the psyche, whose task it is to reveal the unconscious to the conscious, *to reveal the Self to the Ego*, in a reciprocal giving of meaning.

> Without the objectivation of the self the ego would remain caught in hopeless subjectivity and would only gyrate round itself. But if you can see and understand your suffering without being subjectively involved, then, because of your altered standpoint, you also understand "how not to suffer," for you have reached a place beyond all involvements ("you have me as a bed, rest upon me").
>
> (Jung, 1942/1954, 2014, p. 281)

Severino expresses a similar thought when discussing the concept of *wisdom* in Aeschylus:

> Confining oneself to the part means [...] separating oneself from the truth of the All, seeing and experiencing the meaning of the part as truth and meaning of the All [...] Thought is spared pain only if it becomes episteme, thought that glimpses the supreme immutable power of the All.
> (Severino 1989, p. 42.)

The question now is how does the communication between the part and the all, between the Ego and the Self come about in Jung's vision? In the Jungian view, a central role in the communication between Ego and Self is played by the *archetypes*, attractors of the psychic function and actual force fields present in the *collective unconscious*. This last, unlike the personal unconscious, is neither subjective nor a repository for what is removed; rather, it is *objective*, being constituted by the archetypes: *a priori* forms of the mind active in the unconscious of all of humanity.

The *parental archetype* condenses the transpersonal collective image of the "Mother" or the "Father," rather than the personal and individual image of one's mother and father in real life. Hence, the archetypes transcend the subject's *personal* experience and lead him to extend his experience to the *transpersonal*, constituting himself as the homeostatic system of the psyche that compensates the one-sidedness of consciousness and the partiality of his own individual story.

We may therefore suppose that in the aforesaid dream of Serena – the fruit of years of work on the part of the analytic couple – it was possible for a psychic compensation to take place in the patient. The conscious image of her personal mother was rejoined with the unconscious one of the transpersonal Mother, the part was rejoined with the All, and the Ego, center of consciousness, was rejoined with the Self, the totality of the psyche. Then the recognition that was impossible between mother and daughter in reality, became *psychically real* in the dream, and the suffering, linked to the negative maternal complex, was also able to find something to "rest upon" next to the place of loss and lack. Serena was able to remember with her "*conscious mind what was knowledge before the advent of consciousness.*"

Thus, the Individuation process, activated in the course of the treatment, enabled a "re-vision" of her personal story that enabled Serena to access a new *sense of her own destiny*. "Successful therapy is thus a collaboration between fictions, a revisioning of the story into a more intelligent, more imaginative plot, which also means the sense of mythos in all the parts of the story" (Hillman 1983, p. 36.)

In myth, in fact, *Destiny* takes on more colors than *Fate*, and the personal takes on those of the transpersonal. In Fate, as Caramazza states, each individual is placed in a broader structure of the universe, where "the world, gods and men find themselves incorporated in an order that both considers and dominates them at the same time" (Caramazza, p. 149).

Thus, we may sum up with the words of Neumann: "The relationship of the Ego to the unconscious and of the personal to the impersonal decides the fate not only of the individual, but also of humanity" (Neumann, 1949, p. 30).

Fulvia De Benedittis, Sandra Fersurella, Silvia Presciuttini

Note

1 Other words deriving from this root are, in Greek, ιστημι, "to erect," "to put in the scales," "to weigh;"; in Sanskrit: *tisthati* "stands;" in Latin: *stare, stabilire*, "to make stable;" *stativus*, "immobile" and *status*, "attitude," "state," "statue."

Bibliography

Abraham, K. (1911). On the determining power of names. In Karl Abraham, Ernest Jones, Hilda C. Abraham, D. R. Ellison, Hilda Maas, & Anna Hackel (Eds.), *Clinical papers and essays on psychoanalysis*. London and New York: Routledge, 1979.

Aeschylus. (2012). *Prometheus bound* (Ian Johnston, Trans.). https://edisciplinas. usp.br/pluginfile.php/2596054/mod_resource/content/1/PROMETHEUS%20 BOUND%20BY%20AESCHYLLUS.pdf

Albini Bravo, C. & Devescovi, P. C. (2004). *Figli e genitori. Note a margine di un mito amputato*. Bergamo: Moretti e Vitali.

Althusser, L. (1992). *L'avenir dure longtemps. Suivi de Les Faits. Autobiographies*. Paris: Stock/IMEC, 2007; *The Future Lasts Forever* (Richard Veasey, Trans.). New York: The New Press, 1993.

Balsamo, M. (2004). Perché è morto l'uomo dei topi? Destino, evento, struttura, *Interazioni*, 2-2004/22, p. 44.

Bernhard, E. (1969). *Mitobiografia*, Milan: Adelphi, 1985.

Bion, W. R. (1977). *Bion in Rome*. London: The estate of W. R. Bion, 1983.

Boccara, P. (n.d.). Il caso di Alessandro e il completamento di atti psichici incompiuti. Note a margine del concetto di destino in psicoanalisi, *Interazioni*, 2-2004/22.

Bolen, J. S. (1984). *Goddesses in every woman*. San Francisco: Harper & Row.

Bolen, J. S. (1989). *Gods in every man*. San Francisco: Harper & Row.

Bollas, C. (1989). *Forces of destiny. Psychoanalysis and human idiom*. London and New York: Routledge, 2019.

Borgna, E. (1994). *La cura dell'infelicità. Oltre il mito biologico della depressione*. Rome – Naples: Theoria.

Bruck, E. (2021). *Il pane perduto*. Milan: La nave di Teseo.

Buber, M. (1937). *I and Thou*, (Ronald Gregor Smith, Trans.), Edinburgh: T. & T. Clark.

Callieri, B. (2008). *Io e Tu. Fenomenologia dell'incontro. Omaggio al Prof. Bruno Callieri per il suo LXXXV compleanno* (With Angela Ales Bello, Arnaldo Ballerini, Eugenio Borgna, & Lorenzo Calvi; Gilberto Di Petta, Eds.). Rome: Edizioni Universitarie Romane.

Caramazza, E. (1992). L'Ombra. In Aldo Carotenuto (Ed.), *Trattato di psicologia analitica* (Vol. II, chap. III). Turin: UTET.

Caramazza, E. (2017). *Silenzio a Praga*. Bergamo: Moretti e Vitali.

Carotenuto, A. (1977). *Senso e contenuto della psicologia analitica*. Turin: Boringhieri.

Civitarese, G. (2013). *Il sogno necessario* (p. 84). Milan: Franco Angeli.

De Benedittis, F., Fersurella, S., & Presciuttini, S. (2016). Mi resta quel nulla di inesauribile segreto. Legami coniugali e memorie tra le generazioni. In F. De Benedittis & P. Michelis (Eds.), *Figure della memoria. Ricordare in analisi. Una nuova via nella terapia con il gioco della sabbia*. Milan: Franco Angeli.

De Benedittis, F., Fersurella, S., & Presciuttini, S. (2019). *Orizzonti di coppia*. Bergamo: Moretti e Vitali.

de M'Uzan, M. (1984). Les esclaves de la quantité. *Nouvelle Revue de Psychanalyse, 30*, 129–138.

De Santillana, G. (1968). *Fato antico e Fato moderno* [Reflections on men and ideas]. Milan: Adelphi, 1985; 2004.

Dicks, H. V. (1967). *Marital tensions: Clinical studies towards a psychological theory of interaction*. London and New York: Routledge, 2016.

Dumas, D. (1985). *L'ange et le fantôme*. Paris: Éditions de Minuit.

Eliade, M. (1949). *Le myte de l'éternel retour – Archétypes et répétition*. Paris: Gallimard.

Fordham, M. (1994). The importance of analysing childhood for assimilation of the shadow. In Judith Hubback, Michael Fordham, & Rosemary Gordon (Eds.), *Analytical psychology – A modern science* (p. 150). London and New York: Routledge.

Freud, S. (1916). *Vergänglichkeit* [On Transience]. http://www.sophia-project.org/uploads/1/3/9/5/13955288/freud_transience.pdf

Freud, S. (1922). *The Ego and the Id* (Joan Riviere, Trans., p. 36). New York: W. W. Norton and Company Inc, 1962.

Galimberti, U. (1984). *La terra senza il male*. Milan: Feltrinelli.

Gallard-Drahon, M. (1987). Ombre noire – Ombre blanche. *Cahiers Jungiens de Psychanalyse. Le poids de l'ombre*, no. 52.

Girard, R. (1990). *A Theater of Envy. William Shakespeare*. Leominster, UK; New Malden, UK: Gracewing; Inigo Enterprises, 2000.

Gobodo-Madikizela, P. (2003). *A human being died that night*. London: Portobello Books, 2006.

Goethe, J. W. (1808). *Faust: Eine Tragödie; Faust. A Tragedy* (Bayard Taylor, Trans.). Boston and New York: Houghton Mifflin Company, 1898.

Grimberg, L., Sor, D., & Tabak de Bianchedi, E. (1991). *Introduzione al pensiero di Bion*. Milan: Raffaello Cortina, 1993.

Hillman, J. (1979). *Puer papers*. Dallas, TX: Spring Publications.

Hillman, J. (1983). *Healing fictions*. New York: Station Hill.

Homer. (2009). *The Iliad* (A. S. Kline, Trans., Book VI). https://www.poetryintranslation.com/PITBR/Greek/Iliad6.php#anchor_Toc239244954

Homerin, A.-M. (2000). Le couple, creuset alchimique. *Cahiers Jungiens de Psychanalyse*, no. 97, Spring.

Jung, C. G. (1909). The family constellation. In Gerhard Adler, Herbert Read, & Michael Fordham (Eds.), *Experimental researches*, CW (Vol. 2). London and New York: Routledge, 1973.

Jung, C. G. (1909/1949). Die Bedeutung des Vaters für das Schicksal des Einzelnen [The father in the destiny of the individual]. *Freud and psychoanalysis*, CW (Vol. IV). London and New York: Routledge, 2014.

Jung, C. G. (1912/1952). *Symbole der Wandlung* [Symbols of transformation], CW (Vol. V). London and New York: Routledge, 2014.

Jung, C. G. (1913/1954). Versuch einer darstellung der psychoanalityschen Theorie [The theory of psychoanalysis]. *Freud and Psychoanalysis*, CW (Vol. IV). London and New York: Routledge, 2014.

Jung, C. G. (1917/1943). *Über die Psychologie des Umbewussten* [Two essays on analytical psychology], CW (Vol. VII). London and New York: Routledge, 2014.

Jung, C. G. (1919). Instinkt und Unbewusstes [Instinct and the unconscious]. In *The structure and dynamics of the psyche*, CW (Vol. VIII). London and New York: Routledge, 2014.

Jung, C. G. (1921/2014). *Psychologische typen* [Psychological types], CW (Vol. VI). London and New York: Routledge, 2014.

Jung, C. G. (1927). Die Frau in Europa [Woman in Europe]. In *Civilization in transition*, CW (Vol. X). London and New York: Routledge, 2014.

Jung, C. G. (1928). Die Beziehungen zwischen dem Ich und dem Unbewussten [The relations between the ego and the unconscious]. In *Two essays on analytical psychology*, CW (Vol. VII). London and New York: Routledge, 2014.

Jung, C. G. (1934/1954). Über die Archetypen des kollektiven Umbewussten [Archetypes of the collective unconscious]. In *The archetypes and the collective unconscious*, CW (Vol. IX). London and New York: Routledge, 2014a.

Jung, C. G. (1936). *Zivilisation im Übergang* [Civilization in transition], CW (Vol. X). London and New York: Routledge, 2014.

Jung, C. G. (1938/1940). *Psychologie und Religion* [*Psychology and religion*], CW (Vol. XI), London and New York: Routledge, 2014.

Jung, C. G. (1938/1954). Die Psychologischen Aspekte des Mutterarchetypus [Psychological aspects of the mother archetype]. In *The archetypes and the collective unconscious*, CW (Vol. IX). London and New York: Routledge, 2014.

Jung, C. G. (1938/1954). *Four archetypes* (R. F. C. Hull, Trans., p. 27). Princeton, NJ: Princeton University Press, 1970.

Jung, C. G. (1940/1950). Über Wiedergeburt [Concerning rebirth]. In *The archetypes and the collective unconscious*, CW (Vol. IX). London and New York: Routledge, 2014.

Jung, C. G. (1942/1948). Versuch zu einer psychologiscen Deutung des Trinitätsdogmas [A psychological approach to the dogma of the trinity]. In *Psychology and religion*, CW (Vol. XI). London and New York: Routledge, 2014.

Jung, C. G. (1942/1954). Transformation symbolism in the mass. In *Psychology and religion*, CW (Vol. XI). London and New York: Routledge, 2014.

Jung, C. G. (1943/1987). *L'homme à la découverte de son Ame – Structure et Fonctionnement de l'Inconscient* (Roland Cahen, Ed.). Paris: Albin Michel. It. trans. *Introduzione alla Psicologia Analitica. Le Conferenze di Basilea (1934) di C. G. Jung. Trascritte da Roland Cahen* (Elena Caramazza, Prefaced and Ed.). Bergamo: Moretti e Vitali, 2015 (private edition).

Jung, C. G. (1944). Religious ideas in alchemy. In *Psychologie und Alchemie* [Psychology and alchemy], CW (Vol. XII). London and New York: Routledge, 2014.

Jung, C. G. (1946). Die Psychologie der Übertragung [The Psychology of the Transference]. In *The practice of psychotherapy*, CW (Vol. 16). London and New York: Routledge, 2014.

Jung, C. G. (1947/1954). On the nature of the psyche. In *The structure and dynamics of the psyche*, CW (Vol. VIII). London and New York: Routledge, 2014.

Jung, C. G. (1947/1954). Theoretische Überlegungen zum Wesen des Psychischen [On the nature of the psyche]. In *The structure and dynamics of the psyche*, CW (Vol. VIII). London and New York: Routledge, 2014.

Jung, C. G. (1948). *Symbolik des Geistes. Studien Über psychische Phänomenologie*, It. trans, *La simbolica dello Spirito. Studi sulla Fenomenologia dello Spirito*. Turin: Einaudi, 1975.

Jung, C. G. (1950). Concerning mandala symbolism. In *The archetypes and the collective unconscious*, CW (Vol. IX). London and New York: Routledge 2014.

Jung, C. G. (1951). *Aion. Untersuchungen zur Symbolgeschichte* [Aion – Researches into the phenomenology of the self], CW (Vol. IX). London and New York: Routledge, 2014.

Jung, C. G. (1952). Synchronicity: An acausal connecting principle. In *The structure and dynamics of the psyche*.

Jung, C. G. (1954). Zur Psychologie der Tricksterfigure [On the psychology of the trickster-figure]. In *The archetypes and the collective unconscious*, CW (Vol. IX). London and New York: Routledge, 2014.

Jung, C. G. (1957). Gegenwart und Zukunft [The undiscovered self (present and future)] in *Civilization in transition*, CW (Vol. X), London and New York: Routledge, 2014.

Jung, C. G. (1959). Gut und Bose in der analytischen Psychologie [Good and evil in analytical psychology]. In *Civilization in transition*, CW (Vol. X), London and New York: Routledge, 2014b.

Jung, C. G. (1961). *Erinnerung, Träume, Gedanken von C.G. Jung* [Memories, dreams, reflections] (Aniela Jaffé, Ed., Richard and Clara Winston, Trans., Revised ed.), New York: Vintage Books, 1989.

Jung, C. G. (1970). *The symbolic life*, CW (R. F. C. Hull, Trans., Vol. 18, 2nd ed.) London and New York; Routledge: Princeton University Press.

Jung, C. G. & Jarrett, James L. (Ed.) (2020). *Nietzsche's Zarathustra: Notes of the seminar given in 1934–1939* (Vol. 2). Part II, abridged version, Bollingen series. Princeton, NJ: Princeton University Press.

Kaës, R. (2009). *Les alleances inconscentes* (p. 190). Paris: Dunod.

Kafka, F. (1924). *Der Prozess* (David Wyllie, Trans.). https://holybooks-lichtenbergpress. netdna-ssl.com/wp-content/uploads/Franz-Kafka-The-Trial.pdf

Kalsched, D. (1996). *The inner world of trauma. Archetypal defenses of the personal spirit*. London and New York: Routledge.

Kerenyi, C. (1951/1958). *Die Mythologie der Griechen* [The Gods of the Greeks]. London and New York: Thames and Hudson, 1951.

Klein, M. (1946). Notes on some schizoid mechanisms. *International Journal of Psychoanalysis*, 5, 160–179.

Klein, M. (1957). *Envy and gratitude (A study of unconscious sources)*. London: Tavistock Publications, 1969.

Leopardi, G. (1973). Zibaldone di pensieri. In *Tutte le opere di Giacomo Leopardi* (Vol. II). Milan: Mondadori.

Levinas, E. (1982). *Ethique et infini*. Le livre de Poche. Paris: Fayard/France Culture.

Lingiardi, V. (2019). *Venerdì di Repubblica* of 8/11/2019, review of the film *Manta Rey*.

Maffei, G. (2002). *Le fini delle cure*. Turin: Boringhieri.

Miller, A. (1979). *Das Drama des begabten Kindes und die Suche nach dem wahren Selbst* [Drama of the gifted child] (Ruth Ward, Trans., Revised ed.). New York: Basic Books, 1994.

Musil, R. (1965). *Die Verwirrungen des Zöglins Törles* [The Confusions of the Young Törless] (Mike Mitchell, Trans.). Oxford: Oxford University Press, 2014.

Neumann, E. (1949a). *The origins and history of consciousness*. New York: Pantheon Books, 1954.

Neumann, E. (1949b). *Ursprungsgeschichte des Bewusstseins* [The origins and history of consciousness]. London: Routledge, 1954.

Neumann, E. (1952). *Il Sè, l'individuo, la realtà*. Milan: Vivarium, 2000.

Pandolfi, A. M. (2004). Il passaggio dal fato al destino. In *Interazioni*, 2-2004/22, p. 83.

Panikkar, R. (1979). *Myth, faith and hermeneutics: Cross-cultural studies*. New York: Paulist Press.

Panikkar, R. (1981). Per una lettura transculturale del simbolo. In *Quaderni di psicoterapia infantile*, no. 5, *Simbolo e Simbolizzazione*. Rome: Borla.

Panikkar, R. (1981/1984). L'esperienza del tempo. In *Quaderni di psicoterapia infantile*, no. 10, *Tempo e psicoanalisi*, Città di Castello: Borla, 1984.

Panikkar, R. (1985). *Il silenzio di Dio. La risposta del Budda*. Città di Castello: Borla (note).

Panikkar, R. (1986). Verità – Errore – Bugia – Esperienza Psicoanalitica. In *Quaderni di psicoterapia infantile*, no. 13, *Bugia e Allucinazione*, Rome: Borla.

Panikkar, R. (1989). *La Trinidad y la experiencia religiosa*. Barcelona: Obelisco.

Panikkar, R. (1993). *La nueva inocencia*. Navarra: Verbo Divino, 1999.

Panikkar, R. (2004). *L'esperienza della vita. La mistica*. Milan: Jaka Book, 2005.

Pavoni, C. (2009). Dalla colpa alla responsabilità. In *La vita psichica. Percorsi dell'Eros*. Rome: Magi.

Pirandello, L. (1959). *Rules of the game*. London: Penguin Books.

Plato. *The Symposium* (Benjamin Jowett, Trans.). http://classics.mit.edu/Plato/symposium.html

Racamier, P. C. (1980). *Les schizophrènes*. Paris: Payot.

Racamier, P. C. (1992). *Le génie des origines*. Paris: Payot.

Severino, E. (1989). *Il giogo*. Milan: Adelphi.

Stein, M. & Caramazza, E. (2021). *Temporality, shame, and the problem of evil in Jungian psychology. An exchange of ideas*. London and New York: Routledge.

Trapanese, G. (2004). Il destino del tragico nelle generazioni: la clinica e il genere tragicomico. In *Interazioni*, 2-2004/22.

Trevi, M. & Romano, A. (1975). *Studi sull'ombra*. Venice: Marsilio.

Vianello, M., (2022). *La Cappa di Piombo – Capitalismo e Politica: Una Prospettiva Psicoanalitica – Storica*. Rome: Castelvecchi.

Vianello, M. & Caramazza, E. (1992). *L'amorosa utopia – Ipotesi su Sesso, Spazio, Potere*. Rome: Borla.

Vianello, M. & Caramazza, E. (1998). *Donne e Metamorfosi della Politica*. Rome: Editori Riuniti.

Vitolo, A. (2004). Parti d'ignoto. In *Interazioni*, 2-2004/22.

Winnicott, D. W. (1965). *The maturational processes and the facilitating environment. Studies in theory of emotional development* [Sviluppo affettivo e ambiente]. Rome: Armando Armando, 1970.

Zambrano, M. (1979). *I Beati*. Milan: Feltrinelli, 1992.

Zambrano, M. (1997). Il metodo in filosofia o le tre forme della visione. *Aut Aut*, 279.

Index

Pages followed by n refer notes.

Achilles 8
Aeschylus: concept of wisdom 181;
    Prometheus Bound 166–167
affection, expressed by analyst 68–75
affective difficulties 96
affectivity, and the Shadow xix
Alter-Ego, and Ego 56
Althusser, Louis 11, 44, 45, 135–140
ambivalence 44, 46n5
analysis, successful 91
analytic listening 53
Anima 161
Animus 161
anxiety: and freedom 12–17, 76–77; and
    hope 77–80; originary 57–58
archetypal images, splitting of xxvii
archetypal parents, mourning of 169
archetypes 181
Aristotle 128
atonement xxxiv
Atropos 4

Barrett Browning, Elizabeth 53
becoming, paralysis of 8–11
being/thinking polarity 149–150
Bernhard, Ernst 133, 150
Bion, Wilfred 76, 180; *Italian Seminars*
    99
black Shadow xxi
blame 5–6
body, our, encounter with xxiii
Bollas, C. 3; on destiny and fate 175–176
Borgna, Eugenio 124
Bravo, C.A. & Devescovi, P.C., *Figli e
    Genitori* 144
Bruck, Edith, *Il pane perduto* xxxii
Buber, Martin 128

Calderón de la Barca, Pedro, *La vida es
    sueño* 105–106
Callieri, Bruno 5, 56; *Io e Tu,
    Fenomenologia dell'incontro* 52–53
Carpocrates xxxv
Cassandra 98
challenge 105–106
chance 157
Chernobyl 108
choice 89
Chronos 56, 145
Civitarese, G. 180
Clemenceau, Georges xxviii
coincidences 154
collective unconscious 181; and
    collective Shadow xxii
collusion 171
completeness 66
complicity 132
consciousness: symbolic 110, 149–150,
    160, 179; symbolic activity of 52;
    unconscious 36
conspiracy, between mother and son
    74–75
contradiction 103–104
cosmos 153
couple therapy, destiny and fate in
    170–182

Dasein 56, 125
De Santillana, G. 153, 154; on archaic
    cosmogonies 72; on Fate 166;
    Reflections on Men and Ideas 4
death, or illusion 92–93
deception 98–99, 105
de-integration, process of 43
depression 124

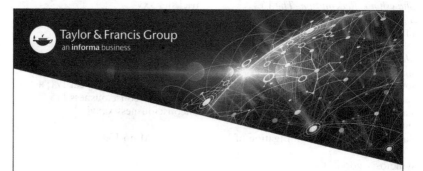